Free Press

Underground & Alternative Publications
1965–1975

Free Press

Underground & Alternative Publications
1965–1975

JEAN-FRANÇOIS BIZOT

Foreword by Barry Miles

Universe

UNDERGROUND PRESS

To offer as many po

Contents

Notes from Underground

A FEW MESSAGES FROM OUR UNDERGROUND FRIENDS
Three founders of the underground press who were crucial to the creation of this book.

John Wilcock was co-founder of **The Village Voice**, **Other Scenes**, the Underground Press Syndicate, and also editor of **The East Village Other**. A leading underground figure from 1954 until today, his huge body of work makes him the co-author of this book:

'I am very amused to see myself popping in and out in this book on the Free Press. From 1954, I was part of that history, editing **EVO** and **Other Scenes**, co-founder of **Interview**, and travelling through the Underground. I got a familiar feeling and, like Jean-François Bizot, I hate copyrights which castrate the propagation of free ideas between free people.'

My first involvement with the underground press came in 1965 when Walter Bowart, founder and publisher of the **East Village Other (EVO)**, asked me to write a London column for them. **EVO** started that year in New York to fill the gap when the **Village Voice** was on strike, and to fill the cultural gap between the increasingly staid old-left Greenwich Village, and the edgy, radical East Village. It was able to get away with much of its provocative language and headlines because its Chinatown printers did not speak English. It was the epitome of an underground paper: psychedelic graphics, anti-Vietnam war news, conspiracy theories, articles on drugs including regular essays by the editor's friend Timothy Leary, articles on happenings, avant-garde events, rock 'n' roll, and sex – in fact, it was the original sex 'n' drugs 'n' rock 'n' roll newspaper. **EVO** was the first to print the work of underground cartoonists Robert Crumb (creator of *Mr Natural*, *Fritz the Cat*, and most of all, his own angst-ridden self as a character), Gilbert Shelton (creator of anti-heroes *Wonder Warthog* and the *Furry Freak Brothers*, whose collections are still in print), Spain Rodriguez, originator of *Trashman*, a Hell's Angel anti-hero. These pages of comics were widely reprinted around the world by the Underground Press Syndicate (UPS) and helped keep many of them in business. The **EVO** office, which was in a loft above Bill Graham's Fillmore East on 2nd Avenue, had a mural across the back wall, depicting all the main characters created by Robert Crumb, Spain Rodriguez and Gilbert Shelton; the way they pooled their talents on this one project symbolized the ethos of the movement: sharing and community came before individual ego. **EVO** realized that they could never distribute further than downtown Manhattan so they came up with the idea of the UPS to disseminate their articles and cartoons across the world. A genuine exercise in subversion. It was very simple: UPS members agreed to send their papers to all the other members and to allow them to reprint anything from them with no fee or even acknowledgment. All it took to join was a letter to the UPS saying you existed. **EVO** became the model for most of the new emerging papers: people liked its irreverence, its underground cartoons, its pro-drug stance, its humour and the way it explored the outer possibilities of what you can do with offset litho before it becomes illegible. They ran collages, handwritten headlines, typewritten copy, printed the thing sideways, superimposed and upside-down. You got the sense of immediacy and the energy of the news as it happened, quickly slapped down on the boards as if it was hot gossip. You got the sense that if they could do it, anybody could. And it was true.

In 1966 myself, John Hopkins and various others co-founded the **International Times (it)**, Europe's first underground paper, using **EVO**, the **Los Angeles Free Press** and the **Village Voice** as models. There was a large enough community interested in news about anti-Vietnam war activities, happenings and the latest developments in the avant garde, music and theatre, about LSD and marijuana for us to survive. We ran articles by William Burroughs, a good friend of the paper, and Allen Ginsberg. I interviewed members of the Beatles who were sometimes called upon for a cheque when things got tough. Articles from most of our issues were reprinted somewhere in the world. At **it** we originated our own cartoon strips, not wanting the paper to become too American, but after about three years,

by Barry Miles

the work of Crumb, Shelton, Spain, S. Clay Wilson and the other American underground cartoonists had become so good that we started to reprint it.

Working at an underground paper was rather like being a starving artist in a garret; most people did it for love. It was several years before I was paid for anything I wrote for **it**, and that was only after it became a workers' co-operative after May 1968. It was wonderful to have my work reprinted across the world, to see something as mundane as a record review appear in a paper from Minneapolis or an essay translated into Dutch or Swedish. The UPS papers ran an ongoing weekly debate on how to live: dozens of models were proposed, discussed and attempted. Some worked, some didn't, and some were a big mistake. Charles Manson was, after all, also a product of the counterculture. **it** was housed in the basement of the Indica Bookshop, which I co-owned, which meant that **it** was more exposed than most underground papers and had a constant stream of visitors from Holland, Germany and the USA, all looking to score drugs and find a crash pad. But we were trying to run an underground paper, not an underground social services office, so we were not always able to help, though we were usually able to find someone to put up runaways. It worked both ways, of course. My most enduring memory of working in the underground press is the warmth and camaraderie of the people who published and wrote them. I remember arriving in Los Angeles in January 1969 and walking unannounced into the offices of **Open City** and saying I was from **it**. Immediately I was offered a place to stay and more invitations to events and meals than I could hope to use. **Open City** was a wonderful psychedelic

broadsheet that ran Charles Bukowski's *Notes of a Dirty Old Man* column; widely reprinted throughout the UPS. It was published from a storefront and had a huge psychedelic mural across the back wall. I thought there was something wrong with it and they explained that, in classic Hollywood manner, the building had previously been used as a film set for an exploitation movie about an underground paper. Reality was often hard to pin down in underground press circles. I received the same warm welcome when I went to the **Los Angeles Free Press**, the first of the underground papers. Editor/publisher Art Kunkin took the day off to drive me around town and show me all the countercultural sights. We tried our best to reciprocate but we were sometimes overwhelmed by the sheer numbers of visitors to Swinging London, all of whom wanted to meet the Beatles.

The spirit of the underground press lives on: in the late seventies there were several hundred punk magazines with wonderful names like **Sniffin' Glue** and **Apathy in Ilford**, produced in Britain on office photocopy machines used out of hours. Then came the internet. The area north of San José, where Ken Kesey and the Merry Pranksters once held their acid tests, became Silicon Valley. Many of the same people went on to found the cyber-revolution, and made sure the internet embodied the fundamental principle that 'information should be free'. The internet, with its great unsorted jumble of facts, lies and misreporting, is in many ways like the underground press, and the advent of personal blogs means that everyone can now publish their own paper.

Jim Haynes co-founded the **International Times** (**it**), in October 1966 in London. He has written *Hello, I Love You*, about sexual liberation, and now lives in Paris:

'I am happy to see that **Actuel** managed to protect those archives which most of us dispersed. This is an historical underground book that should please everybody who was concerned and more. As the UPS dissolved around 1975, it is not easy to find those papers.'

You can get in touch with him and order his very underground book by sending 20 euros to Jim Haynes (83 rue de la Tombe-Issoire, 75014 Paris, France).

Richard Neville founded **Oz** in London, which inspired **Actuel**:

'I LOVED the proofs – thanks, what a reminder. I got a sweet sad letter today from John Wilcock, the unacknowledged, unassuming catalyst. Sometimes I wish I'd turned **Oz** into an **Actuel**, but the butterfly drifted into history, and I still write for a living.'

We are the future!

THE FREE PRESS IS EVERYWHERE

Pop art, irony, collages
surrealism, cybernetics
happenings, road movies
activists, poets, angry young men, psychedelia
beatniks, Situationists
Buddhism, Native Americans
revolution, ghettos

THE REALIST

Case History of the Manchester Caper

by Paul Krassner

Once there was upon a time a face painted on the hand of Señor Wences that magically became a real person named Jacqueline. She kissed a senator in a Spearmint ad, and he in turn became a real person named Jack. They were married by Chief Justice Earl Warren and lived in good taste for not quite ever after.

Suddenly he was slain by the man who had most to gain—Mark Lane—who in turn was killed at the police station by Vaughn Meader.

(Continued on Page 13)

Legal and Actual Concentration Camps in America

by Charles R. Allen, Jr.

While fascism is many things, reflected in unnumbered manifestations, it is, quintessentially, the art of the end square—carried to a terrible science. Hitler, Mussolini, Trujillo, Batista, Franco—and, of course, today's variant, Johnson—were, and are, above all proto-type squares.

It's not only that each in his own way — Mussolini with his castor oil 'treatment' Hitler with his concentration camp system leading directly to the 'Final Solution' (the last, desperate

(Continued on Page 5)

Blow-Up, Psychedelic Sexualis and The War Game —or, David Hemmings Is Herman Kahn in Disguise

Ready for another little trippypoo?

Start with this letter from a subscriber: "I've recently heard rumors that Paul Krassner doesn't exist and that he is, in fact, a composite of a number of fulsome individuals. These people, it's said, each subject themselves monthly to a strange experience, then everyone's experience is compiled into one story which is subsequently given some idiotic moral (much in the same way *Time* magazine writes its articles). In issue #74, for example, the *Crazy SANE to Loving Haight* story was actually written by a Krassner who attended SANE's rally, another who's an ascetic but takes acid, another who visited Haight-Ashbury, another who

reads *McCall's* ads in the N.Y. *Times*, another who insulted Joe Pyne, etc. In this way, the story appears to be the exploits of one man, the mythical Paul Krassner. I've also heard that a conspiracy has developed by which one faction of Paul Krassners is seeking to gain control over the rest through the use of CIA terror tactics. Is this the reason I haven't received issue #75?"

Now the whole world knows.

This has been Vietnam Summer, a men's cologne, more fragrant than Spring Mobilization, which sponsored an anti-war march on April 15, in San Francisco, where then-*Ramparts*-publisher-not-to-be Ed Keating

(Continued on Page 17)

No. 75

35 Cents

ABOVE: **The Realist.** The granddaddy of the underground press, founded in 1958.
OPPOSITE: Collage by Claes Oldenburg for **Other Scenes**, John Wilcock's paper.
OVERLEAF: Collage by Charles Henri Ford, New York, 1966.

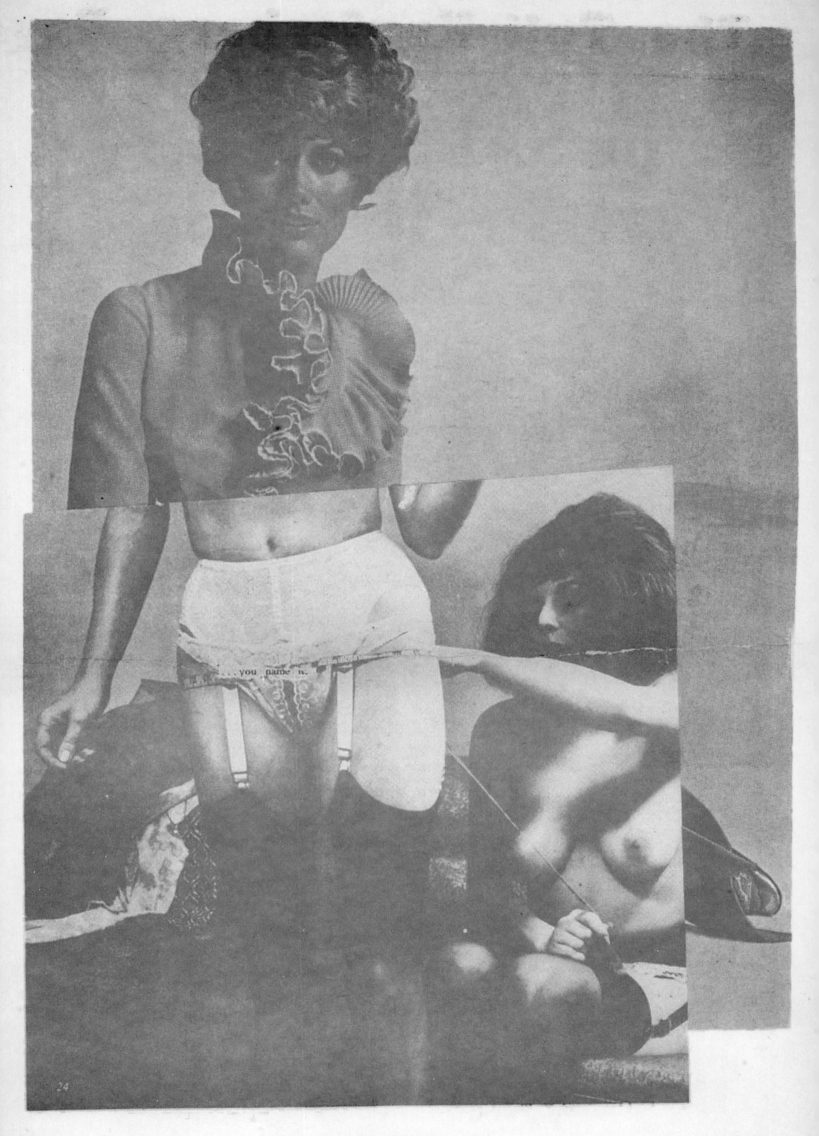

...you name it.

cloes oldenburg

'This is about me'

to Gide—

bashful

Properly conducted,   the impat

HOT DOG Begat

Blue Meanies   Oh la la

He calls it

Pssst!   Morrison's Penis
Is

ISTORY running young

e can't lose

Elusive

baby-faced   emptiness   rarin' to go

JOIE DE VIVRE

Hooray For

hibitions

crime-fighting

od-given Form Is far from

Glamor B

u haven't seen

o's *Country of*

NO

did you , Mini-basket Marauder,

After that Revolting Son

Superstars

KEEP BITING
EVEN WHEN BITTEN **?**

rs Muffle a leader whose ideals

it would have paid you

Tape it

TO

ollate
slit
forate
duce
store
large
nd seem to

tangle

Chicken 'n Dumplings

13

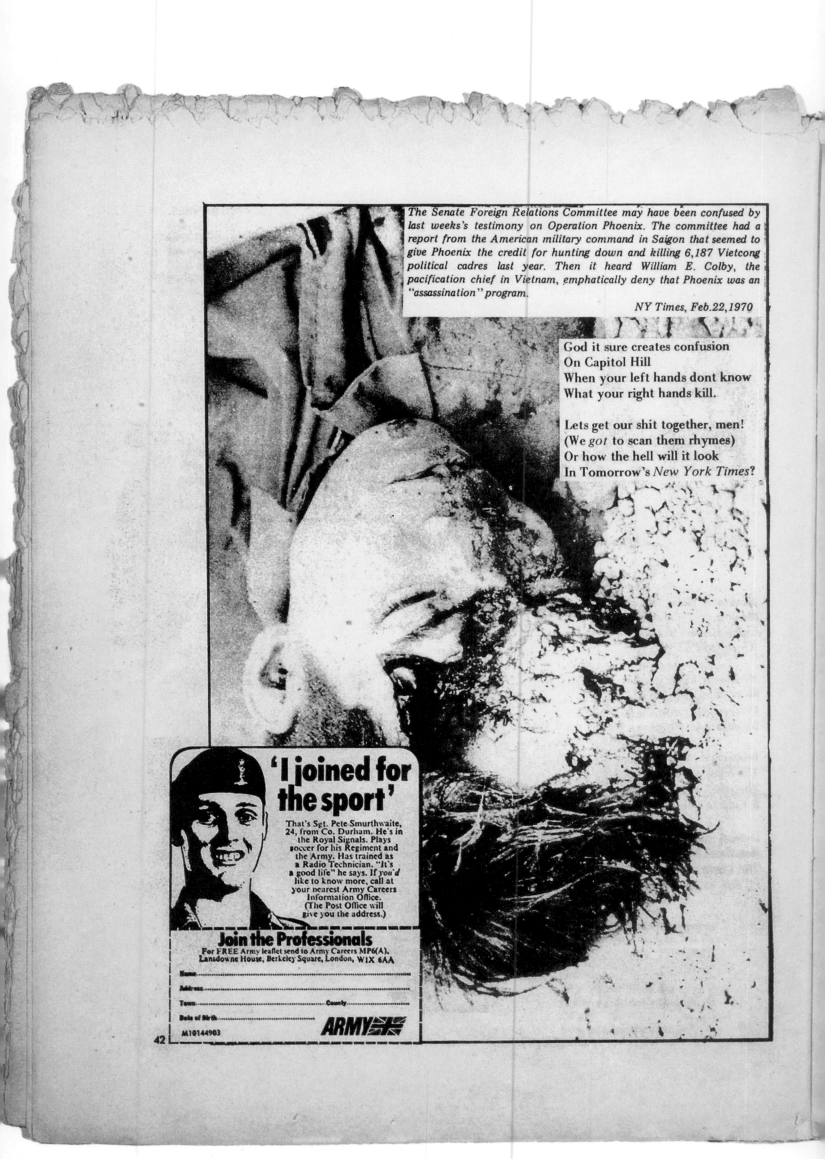

The Senate Foreign Relations Committee may have been confused by last weeks's testimony on Operation Phoenix. The committee had a report from the American military command in Saigon that seemed to give Phoenix the credit for hunting down and killing 6,187 Vietcong political cadres last year. Then it heard William E. Colby, the pacification chief in Vietnam, emphatically deny that Phoenix was an "assassination" program.

NY Times, Feb.22,1970

God it sure creates confusion
On Capitol Hill
When your left hands dont know
What your right hands kill.

Lets get our shit together, men!
(We *got* to scan them rhymes)
Or how the hell will it look
In Tomorrow's *New York Times?*

42

NEWS photo by John Pedin

Ranger Won't Be Lone. Staff Sgt. Joseph Rizzi, 20,
and fiancee Janice Cubbitt check luggage in his Bronx home. Rizzi,
graduate of Army ranger school, and Janice will wed Saturday.
Pentagon has given him extra leave for honeymoon. He was to have
reported after wedding for tour of duty in Vietnam.   —*Story p. 4*

*I tell her daddy's plane fell down out of
the sky*

*wife of missing
US Air Force pilot
on CBS-TV, Xmas 1969*

And what was daddy doing there, mommy?

Burning little children like you, dear
in the arms, legs, eyes, mouth, body & cunt, dear . . .
Burning them to death.

Now go out and play, dear.

News Poems, Tuli Kupferberg, New York, 1970.

What are YOU doing to protect yours...

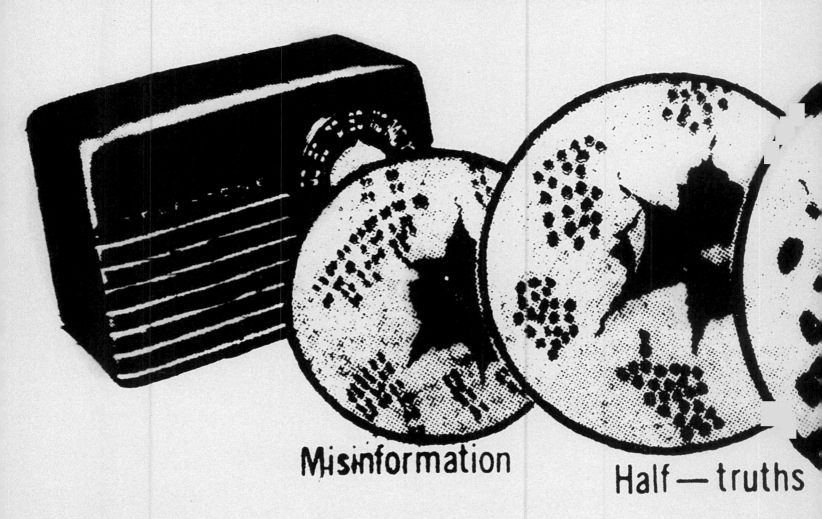

Misinformation

Half—truths

MEDIA
BURN
The Nation's
leading men

from:

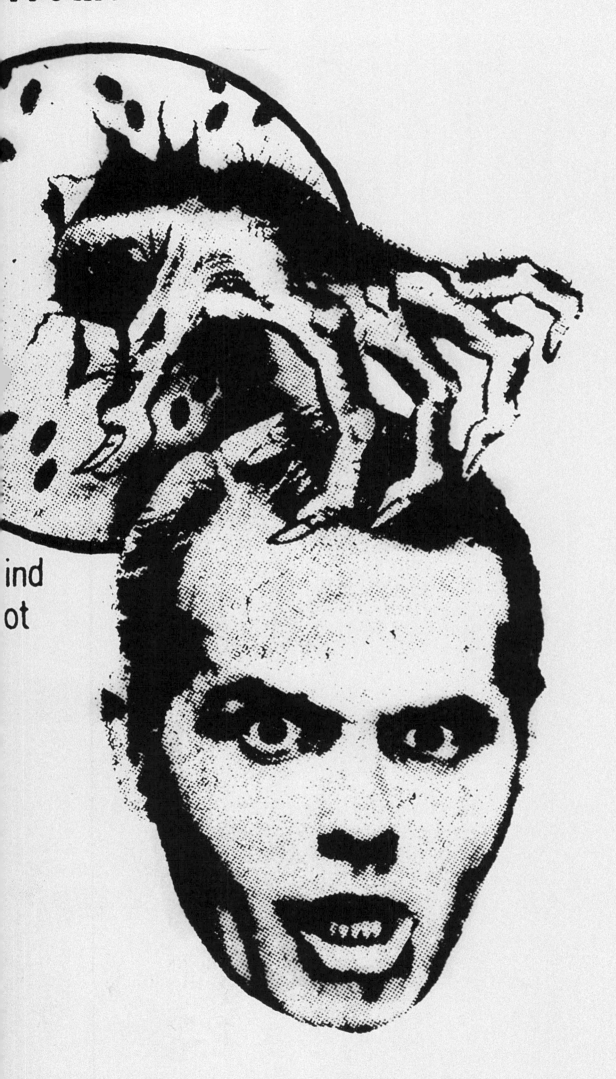

ind

ot

al crippler

An adbusting ad from
Counter Culture by
Joseph H. Berke, 1969.

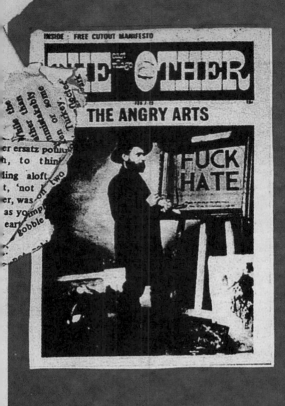

THE OTHER
INSIDE: FREE CUTOUT MANIFESTO
THE ANGRY ARTS
FUCK HATE

EXTRA!!
THE OTHER
"My God! My God!
Where is this happening?
This is America!"

THE OTHER
ON YOUR PROMOTION... AND MERRY
CONGRATULATIONS CARDINAL

THE east village OTHER
SPEED KILLS
UNCLE SAM TURNS ON IN VIETNAM
SENDS OUR BOYS UP JUNKIE TRAIL

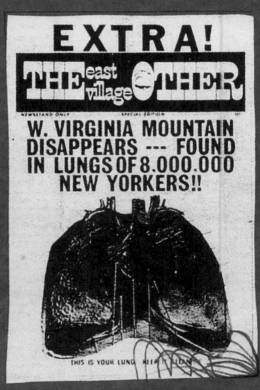

EXTRA!
THE east village OTHER
W. VIRGINIA MOUNTAIN
DISAPPEARS --- FOUND
IN LUNGS OF 8,000,000
NEW YORKERS!!
THIS IS YOUR LUNG

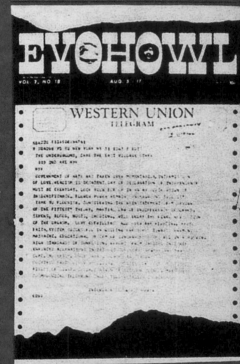

EVO HOWL
WESTERN UNION
TELEGRAM

THE OTHER
"BURNED OUT"

Inside: All About The Revolution
THE OTHER
THE SHIT HITS THE FAN

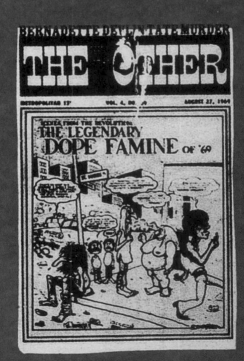

THE OTHER
THE LEGENDARY
DOPE FAMINE of '69

18

VOL.2 NO.10   © 1967 by The East Village Other Inc   APR. 15- MAY 1   20 cents outside N.Y.   15¢

SAN FRANCISCO

In the late fifties and early sixties after the "beat generation" had been incubating for ten years, it stuck its head out of its cloistered womb and ran into the ominous status quo. The Health, Police and Fire Departments, acting on the advice of a sensational press, representing a frightened and lost power structure, launched what appears in retrospect to have been a carefully laid plan to harrass the beatnik communities in New York and San Francisco.

Inspectors scurried over MacDougal Street issuing summons for infinite "violations" which had previously remained undiscovered. Artists were thrown into the streets when they were discovered living in lofts — places which because of their condition could not be rented to commercial establishments, yet were not ramshackeled enough to be condemned.

In New York the exodus began from Greenwich Village, which had become a political plum for the Village Independent Democrats, to the un-aligned, un-desirable Lower East Side where the rents were still cheap.

In North Beach, gangster elements took over as the beatniks moved out, leaving today a quieter craftsman's community surrounded by topless joints.

Like a cue-ball scattering the opening shot, the establishment broke the cluster and spread the beat generation across the country. It took the seeds carried by poets, painters, and psychedelic holy men ten years to flower into the gigantic minority of gypsy drop-outs currently imploding from the middle-class vacuum.

Story and Photographs Copyright 1967 by Walter Bowart

Continued on page 3

The International Times   No 8   Feb 13-26 1967/1s

ginsberg • *townshend (who)* • *snyder* • *mandrake root*

it

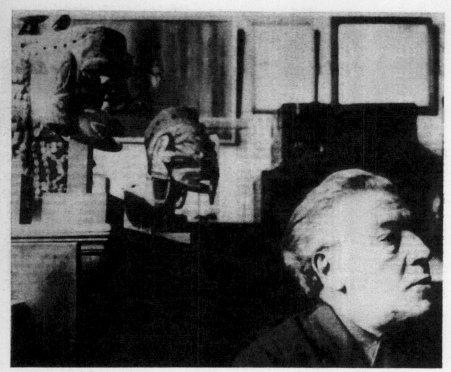

Andre Breton in his studio (masks from New Hebrides).   Photo: P. Volta.

PARIS . . .

On the Death of Andre Breton, 70

BY JEAN-JACQUES LEBEL

ANDRE BRETON died a psychosomatic death. They call it asthma. He was 70. That man was quite different from his legend, far more occult. It will take years to appraise the range of his artistic and human influence, but none, not even his worst enemies, deny that his was one of the great revolutionary minds of the century.

His failures were great too. They were mistakes of the heart. When asked in 1948 what his hopes and fears were for the future, he answered: "I believe we will soon come to the United States of the World."

Unlike those ex-surrealists who sold out to the cultural industry in exchange for power, like Aragon, or in exchange for money, like Dali, his intellectual integrity will remain for many of us (as well as for the coming generations) an everlasting source of inspiration. Along with Bataille, Joyce, Artaud, he was one of the main lighthouses of his time.

I am not capable at this point of painting a panoramic picture of his life and work. All I can say is: he was my friend for fifteen years. My vision of him is purely subjective. How could it be otherwise? The tremendous importance of his writings is itself eclipsed by the beauties of the man.

As an adolescent they had me in a reform school and very near suicide — the darkness of that "social order" was too much to endure — but his answer to an SOS letter was the most illuminating gift from a poet of his calibre to a young man. Of course, later we had our fights, mostly about revolutionary tactics, but never was the high-power current of affect interrupted between us.

As I walked around him at the hospital morgue — with most of those who, in this damn country, ever wrote, painted or did anything worthwhile — he was concentrating and didn't want to be disturbed. He was in the company of his peaceful deities, lit by the Bardo of Liberation.

The next day, he had changed. Not only had his beard grown slightly, he showed psychic pain. He had the horrors. He was burning at the stake. I kissed his forehead and fled in despair.

Saturday, before the burial, I saw him for the last time. His peaceful deities had again taken over his body. But this time he was gone.

He was buried with the postcard of the aztec crystal skull I had laid at his feet amidst the flowers. Someone later slipped the card in the chest pocket of his pyjama. He rests with his best friend, the poet Benjamin Peret, at the cimetiere des Batignolles. Along it runs the rue St. Just.

International Times hopes to live up to its title by publishing as much news of happenings in countries other than Britain as possible. To do this we need the help of people close to the "scenes" in other countries. If you have anything to report on or blast off about from your part of the world, please do send it on to us. Copy can be in any language. Photographic material would be much appreciated, handled with care and returned when used. So lets hear from you, wherever you are—Peking or Wigan.

As a member of the Underground Press Syndicate, IT will from time to time reprint from overseas, particularly American publications. If you come across any article, cartoon, explosion, that might suit us, please send it on. Anyone who would like to act as a distributor for the paper is an angel.

AMSTERDAM . . .

—PROVO SUGGESTIONS

BY SIMON VINKENOOG

DIAS — organiser Metzger invited Amsterdam provos to participate in his positive destructive purposes: I gather that he even announced their appearance. They didn't show up — for several reasons: it's like asking soldiers to come and fight a battle (but bring your own battlefields along!). Also: they are the poorest nomads in Western Europe!

The provo happenings are strictly bound to the Amsterdam environment, where authority built up the necessary provocative circumstances: cruel beatings, police hound dogs, a Royal marriage, and unwise decisions, of a Lord Mayor who lost his head (without afterwards using his mind) and a Police Commissar who became fall guy.

The great thing about provo activities is that a number of reasonable persons realise that no blame or guilt or responsibilities can be shovelled down someone's private back. A criminologist will announce that crime is a neurosis, as we all know, and the well-known novelist Harry Mulisch wrote in a three-week fit of anger and laughter a Report to the King of Rats in which he gives a detailed follow-up of events leading to the street riots of June 14 last.

There is not so much a "class struggle" as a "caste struggle" typically Dutch, he portends: the regent's mentality which gave the Dutch Establishment its public figures since the 17th Golden Century, a mentality which takes democracy in its stride and still has to learn some basic rules.

A provo happening in London would mean a number of things for which London activists have not shown enough initiative, energy and courage as yet. At least, I haven't heard of anything like the following: throw a smoke bomb at the Queen passing by, make the horses of any parade nervous by spreading their way with lion's shit, ridiculise the bowler hats, poke fun at tradition, empty the House of Lords, throw flower parties instead of tea parties, declare someone to be Imperial Wizard, Magician, have him take over the ceremonial functions, baptise slums, perform fake rituals, go with a dagger of hoaxes deep into the heart of dusty tradition, lay open the fact that most of what's being shown to English audiences is nonsense, tell to the TV audiences by visual means that the colourful, tourist-attracting by Age and Pomposity sacred traditions are Empty Meanings.

This just a friend's suggestions: we all know these things — but as soon as you give some kind of public open form to the knowledge, you create a provocative atmosphere in which there is place for some changes.

Or at least: some reappraisals by those who haven't discovered yet that the kicks within them can be ignited again into a flame bursting out into action, the kind of surrealistic (but REAL) agitation, that Breton — in liberty at last! — tried to weld together from Marx's changing society and Rimbaud's transforming man.

The actions are interlocked, man projected in the structures of the society he created himself, and within the context of evolving revolutions around to be changed by all means. Rochefort's two constitutions are very valid nowadays: One: everything must go. Two: nobody is charged to execute this law.

You cannot change anything but yourself. Hans Tuynman, who got a three months prison sentence for having distributed pamphlets (he offered two to policemen-in-uniform who purposefully took him away) invited people to individually witness a forbidden demonstration, wrote a beautiful book in jail: Full time provo.

The Dutch publisher took a part-translation along to the Frankfurt Book Fair. It served one purpose: from the fees collected by sales, the provos bought a boat in which at least fifty people can sleep. They called it Hashimin and it's still moored opposite number 25, Jacob Catskade, Amsterdam.

They needed some place, and what with the housing-shortage — one of the war-neurosis which twenty-one years of "progressive" government wasn't able to eradicate — this solution is a gift from heaven.

Tuynman's sentence which was the more offensive since at the same time a number of students got a fine (money: Mammon) for having caused the death of one of their "noble" colleagues during one of their ancient rituals (his head covered with a sack full of coal dust, he asphixiated on the way in a horse-driven carriage to the cesspit where he was going to be dumped for his "initiation" . . .).

More than a thousand artists and intellectuals put their signature to a text, published as an announcement in several newspapers, asking for a re-appraisal of JUSTICE. That's what provo is and means!

new deal in IMAGE magazine! out end this month! n.y. portfolio, usco! art and inner space! reappraisal of astrology! electron microscopy! 5s! at all doog bookstores! etc.

Think

by R. Buckminster Fuller

The author—inventor, engineer, architect, philosopher—is best known for his geodesic domes; thousands have popped up all over the earth, one of the most recent at Expo 67. Here, he offers a prophetic glimpse of the future, how man may live and travel.

Those who have had the pleasure of walking through the great skylighted arcades, such as the one in Milan, Italy, are familiar with the delights of covered city streets, in which outdoor restaurants and exhibits are practical. They can envision the effect of a domed-over city, where windows may be open the year round and gardens bloom in the dust-free atmosphere. From below, the dome would appear as a translucent film through which the sky, clouds and stars would be visible. It would not create a shut-in feeling any more than carrying a parasol above one's head on a sunny summer day.

There are other persuasive arguments in favor of domed-over cities. (It is no aesthetic accident that nature gave us no cubical heads, eggs, nuts or planets, but encased the contents in curvilinear structures.) There is, for example, no method more effective in wasting heating and cooling energy than the system employed by New York and other skyscraper cities of the world. A dome over mid-Manhattan would reduce its energy losses approximately 50-fold. Such a dome would reach from the East River to the Hudson at 42nd Street on its east-west axis, from 64th to 22nd Street on its north-south axis, and would consist of a hemisphere two miles in diameter and one mile high at its center. The cost of snow removal in the city would pay for the dome in 10 years.

Studies made at the Snow Institute of Japan and by Japan's Mitsubishi company indicate the cost of heating the surface of the dome with electric resistance wires imbedded in the skin. To maintain a temperature sufficient to melt snow and ice (with the heat turned on only during the time of snow and ice formation, for cities in the snowfall magnitude of New York) would cost

(Continued on Page 15)

23

Cybernetic Serendipity

the computer
and the arts

held at the Institute of Contemporary Arts
Nash House, The Mall, London S.W.1
August 2–October 20, 1968
Organized by Jasia Reichardt

There are three sorts of exhibits: 1, very good IBM models (with earphones) demonstrating how computers work; 2, artworks produced by machines; these include drawings, there are numerous machines (computers down to Meccano) producing curved-line patterns. More visually developed are the film cartoons (especially the one by Stan Vanderbeek). There are also poems (and Manchester University Computer does love letters: 'Honey dear ... My fellow feeling breathlessly hopes for your dear eagerness.... yours wistfully, MUC'). There are fibreglass spheres for listening to taped electronic music; there is an amazing machine by Vladimir Ussachevsky that produces visual and audial variations on tunes whistled into its mike. There are TV pictures, some reacting to sound impulses, others to forms of mechanical interference. 3, machines that are artworks in themselves; they include strobe-lit sound-vibrated metal rods; a mechanical flower that tosses when you speak to it; 7-foot radio-controlled Rosa Bosom who shrieks and swipes at people with her red foam-plastic lips, and, also by Bruce Lacey, a sex simulator (3½-minute treatment) and a photosensitive owl....

In conception and layout the exhibition is like a funfair with an arbitrary assortment of sideshows. It demonstrates that cybernetic machines are a drag in finite art situations where they merely take over a human activity (as in drawing and writing). On the other hand, where there is interaction with people and with other events, they are capable of infinite development.

Biddy Peppin IT

A computer metamorphosis. A square is transformed into a profile of a woman and then back into a square

```
jollymerry
hollyberry
jollyberry
merryholly
happyjolly
jollyjelly
jellybelly
bellymerry
hollyheppy
jollyMolly
marryJerry
hoppyBarry
heppyJarry
boppyheppy
berryjorry
jorryjolly
moppyjelly
Mollymerry
Jerryjolly
bellyboppy
jorryhoppy
hollymoppy
Barrymerry
Jarryhappy
happyboppy
boppyjolly
jollymerry
merrymerry
merrymerry
merryChris
ammerryasa
Chrismerry
asMERRYCHR
YSANTHEMUM
```

Computer's first Christmas card

Kennedy in a dog

Data from a photograph of Kennedy is inserted into data from a photograph of a dog. The final output looks like the face of Kennedy in the shape of a dog's head. Thus there are three contributing elements: Kennedy, dog and the square which forms the element of the overall pattern.
Idea by Masao Komura, programme by Fujio Niwa (CTG)

COMPUTER
Any system which operates on information to produce an output.

Computer art

A fascinating experiment was made by Michael Noll of the Bell Telephone Laboratories whereby he analysed a 1917 black-and-white, plus-and-minus picture by Mondrian and produced a number of random computer graphics using the same number of horizontal and vertical bars placed within an identical overall area. He reported that 59% of the people who were shown both the Mondrian and one of the computer versions preferred the latter, 28% identified the computer picture correctly, and 72% thought that the Mondrian was done by computer. The experiment is not involved either with proof or theory, it simply provides food for thought.

Jasia Reichardt

A 35-mm transparency is made from a photo of some real-world object and scanned by a machine similar to a television camera. The resultant electrical signals are converted into numerical representations on magnetic tape. This provides a digitized version of the picture for computer processing.

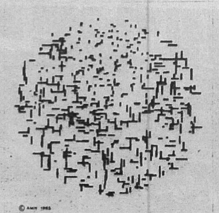

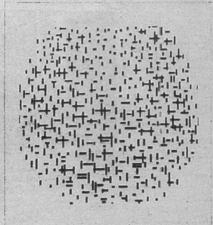

Piet Mondrian's *Composition with lines* 1917

SCOTT RUNYAN

How to be a Magician in Your Spare Time

by Deblin LeMohle

Pop Magic is, sad to say, here. It has become as inescapable as Herb Caen, and it looks as though the old guard of Occult freakdom is just going to have to tolerate all you brand-new witches who are bursting into that once exclusive sanctum of the truly weird. Many of my fellow craft-members are "right this minute, folks!" chuckling under their breath, murmuring things like "Never fear, these naive assholes will blow up their friends, freak their minds, and it will all be over in six months." I think that would be monumentally tragic. As I see it, this so-called fad is the first, and quite possibly the last, opportunity Witchcraft will have to make it for a long time. I am, therefore, in the interest of public safety, breaking the silence of centuries (WAZOO!).

LESSON 1. *Forget everything you have learned or heard about Black versus White Magic symbolism.*

Let us examine, for instance, the color Black, a shade much associated with Dracula. Black, in genuine occult circles, is symbolic of infinity of the Universe before creation. It is the *Mother* color, as all other hues are contained in it. As such it is sublimely sacred and is thus used more than any other color for the robes of the Magician. It is also the color of the planet Saturn, which in Magic contains the wild forces of the four natural Elements: Air or wind and sky; Earth, i.e., earthquakes and volcanoes; Fire, as lightning; and Water, the waves of the sea, rain, etc. You can replace Black with extremely dark Indigo Blue, which is exactly what our Northern European ancestors did.

Human blood, nakedness, and ritual highs were used for benificent purposes long before anyone thought about being a bad kid with them. Death, Sex, Birth, and Ecstacy are the elements of religion itself, and whether they are sublimated or out front, they are still there, even in Christianity. To confront some of the symbolism of Death and Birth in Magic, one could use skulls, the color Black (Death is after all union with infinity), blood, and the color Red. The blood, if it is not an animal's, is *the magician's own.* I have drawn my own blood in healing rituals many times. Human sacrifice does occur, for the magician who has taken on godhood during the spell symbolically offers his semi-devine life for that of the sick person, by spilling some of his own blood in propitiation to the universal balance, "A life for a Life." If you expect potent magic to be painless, turn back now. Obviously, killing someone else for magical purposes doesn't make it, and if you wish to be a great wizard, your ass will have to go on the line, just like the Baby Jesus said: "He who would lead must be the servant of all." To offer an animal as a sacrifice of thanksgiving is time honored, but it cannot replace the personal offering of the magician. If you need a part of an animal's body for your magical equipage, you must kill the animal yourself, and you must do so swiftly and humanely. You must also bury the remains, or eat them, as the case may be, with respect and reverence. If you believe that it is immoral to harm any living thing, an animal sacrifice is not necessary.

Ritual nakedness has been a symbol of communion with, and acceptance of, nature for a long time, indicating "I like me just as you made me." Ritual Sex has its place too, and is very holy. However, your body is not a toy, especially in a spell. If you are a female, you symbolize the Earth as the Mother, if male, the Sky as the Father; and if you conduct psuedo-magical orgies for kicks, expect to be shafted by whatever you have invoked. During orgasm we glimpse, for a few moments, where we stand as part of the Universe. Sex is therefore as much Union with God as with your partner. In the good old days the sacred and the so-called obscene

ROBERT ALTMAN

11

LIVING THEATRE

MAT PIECE

FOCUS ON THE LIGHT

let flow the life energies
    in abundant
      glow
      and
      Radiation

penetrate into the acid lucidity
  clarify the focus
  make the destination clear

PLAN THE RITUAL OF EXORCISM

dissolve into the directionless
  create the floating
  make the direction the moment
let go the static tenseness
  in sighing submission
    to the power heavy universe

let Resistance and strength
  dissolve into earth particles
the pulse Reminds us
  that we can be Reminded
    of the infinite

    the pain
    the unbearable pain
    THE SILENT SCREAM

sink under -breathe- and when the stomach is still pained
with the fear, and blood is Rushing and the pressure
mounts in the forehead — THE FULL BREATH — the
silent scream that lites up my head — THE INCANDESCENCE —
the light- focus on the light- focus on the focusing
on the light.

"Theatre is rather the crucible of fire and real
meat, where by an anatomical trampling of bone,
limbs, and syllables, bodies are renewed and the
mythical act of making a body PRESENTS ITSELF PHYSICALLY
and plainly."

"... OPERATION by which the human
body when it was RECOGNIZED as EVIL
WAS passed, transported physically
and materially, objectively
as IF MOLECULARLY
FROM ONE BODY TO
ANOTHER."

Antonin Artaud
Artaud Anthology

MALINA: The Yom Kippur service exists on a much realer and higher level in the Hassidic service where, to the Christianized eye, the service is totally disorganised. The services in the Orthodox synagogues tend to be messy events, very holy events, in which the people stand around and participate in various degrees of centralised involvement. But unlike your running out and copping a sandwich on Yom Kippur, discussion is not outside the framework and it's not considered escape or diversion. You could be arguing about some part of the service or you could be arguing about some theoretical issue. Or having discussions about

'Why does he sing the word eloheem so loud?' In 'Paradise' we make the rule that whatever we're doing — if we're sitting in the dressing rooms and smoking — especially with a member of the audience, is part of the event. Anything I say to you in the lobby is very much part of the play. If 'Paradise Now' can be said to have a direction, it is that I don't have to put on any kind of an act. I say to you exactly what I have to say to you, with possibly the one super-direction that it should be paraphysical, which doesn't always mean nice-sweet, of course. But it means that if I'm talking to you in the lobby I should have what used

to be called a super-objective, taking whatever we're talking about into the level of what Paradise is as far as I can at that moment.
BECK: It's part of that unification that pervades Judaism, the constant sanctification of all meals and the way that you treat the household. Their passionate love for being alive and making all the daily acts very holy and seeing the holiness in the way a man picks his nose or scratches his ass.
MALINA: Ultimately, it's very holy.

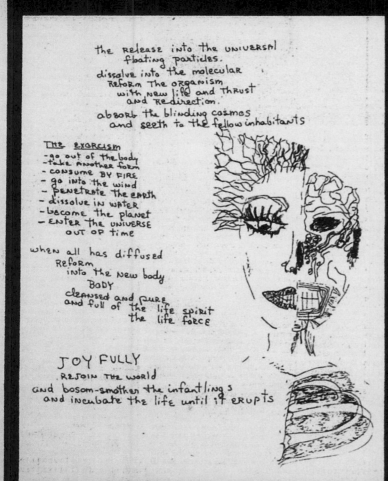

the Release into the universal
  floating particles.
dissolve into the molecular
  Reform the organism
    with new life and thrust
    and Redirection.
absorb the blinding cosmos
  and seeth to the fellow inhabitants

THE EXORCISM
- go out of the body
- take another form
- consume BY FIRE
- go into the wind
- penetrate the earth
- dissolve IN WATER
- become the planet
- ENTER THE UNIVERSE
  OUT OF TIME

when all has diffused
  Reform
    into the new body
      BODY
    cleansed and pure
    and full of the life spirit
      the life force

JOY FULLY
  RejOIN THE world
and bosom-smother the infantlings
and incubate the life until it erupts

devour the siggling forces
emanating from creation

listen to the silent laugh
of the belly

penetrate the internal
emerge the dark fantasies
pillow the soft eye and

OBSERVE.

Karen Weiss
'68-'69

PREVIOUS PAGES, LEFT: **In the summer of 1968, Other Scenes checks out the cybernetic future.**
PREVIOUS PAGES, RIGHT: **Bringing magic into everyday life.**
OPPOSITE: **it provides a forum for the Living Theatre, London, June 1969.**
ABOVE: **Actuel, Paris, 1971. Pacifism, anti-militarism and liberation of the body: a New York happening by performance artist Yayoi Kusama.**

AND THUS MAY YOU SEE RA

Poster from **The Seed**, Chicago, 1969.

Oz, London, 1970.

Actuel, Paris, 1971. The naked truth. Who's influencing whom?

ABOVE: Mel Lyman, notorious cult leader. **Avatar**, Boston, 1968.
OPPOSITE: The Diggers celebrate the death of hip. **Berkeley Barb**, October 1967.
OVERLEAF: Situationist pamphlets from Paris cross the Channel and get reprinted in **it**, 1967.

Berkeley Barb

Vol. 5 No. 12 Issue 110 (Pub Fridays) September 29-October 5
2886 Telegraph Ave., Berkeley Calif. 94705. 849-1040

15¢ BAY AREA   **20¢ ELSEWHERE**

DEATH OF HIP

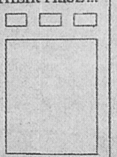

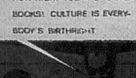

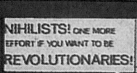

THE ORGAN

LICK THIS SPOT

SEPTEMBER, 1984   Volume I, Issue II

ERIC KROLL

TRUCKIN' TOWARD TAOS WITH TOOTSIE

by Jon Stewart

About 10 miles east of Barstow, California, is a desert town that nobody ever heard of, because nobody ever stops there. Highway 66 runs by the town, very fast. I know; I was there. Where the ramp meets the highway there is a "no pedestrians" sign on which is carved, probably by some ancestor of mine, a skull and crossbones over the words, "Death and Damnation —I have been standing here for eight days—Oh bury me not on the Lone Prairie." The attendant at the gas station near the freeway assured me that many hitchhikers were buried in that scalding sand. "You might as well become a resident," he said.

Of course, the attendant wasn't aware that I was on assignment for *The Organ*, and that being in such a position naturally engenders good karma, not to say great luck. So he was probably astonished when, after only three hours of the vicious afternoon heat, a gigantic four-ton refrigerated semi-truck pulled off onto the shoulder and the driver indicated that if I would run the half mile or so down the highway I could ride with him.

I vaulted into the seat, gasping for breath, and we were off. By the time the driver had ground through the full ten gears I'd recovered enough to ask where he was going.

"Albuquerque," he said.

"What are you carrying?" I asked, just for the hell of it.

"Two tons of Tootsie Rolls," he replied, never glancing up from the road.

You get your kicks on Route 66.

 5

1

ABOVE: After the Summer of Love, the freaks left the cities and headed out to New Mexico. **The Organ**, Berkeley, 1970.
OPPOSITE: **it**, London, 5 April 1968.

it

The International Times

NO.28   LONDON **1/6** ENGLAND   APRIL 5-18, 1968

WHY TRIBE?

We use the term "tribe" because it suggests the type of new society now emerging within the industrial nations. In America of course the word has associations with the American Indians, which we like. This subculture is in fact more similar to that ancient and guage and religion, no matter what country it may be in.

More basically the "tribe" implies a different sort of social order from that by which most people live today: based on community and comradeship, personal relations and responsibilities rather than abstract centralized govern successful tribe the European Gypsies: a group without nation or territory which maintains its own values, its language and religion, no matter what country it may be in.

In the United States and Europe the "tribe" has evolved gradually over the last fifty years—since the end of World War I—in response to the increasing insanity of the modern nations. As the number of alienated intellectuals, creative people, and general social misfits grew, they came to recognize each other by various small signals if nothing more impressive than a beard or rough clothes. The movement was much attracted to Marxism in the thirties and early forties; all the anarchists and left-deviationists were clearly tribesmen at heart. After World War II another generation looked at Marxism with a fresh eye, and saw that within Marxian political systems there are too many of the same things as are wrong with "capitalism." Too much anger and murder. The idea came: Perhaps it is the whole "western tradition", of which Marxism is but a part, that is off the track. This led many people to study other major civilizations—India and China— to see what they could learn.

It is an easy step from the dialectic of Marx and Hegel to an interest in the dialectic of the ancient Chinese yinyang theories; and early Taoism. Lao-tzu and Chuang-tzu. From Taoism it is another easy step to the philosophies

and mythologies of India—vast in scope, touching the deepest areas of human psychology, and with a view of the ultimate nature of the universe which is almost identical with the most sophisticated thought in modern physics—that truth, whatever it is, which is called "The Dharma".

Next comes a concern with deepening one's understanding in an experiential way: abstract philosophical understanding is simply not enough. At this point many, myself included, found in Buddhism a practical method for clearing one's mind of the trivia, prejudices and fallacies that lay a net on us—and more important, an approach to the basic problem of how to penetrate to the deepest non-self Self. Today we have many who are deep into the Ways of Zen, Vajrayana, Yoga, Shamanism, Psychedelics. Buddhism is a long, gentle, human dialogue—2,500 years of quiet conversation—on the nature of human nature, and the eternal Dharma. In the course of these studies it became evident that the "truth" in Buddhism and Hinduism is not dependent in any sense on Indian or Chinese society, and that "India" and "China"— as cultures— are as burdensome to human beings as any others; perhaps more so. It became evident that "Hinduism" and "Buddhism" as social institutions had long been accomplices of the State in burdening and binding people, rather than serving to liberate them. At this point looking once more quite closely at both East and West, some of us noticed the similarities in certain small but influential esoteric-mystic-semi-heretical-esoteric "inside" movements—"outside" worthodox-heretical. These schools of thought and pra

CONTINUED ON PAGE 10.

Yoga Sex : Stay High Forever.

37

ACTION

N° 14 ● JEUDI 20 JUIN ● PRIX MINIMUM : 0,50 F ● Ce journal a été réalisé au Service des Comités d'Action, avec le soutien de l'UNEF, du SNESup et des Comités d'Action Lycéens.

CITROËN ne désarme pas !

OPPOSITE: **Action**, Paris, June 1968. Industrial unrest is a real bolt from the blue.
ABOVE: The hardline tactics of the French CRS riot police make them targets themselves.

OVERLEAF, LEFT: The circus is in town, and everything's moving.
OVERLEAF, RIGHT: **Other Scenes**, New York, November 1968. Here's what we thought of Nixon, his Democrat opponent Humphrey and the corrupt governor of Alabama, George Wallace.

OTHER SCENES

VOL. 1, NO. 6   SEPTEMBER 1968   25 cents

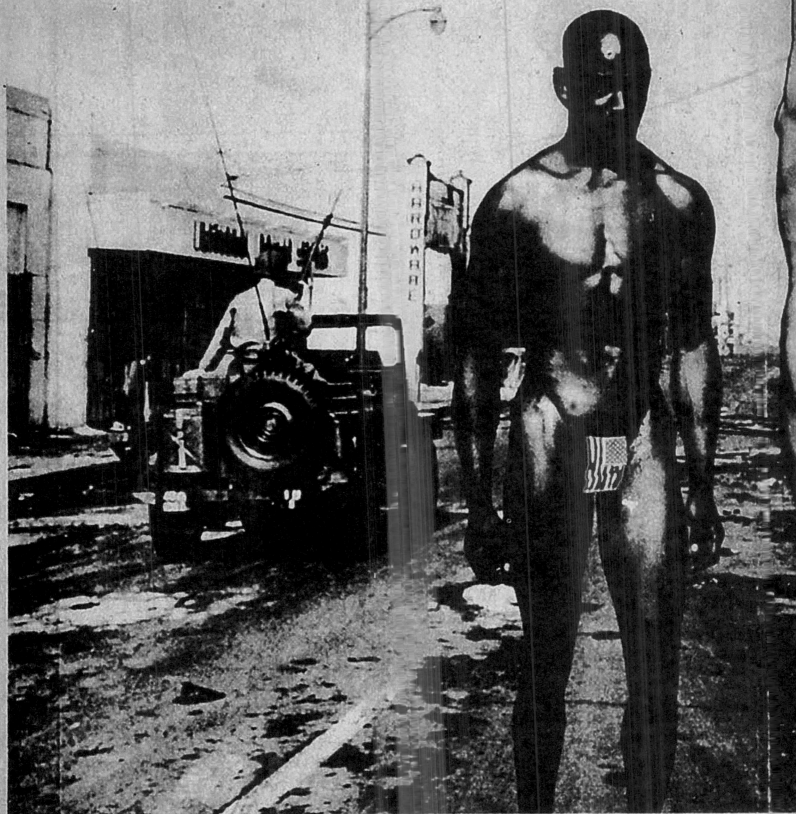

Other Scenes, New York, September 1968. Danger and desire in the ghetto: a collage by Philip Proctor.

OZ
FIRESIGN
COMBINAGES
BY
PHILIP
PROCTOR

43

"YIPPIE"
OZ

31   4/-

Brave
New
Morning

He drives a Maserati
She's a professional me
The boy is the son of th
art editor of Time mag
Some revolution!

47

NOLA Express

a product of 6 grand

BOX 2342
NEW ORLEANS, LA. 70116

July 30 – August 12, 1971.

NATIONAL DISTRIBUTOR:
J & A Distributing Co. 1133 Broadway,
Rm 506, NY NY 10010. (212) 242-4741.

NOLA Express is published every other week
at 606 Common, New Orleans LA,
by the Southern Louisiana Media Corp-
a non-profit corporation. Second Class
postage paid at New Orleans LA.
Subscriptions are $6.00 for one year.
Address all correspondence and
remittances to P.O. Box 2342,
New Orleans, LA 70116. (504) 524-6798
(c) 1971 Southern La Media Corp

NOLA Express is available on microfilm
of the Underground Press Package from
Micro Photo Division, Bell & Howell,
Mansfield Rd., Wooster, Ohio 44
Box 26, NY NY 1

Freak out!

FIRST SLOGAN OF
THE FREE PRESS

FIRST SLOGAN OF
THE FREE PRESS

Turn on, tune in, drop out
Get naked, get out there, go crazy
Find a guru and blow your mind
Magic wands and magic mushrooms
You're never too far from a joint

A NEWSPAPER OF DETROIT

15¢

20¢ Outside Detroit

"The path of Love is the right royal road that leads to the abode of immortality and eternal bliss — Parama, Dharma, where time cannot exercise its destructive power, where Maya cannot show her face. It is the clear and open way to God.

There is no virtue higher than Love; there is no treasure higher than Love; there is no knowledge higher than Love; there is no Dharma higher than Love; there is no religion higher than Love. Because Love is truth. Love is God.

This world has come out of Love, this world exists in Love and this world ultimately dissolves in Love. God is an embodiment of Love. In every inch of His creation you can verily understand his Love. Live in Love. Breathe in Love. Sing in Love. Eat in Love, Drink in Love. Talk in Love. Pray in Love. Meditate in Love. Think in Love. Move in Love. Die in Love. Purify your thoughts, speech and action in the fire of Love. Bathe and plunge in the sacred ocean of Love. Imbibe the honey of Love and become an embodiment of Love."

Yogirag Sri Swami Satchidananda

actuel

SPECIAL LE TOUR DU POP
LES SILENCES DE DYLAN·UN POEME
BLACK PANTHERS PARTY
JOURNAL D'UNE COMMUNAUTE

N°13/3.50 F/40 FB

OPPOSITE: Love is God and God is love on the cover of **Fifth Estate**, Detroit.
ABOVE: **Actuel** gets switched on, June 1970, issue 13.

Berkeley Barb

20¢ ELSEWHERE   Vol-5 No. 21 Issue 119 (Pub. Fridays) November 24—2856 Telegraph Ave., Berkeley, Calif. 94705 849-1040   15¢ BAYAREA

GANDALF GROOVES

OTHER SCENES

NEW YORK CITY   Vol. 3 No. 14   UPS   25 cents

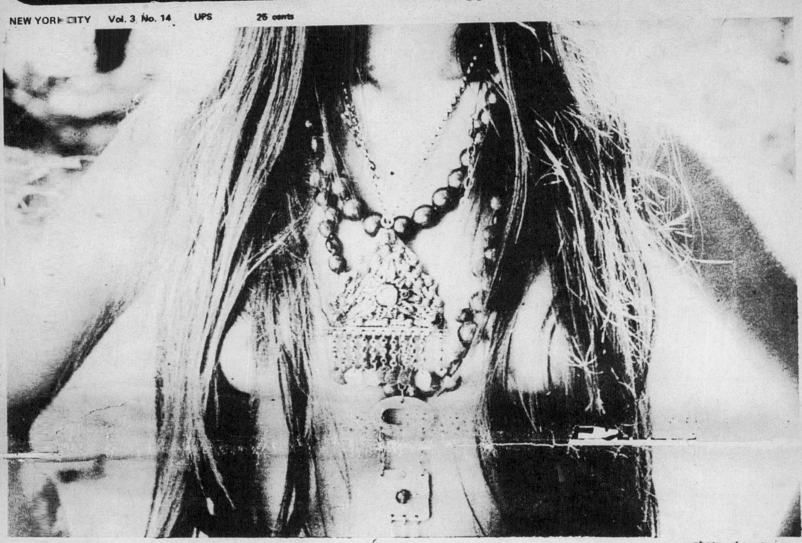

photo Luis Vairla

55

At the beginning of anything, there is a certain lust to creation, that's how we got started, it's why Eve ate the Apple so eagerly. She ate everything eagerly. When music -- our music: spontaneous, ballsy, rock--began, there was that kind of lust and joy in its creation, even the quiet creations. Now music has become a little more sophisticated, mainly institutionalized, like trilobites (and with equal guesses as the the First Cause. Music criticism, now that it's an Art we are discussing, is the same frowzy, cluttered party conversation poop as the others. The critic gives a fast rundown of quotables: "blend of jazz and baroque pop cascading down like a do-right waterfall", etc, followed by the real meat, the anecdote, letting you know that the writer is this tight with the musician(s). This is because everyone who owned a transistor radio when "Naughty Lady of Shady Lane" (Rock Around the Clock, Ricochet Romance, even Chantilly Lace) first blared, is now a music expert, thanks to years of long exposure. Writers, therefore, have to prove their greater, closer identification with the music. (Pass the mustard, will ya...?)

Jean Louis Barrault said (in Cue) the most important quality of life is "to be a virgin every morning. To kill (your) self each night and to be reborn again each morning." To take joy and grow

FILM-ELF

Too many people have forgotten the joy of living and are content with the word of others.

This is not a cinematic landmark; scene piled upon scene does not create a fine necklace or tapestry, the overall is too uneven. Still the movie is extraordinarily powerful in its effort to communicate the richness of that century some of the battle glory and the violence, pristine private moments. The battle scenes are wonderful, as is all of the photography on location in Ireland. Those scenes set around the main story are also, perhaps because of lack of tension, quite compelling, as when Alfred realizes that many 'outlaws' are more just than his nobles. There are moments of skill and technical sophistication, which prevent this movie from being just another epic; it's an epic with subtlety.

John Vaccaro and The Playhouse of the Ridiculous are much fun, but fun with the necessary complement of professional goodness (what does it mean...?) The latest production is Heaven Grand in Amber Orbit by Jackie Curtis, which phrase alliterates beautifully; is a short poetic statement unto itself, being equally reminiscent of Heaven Grand-ness, the lustrous beauty and value of Amber and as modern as space age Orbit. If that seems far-fetched:

1. You haven't seen the play.
2. It is.

The beauty of Theatre of the Ridiculous, as a whole, is the non-consequentiality of stage action; this is the major non-linear theatre created in America. Unlike the more serious Living Theatre, Grotowski (who is in New York at BROOKLYN ACADEMY OF MUSIC) or Joan Littlewood's troupe, T. of R. has values quite different, not concerned with affecting change in the audience against their conscious will so much as it desires to amuse--with reservations. This funny theatre's essential menace derives from its very freedom, a concept which has taken modern theatre down a strange trail. There is foreboding to a theatre which says, "laugh--if you know when and at what. Remember, we will be the judge. All of Us." Emphasis is on costume, makeup, and embroidery of theatre. Characters are fantastic and confusing as possible, even multi-sourced. One basically male (you can tell by the distribution of muscle) will utilize 40 well known one-liners from different stag and screen actresses, plus gestures, in order to (re) create a character role. The characters are fantastic because they are based on the marvelous, perfectly paced insane reality of the people who are the theatre.

It is impossible to mention each person who helps to make this play so outstanding (and it is, especially when you look at the competition). Major roles are played by Frank Dudley, Ruby Lynn Reyner, Jaime de Carlo Lotts, Morris Chevrolet, John Harry Christian and John Vaccaro. The play is at the Gotham Art Theatre, 455 West 43rd, Thurs-Sun. at 9 PM, call 581-5011 for reservations.

JOHN SINCLAIR IS STILL IN JAIL.
John loves music as he love life; he is not a symbol of the recurrent phenomenon, 'fuck the system and it will fuck you,' he is John Sinclair, very much a man and very much a man and very much in jail. Denied right to appeal, denied right to bond, denied but in no way negated. Please, start talking and give to the defense fund:
There is no way to criticize the action taken against him, there is only action to be taken.
lesser wrongs are only lesser in magnitude, not quality. Alfred the Great is a movie whose substance is too great for the

supporting structure, and director Clive Donner has been able to find the center of this... The film attempts to create an Alfred torn by his greatest passions; either to be a priest and serve God or to unite England and save his people, the country. David Hemmings as Alfred gives a curious performance, finicky at some moments, overwhelming in others. Michael York plays the Viking warrior who is his opposite in every way, lusty and unashamed of it; proud of his warrior god who is the god of life, linking men with animals, or whatever he roars in the mead hall. Alfred's queen, is so much in love with him that she comes to love him for spurning her. She never really understands his fear of his own nature.

Another play by Tom Murrin, whose Cock-Strong was performed by P or the R, Myth (or maybe Meth). This time directed by La Mama's Ed Setrakian at The Lot Theatre, Bleecker. Murrin pits words, endless streams, against dissimilar, baffling counterpoint actions, the play seeming a dream sequence in which each character tries to interact with the others: sometimes called reality. A man, an innocent stranger, Kenney, comes upon a strange family of a slightly fanatic Latin Military type, Pa; three daughters who are like the whiter shade of pale and beyond; and a general frenzied outsider, rather maniacal boyfriend, Corporal Goodhart. Mari-Claire Charba as the older, worn too smart to be idealistic sister, her usual professional self, giving the part a subtlety it needs; Gloria James as the black sister who wants to go to Haiti also uses her role quite well.

Much talk, on various levels, people trying to talk to with one another, tell of fears and pasts, hopes and nightmares, sprinkled with dialogue which is just too obtuse, too far away from whatever themes are even tenuously established: "Let there be light, and there was music" was not at all helpful as lines go, Setrakian's direction was especially good in the second act, when much of the play.s mood was established, allowing the actors to use the structure as set up. (Continued on Page 17)

OZ talks to DR G — the only groupie with a Ph.D in captivity.

Why the Press Council is a dangerous hoax.

Why Portugal — the poorest country in Europe — has a defence budget second only to the United States.

What the man who discovered that cannabis is non addictive said to Caroline Coon.

Millions are starving...Millions of pounds worth of food is dumped each year. Why?

You've never seen Ophelia looking like Marianne Faithful looking like this.

Led Zeppelin...Murray Roman...Everly Brothers...The Incredible String Band ...Two Virgins...BOB DYLAN

For those who find OZ hard to read this issue is the next best thing to braille.

OZ
19 3s

USA 60c.
DENMARK 3Kr.
HOLLAND 2G.
GERMANY 1.8 DM.

VIVIAN
BONZO DOG BAND

OPPOSITE: A hardcore view of the art scene from **EVO**, New York, October 1969.
ABOVE: **Oz**, London, March 1969. Germaine Greer catches Vivian Stanshall on the fly.

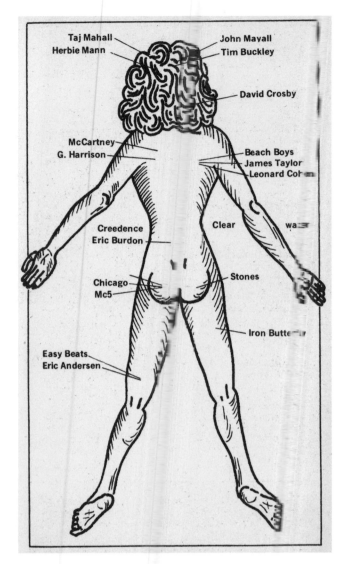

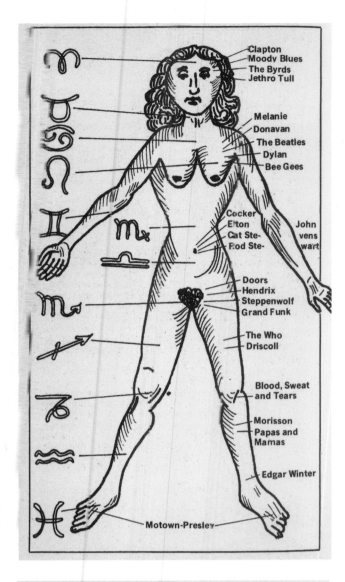

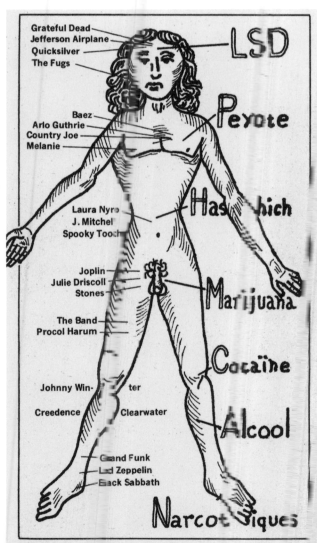

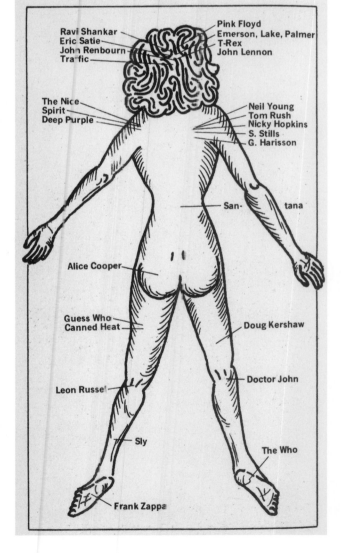

ABOVE: **Mainmise**, Montreal, 1970. A tarot that
maps out some little-known erogenous zones.
OPPOSITE: The cover of **EVO** is a bullet to the brain
for traditional values.

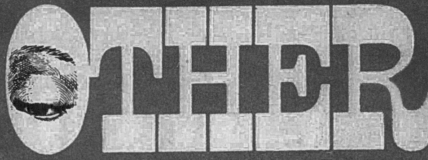

TRASHMAN INSIDE

THE east village OTHER

VOL. 6   NO. 6   JAN. 5, 1971   25¢ N.Y.C. 35¢ OUTSIDE

CELEBRATING THE DECLINE OF TRADITIONAL VALUES

ABCVE: **Parapluie** Paris, 1970. **Actuel**'s more glamorous cousin.
OPПOSITE: **Mainmise**, Montreal, 1971. A dead ringer for David Bowie.

grand bazard freak où tu
des vêtements plein de couleu
et de fantaisie
On est ouvert de 13H. à 20H.
CROCHE

WANTED

HIP COPS

We know it's a heavy trip, but there are more than 30 vacancies on the Berkeley Police force. If hip people do not apply and go on to fill those vacancies, we'll get more of the same old stuff and have the same old hassles! Put yourself on the line—and get some change for it, too. **Starting pay for Berkeley officers is $782 per month.**

We want PEACEmen, not POLICEmen
If you are one;
If you love children and other growing things;
If you do not like the use of force when gentleness will work;
If you will defend justice for all, regardless of race, appearance or politics;
If you believe that all people should be free to live their own lives if they do not harm others;
If you value people for themselves, not for their money or dress—
THEN WE NEED YOU TO REMOLD "THE MAN" AND HIS JOB.

MINIMUM REQUIREMENTS—Applicants must:
1. Be between 20 and 29 years old.
2. Have completed two years of college.
3. Be 5'-8" or taller and of proportionate weight.
4. Have a valid driver's license.
5. Be in good health and physical condition.
6. Have at least 20/70 correctable or 20/30 eyesight.
You must also be willing to undergo a medical examination, take a loyalty oath and have a background check. You must be a United States citizen but need not live in Berkeley.

TO MAKE APPLICATION— Write to: Berkeley Police Department, Personnel Dept., 2100 Grove Street, Berkeley
Call: 841-0200
Recruiting information is available free from the Berkeley Police Department.

IF YOU APPLY—If you are hip (black, white, red, yellow or brown) and decide to apply, please notify the BBC or the Berkeley branch of the ACLU. We want to be sure that you are hired without prejudice as to your appearance, race, or background. BBC Patrol can be reached at 526-6370. ACLU can be reached at 548-0921, or at 1919 Berkeley Way.

Published as a public service by The Better Berkeley Council, 1534 Grove Street, Berkeley

OPPOSITE: **Parody ad from the US, 1968.**
ABOVE: **A San Francisco small ad from 1970. The clean-cut look can work wonders.**

ABOVE: **A waterbed for all the family, 1970.**
OPPOSITE: **Mainmise**, Montreal, 1972. A map to show you where it's at.
OVERLEAF: **Actuel**, Paris, October 1970: Jimi Hendrix, Jérôme Savary,
Michel Le Bris, John Cage.

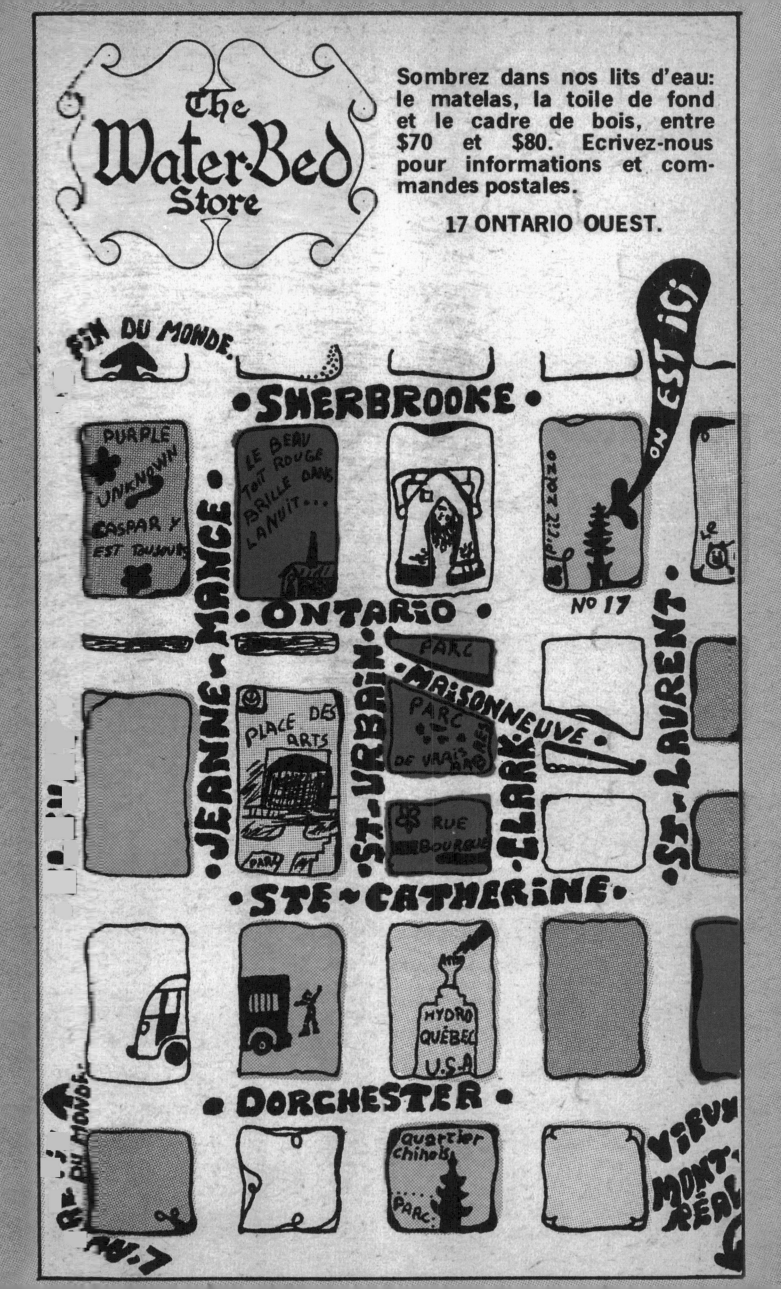

allez en Cage

Pour toutes les oreilles ouvertes sur le monde, avis : il y aura à entendre, à voir, à vivre.

Il est temps de découvrir les œuvres de Sylvano Bussoti, un Italien férbile et théâtral. A ne pas manquer : un film mis en scène et en musique par Bussotti (22 octobre — 14 h 30 — Musée d'Art Moderno).

Aussi, une rétrospective complète sur bande de l'œuvre de Luis Pablo, œuvres électro-acoustiques et instrumentales. Une sorte de défense et illustration de la conscience déchirée de la musique nouvelle. Surtout John Cage, le pionnier de la musique visuelle, aléatoire, et du happening aux Etats-Unis. Le versant extraverti de l'expression musicale. Musique éclatée. Pouvoir du son. Les bruits imprévisibles, la rue, le dehors.

Musique ouverte. L'humour, la subversion, la bonne humeur, la sensibilité jouent ensemble. La représentation visuelle

D.R.

ou son est inséparable de l'audition. Pour les song books — création mondiale — 90 petits solos. Les interprètes Cathy Berberian et Simone Rist disposent d'un tas d'accessoires : cabines en bois pour changer de robe sur scène, en gardant la tête à l'air, trappes pour descendre, suspensoirs pour s'élever, machines à écrire, verres de cognac, etc...

Grâce à Cage, après le *Roland Furieux*, c'est *Musicircus* (mardi 27 octobre de 18 h 30 à 23 h). Pour cette fête qui fait revivre les Halles : un quatuor, un pianiste, un orchestre d'enfants, un groupe folklorique, un gymnaste, des lutteurs, des phoques savants, un chœur d'église, du jazz, de la pop-musique, une chanteuse des rues, un accordéoniste aveugle, des personnages de cirque.

F.S.

(1) Théâtre de la Ville, Musée d'Art Moderne de la Ville de Paris, Cinémathèque française (Chaillot).

LIBÉREZ LEBRIS

François Tusques, accompagné de Bernard Vitet, Jouck Minor, Beb Guerin et François Tusques, a donné un concert le mercredi 3 septembre dans le cadre des *Féeries des Tuileries*. Pendant trente minutes, Tusques et ses musiciens ont joué devant une assistance nombreuse un morceau intitulé « Libérez Michel Lebris ». Ces soirées « dites de variétés » sont enregistrées par l'O.R.T.F. D'autre part, François Tusques doit sortir un disque produit par Gérard Terrones : « La révolution est une transfusion sanguine, voilà la mer, voilà la vie... ».

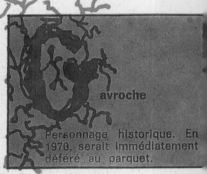

John Sinclair, le leader Yippie, fête son premier anniversaire d'incarcération : il avait été condamné en 1968 à dix ans de prison pour « possession de stupéfiants » — deux joints dans sa poche. Il est enchanté : « La prison, c'est ce qui m'est arrivé de mieux : j'ai le temps d'étudier, de lire, de penser. C'est terrifiant quand on est libre mais en fait, c'est moins terrifiant que l'usine. Au moins, on ne peut pas, en prison, vous empêcher de penser. »

Gavroche
Personnage historique. En 1970, serait immédiatement déféré au parquet.

Le droit à la paresse
La France détient le triste record de la durée du travail. Selon un rapport de l'I.N.S.E., elle diminue dans tous les pays d'Europe. En Norvège, déjà le palier des 40 heures est franchi. En France la durée hebdomadaire du travail était en 1968, plus longue que celle de 1955 : 46 heures. Elle a un peu baissé depuis : 44 heures depuis le 1er avril 1970. A quand les 30 heures ?

oi
A exception de ceux qui la modifient, nul n'est censé être à l'abri de la loi.

Le département de la Justice de Washington vient de publier un rapport sur le quotient intellectuel des agents de la force publique. Conclusion : les policiers américains sont de moins en moins intelligents.
En 1962, leur Q.I. dépassait la moyenne nationale, avec une cote de 107,7. Aujourd'hui, à l'aurore des belles années 1970, le Q.I. s'est effondré en dessous des 100 : 93,19 seulement.

éfiance
Devenue une vertu nationale, elle permet aux maîtres-nageurs, aux appariteurs musclés et au ministre de l'Education nationale de confondre Voltaire avec Nanterre, les cheveux longs avec les délinquants, la jeunesse avec une menace.

La mort de l'individu
Pour les rebelles, les insoumis, les asociaux, les hippies, une nouvelle invention à leur intention. Une drogue qui rend docile et sociable est expérimentée dans les prisons américaines. Les volontaires reçoivent une injection d'anectine qui paralyse leur volonté soixante secondes. Le sujet éprouve une violente sensation d'étouffement et de profonds sentiments d'horreur et de terreur qui lui donnent l'impression d'un long cauchemar. Les experts pensent qu'un traitement à l'anectine vaut bien une longue peine de prison.

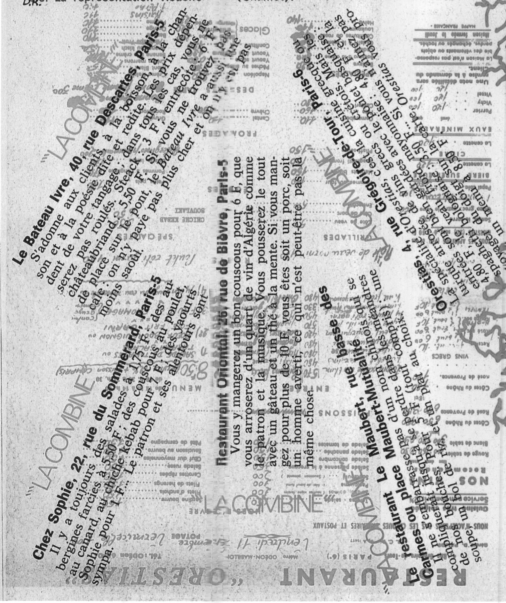

(JÉRÔME) (PARENTHÈSE)

Jérôme Savary et son grand Magic Circus sont une parenthèse, une restriction mentale dans la tête des critiques français. Savary est le type qui a fait l'an dernier au Théâtre de Plaisance — encore un truc qui n'existe pas — le bide le plus flasque avec le spectacle le plus fracassant. Notre critique nationale n'aime pas Savary pour un tas de raisons qui mettent en jeu un tas de choses. Les structurs de la Kultur entre autres. Donc Savary, matière extrêmement volatile, ne « prend » pas sur le sol français et s'évapore tout de suite. On le retrouve à Francfort, à Londres, à l'Université de Brandeis (U.S.A.), ou bien à Toronto où le Grand Magic Circus vient de produire ses « tableaux vivants sur le thème du colonialisme ». En France on devine parfois Savary dans la salle enfumée d'un bal de province en train de jouer de la trompette, dans la poussière d'une kermesse jouant du tambour, ou dans la pénombre d'une soirée gaie chez un éditeur de la rive gauche préparant un feu d'artifice. Vous le sentirez peut-être aussi passer dans le film de Pierre Barouh intitulé Ça va, ça vient, ce qui convient parfaitement à un courant d'air.

A peine rentrés de leur tournée dans les pays de l'Est, trois des membres du Blood, Sweat & Tears invités à Paris par R.T.L. fin septembre, ont déclaré lors d'une conférence de presse : « La propagande anti - communiste américaine correspond très bien à la réalité stalinienne ».

abac (passer à)
Opération de simple routine accompagnant la lecture de vos papiers d'identité dans une maison faite tout exprès (à suivre n° 2).

Jimmy Hendrix **expire**
Jimmy Hendrix **ils vont te bouffer**
Jimmy Hendrix **ils n'aiment pas**
                  seulement le fric
Jimmy Hendrix **ils aiment le sang**
Jimmy Hendrix **encore tout frais**
Jimmy Hendrix **ils vont t'exposer**
Jimmy Hendrix **à l'analyse**
Jimmy Hendrix **idéologique**
Jimmy Hendrix **ils disent**
Jimmy Hendrix **mort de drogue**
Jimmy Hendrix **ils crèvent aussi**
                  ils sont malades
Jimmy Hendrix **on va les achever**
Jimmy Hendrix **on se lève**
Jimmy Hendrix **on te porte vivant**
Jimmy Hendrix **germe**
Jimmy Hendrix **ton sperme**
Jimmy Hendrix **éjacule**
Jimmy Hendrix **tu as trouvé**
                  un réceptacle
          La veuve joyeuse

Horace

Jimi Hendrix est mort le 18 septembre 1970. Je l'avais rencontré il y a quelques mois, dans un cabaret de Londres, à l'aube. Ses impresarios l'appelaient « l'homme de l'an deux mille ». Sa poésie m'a ébloui.

Il parlait : « La guitare est une arme pour changer les esprits. Je ne suis pas un politicien : je lutte avec ma musique. Nous vivons une sorte de Renaissance, une Renaissance menacée par la violence, la répression, la bombe H. La guitare est l'arme du moment, l'arme de l'homme libre. Ma musique, c'est ma façon de dresser des barricades. »

Et la drogue ?

« Ce n'est pas un but en soi, mais un moyen d'aller vers l'Inconnu — plus loin encore — pour trouver des sons nouveaux. J'entends parfois ces sons. Lorsque je casse mes guitares et mes amplificateurs sur scène, ce n'est pas par goût de la violence, mais par désespoir : je n'arrive pas à reproduire cette musique. J'utilise la drogue pour faire un trou dans le mur. Tous les moyens sont bons pour créer l'homme demain. La génération qui nous succédera n'aura peut-être plus besoin de drogue : tant mieux — je ne conseille ces voyages à personne. »

Vous parlez d'expérience dangereuse...

« Je suis l'un de ceux qui vont à l'avant-garde pour explorer le danger, une sorte de boy-scout. Je sais les périls que je cours, je sais que je peux mourir pendant ma mission. Je sais aussi qu'il y a des gens derrière. Mais j'ai vécu de nombreuses expériences : cela me donne le droit de prendre des risques. Il ne s'agit pas simplement de la drogue. Lorsque je me rends aux Etats-Unis, on me regarde encore de travers, on cherche parfois à provoquer un incident : je suis un homme de couleur. »

Pourquoi cette violence dans votre musique ?

« Quand on est frustré, on joue fort, trop fort. Si l'on joue normalement, les gens n'écoutent ni les paroles, ni la musique. Et la musique pop doit rendre conscience aux gens, les transformer. Elle trouve un public qui ne prêterait pas attention à des chansons ordinaires. Le temps de la mesure et du cœur viendra plus tard. Il faut heurter l'ordre établi. Et pourtant, la violence ne suffit pas. Je travaille avec les non-violents, d'autres font des barricades. Ma violence sur scène veut servir l'amour. Quand les hommes rentrent chez eux au sortir du concert, ils n'ont pas besoin de battre leur femme : ils font l'amour. »

Pensez-vous que la jeunesse va créer un monde nouveau ?

« Etre jeune, c'est être mécontent. Le monde du pop ne cherche pas le pouvoir politique, mais le vrai pouvoir, celui du cœur, de l'esprit, de la prise de conscience de l'homme, toutes races et couleurs mêlées. Ce sont les jeunes qui ont les premiers le droit à la parole : ils sont plus purs, ils indiquent un chemin. Nos disques et nos groupes ne représentent que des véhicules.

Il faut aller du négatif au positif : nous parlons de l'homme de demain. Aujourd'hui, nous ne sommes que ces gitans. L'avenir : qui sait ? Nous aurons le pouvoir. Ça prendra peut-être mille ans. Je m'en fiche : j'ai le temps. »

ACTUEL
60 RUE DE RICHELIEU
PARIS 2E, FRANCE

OPPOSITE: Qu*** re cover art from **Nola Express**, New Orleans, 1971.
ABOVE: In In***, **Baba** means 'sage' or 'spiritual father'.
OVERLEAF, LEFT: **Mainmise**, Montreal, 1971. A recipe for eternal youth.
OVERLEAF, RIGHT: **Actuel**, Paris, 1973. The fast track to enlightenment.

Prenez trois livres de cinabres véritable, une livre de miel blanc et une poignée de graines de chanvre indien. Séchez cette mixture au soleil et rôtissez-la sur le feu en y ajoutant de l'eau jusqu'à ce qu'elle soit de la consistance voulue pour pouvoir être roulée en petites pillules. Prenez dix pillules chaque matin; en moins d'un an vos cheveux blancs redeviendront noirs, vos dents abimées repousseront et votre corps redeviendra souple.

Celui qui prendra de cette mixture d'une façon constante se réjouira dans la bénédiction éternelle; sa vie sera faite de beauté et il ne mourra jamais.

Attribué à Confusius.

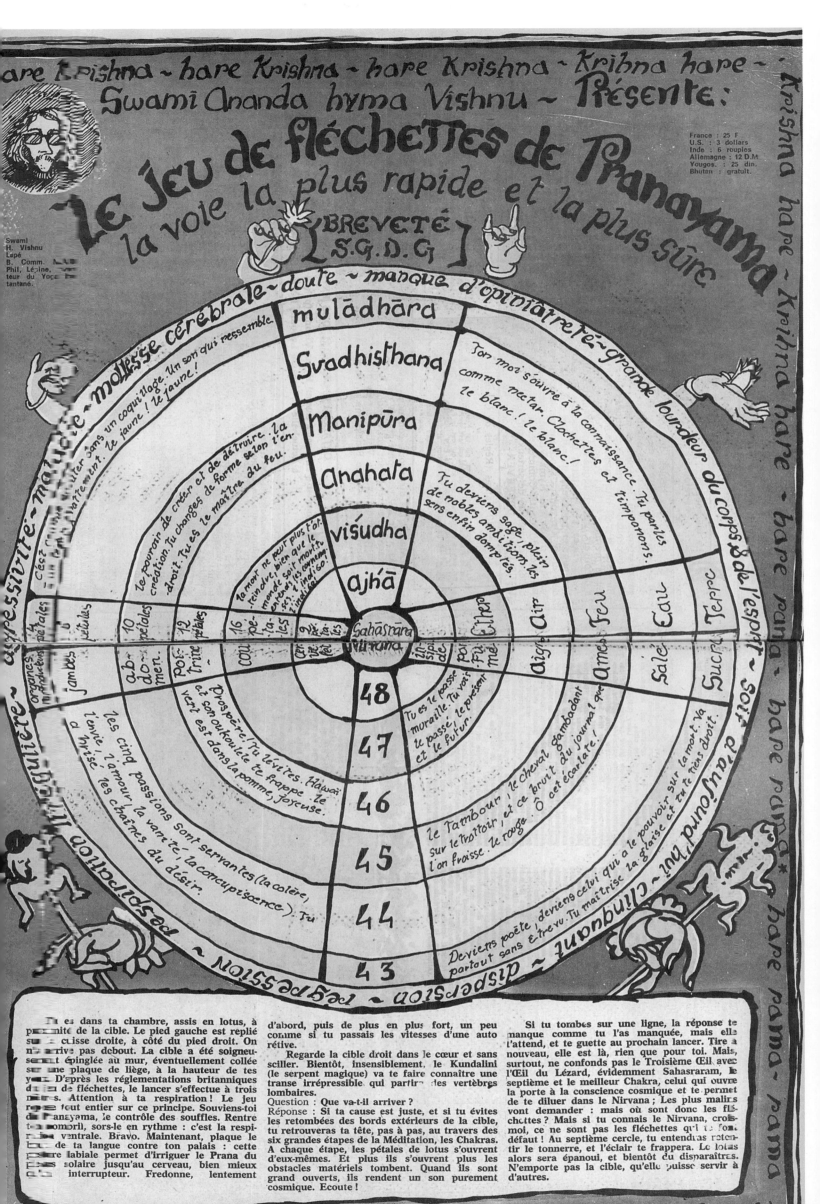

THE SERP

In the last thirty years the East has been seeking out the West and vice versa. Indian culture has been exposing its wares, disciplines, music, religions and philosophies to American curiosity. And in turn, America has been exposing itself, its material wealth and meaningless advanced technology.

Pacifism by Gandhi, meditation by Mahareshi, and music by Shankar have now solidly entrenched themselves in young America's vocabulary as well as militarism by Johnson, activism by Westmoreland, and music by the United States Marine Corps Band.

But recently some Americans, really, breaking through the secondary, illusion of media pablum to the bubble gum mentality of the all-pervasive American consumer consciousness, have begun to join and embrace the psychic cure-all of these ancient traditional Indian beliefs and disciplines hold.

Freud, Jung and Kundalini... has become a new battlecry for a new generation of evolving americans. If we include, as we must, Buddhism, which has its roots in India, we have it all, the great sweep of practically all that... has learned about where he really lives — his inner self. And even if American had learned across her fat belly, and then touched the navel of Buddha, Americans have been easternizing; uncoiling "the serpent power" of their own individual consciousness.

Some Americans, and more every day, have been taking the psychic cure, the "inner trip" to a...ment. And one man who has been actively at work to see that the meeting takes place at the highest possible level, where East is no longer east, nor West West, is a thirty two year old "psychic therapist" from Bombay, India by the name of Shyam Bhatnagar.

Shyam's life is not unusual to a westerner but for a Hindu and an Indian, it is thoroughly... Born of fairly well-off western-... parents, he received a... in philosophy from the University, Bombay. He came to the United States about eight years ago and ...ned up his own Indian ex...t business. He accumulated wealth but ...t it he also accumulated ...m and guilt and a bad stomach which ...tern societies are natural...ve... A few years later, he decided ...ive it all up and went... India to seek out his spiritual guide ...teacher since the age of ... Babaji, a "guru" reputedly re...ted to be 178 years old... lived in one of the many valleys ...the Himalya mountains. ... Shyam found him, and the... his own self; all the wisdom of ... and the reality of the... In 1966 he established his first ...Development Institute, the Shyam Shivam Sundaram (Truth-...ity-Good) Institution, at... Second Avenue in New York as well ...in Bareilly, India, along with... teacher of philosophy, a man named ...ch. He decided to sta...himself in America, seeking out the ...who needed him and to ...his services, at first free and later ...reasonable price.

...ough he has ultimately...ned his program at children, all Shyam's ...dents — 22 in New York City, 20 in urban New Jersey and six in ...Ohio — are adults 20... 40.

"... I had to sum up the Insti...ion's purpose," Shyam has said, "it ... expose the intelligence of the West to a higher level of awareness ...ugh natural means. There is... tremendous potential in this country ...self-fulfilling disciplines.

...ery culture that has ever achieved material satisfaction has fallen

into very high philosophies ...into a great deal of pervers... ...over and the culture has di... "My basic aim is to prev... victims of deterioration."

New Shyam has managed ...tion have been through the ...India. As he has stated it si... the movement of the sun... sible. Most of all it would re... of safe storage, we eat food... if we didn't have these stor... has created a strain on our...

Discipline involves the si... that food, we shouldn't be. Y... techniques were written dow... by a man named Charak, th... He wrote a huge epic on the...

As far as the macrobioti... for monks who are living... in New York City unless... live on it.

Shyam has also gone on to... foods and the fact that, "the... which in present society is a...

"Natural foods are not of... create off balance...wards... to us in the industrial age... taboos on executing this en... ...ie...sexual activity of a 12... ...suppressed. It is why peo... harmful to the genitals espe...

One of the most all-inclu... Shyam has used as an all-ar... Yoga exercises as Shyam ha... lies at the bottom of the sp... cipline, and exercises."

"In the West it is called... that lies dormant in everyth... the spine. Once this serpe... cere-brum, one attains a sta... consciousness. But one must ...centers of consciousness tha... rise through)

"The first chakra is the... vival and is situated at the... the genitals at the point wh... to be satisfied before the s... Svadhishtana or procreation... center of procreation. Both ... gravitational chakras and, o... The third chakra is the... gravitational chakras and, o... The 4th, 5th, and 6th... heart chakra. The Visuddha

NT POWER

by Allan Katzman

...located between the two eyebrows near the pineal gland.

Kundalini Yoga exercises give an exercise to every tissue of your body for every center of consciousness gives natural balance and natural expansion to the tissues which in turn become more sensitive and strong. This reflects on all our diseases and on account of the natural diets, natural body movement tunes into the cosmic intelligence and awaits the natural elimination rather than take laxatives, drugs, or masturbate while looking at a naked woman's poster in Playboy.

Swami has counselled his patients, or as he refers to them, "students, that "it is a pleasure to work with your own body but one must remember that no one single group of people can be tuned into a group of exercises in general. Only by a serious one can they be exposed to their energy levels."

This is the part of his teachings that Swami has referred to as psychic therapy, as he has explained it, "I work with the mischannelized psychic energy of the individual which causes psychosomatic ailments. After measuring the moon and the sun through sympathetic and parasympathetic nervous systems, I determine the energy level of the student and prescribe exercises and mantric disciplines. I do not ask personal questions other than medical. In turn I make people aware of their psychological ailments and which chakra or center of consciousness, its energy is blocked or I play mantras appropriate for each chakra and by playing I activate the chakra and by feeling the sun and moon fluids in the pulse I determine the tension. To most of my students surprise, they identify with my diagnosis and cure. If it were my choice though, I would only work with children, as we started out in our institution in New Harry, New Jersey and Akron, Ohio. I wish there could be more institutions to help children in various parts of the world. Contemporary or apple education, which is objective knowledge, is not sufficient enough to live life by. I believe this is the main cause of our individual, social, national and international tensions. In short, tuning into one's body and the various levels of consciousness is the prime aim of our work."

This then has been the state of the soul in America circa 1968 and the possible cure held out to American "serpent power" known as Kundalini Yog.

Young people have been rising up their only way to survive in the world of the future. They have been going back to plug in and tap the Cosmic energy that lies dormant in everything, especially themselves, and by harnessing it, witness the fields they have been seeking the youngest instinct of consciousness, the oldest law of nature: what Darwin saw as Evolution, what Marx proposed as the "Classless State," what scientists have termed the "Secrets of the Universe," what Christ prophesied as The Kingdom of Heaven, what mystics long ago referred to as "Godhead."

It has all been the same trip, and this movement towards man's own many-leveled facets of energy, or what God made in his own image, has been nothing new in the world. In the case of Americans, it has been a natural consequence of every culture that has ever achieved material satisfaction and success for some and not for all. In the case of Mankind, it has been the oldest battle of all, of one between matter and spirit but with one exception and the one that ancient cultures have always understood and now hold out to us: "We are all One and One is all."

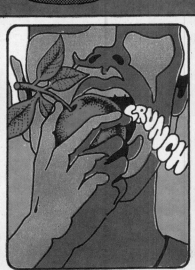

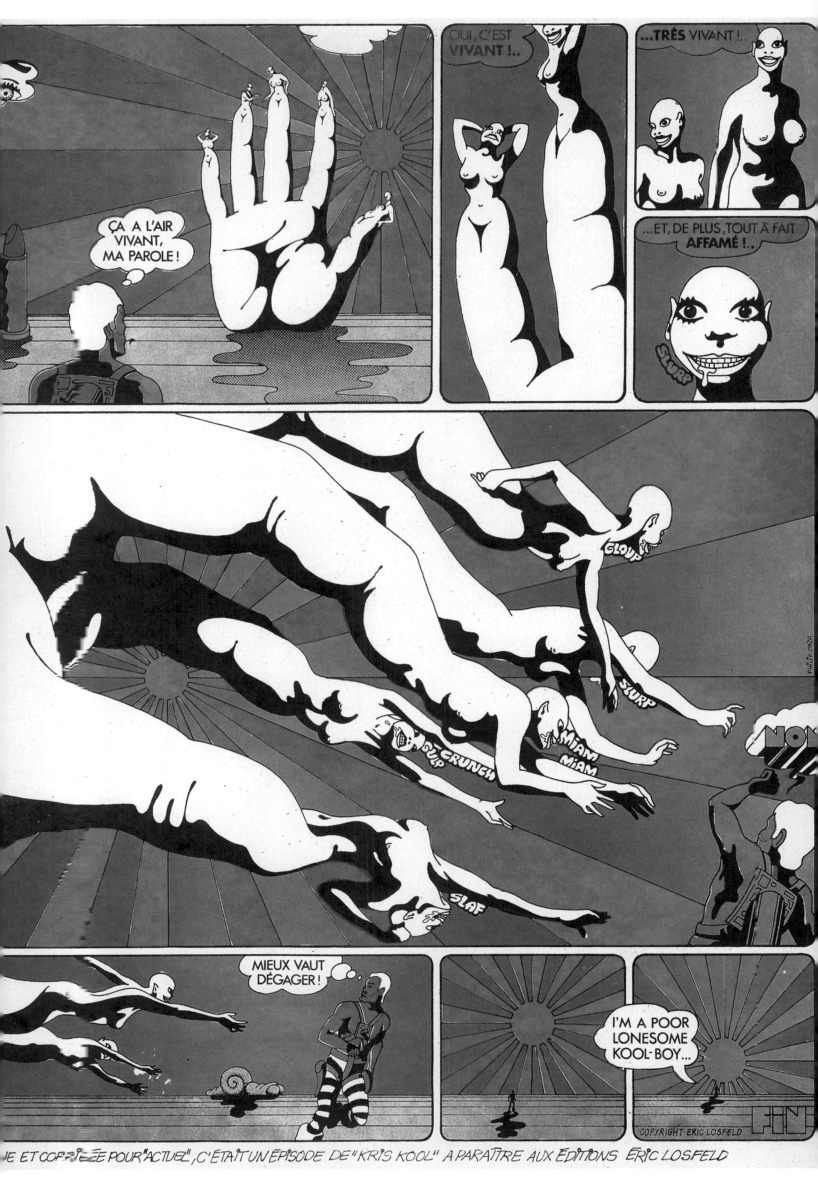

ABOVE: *Kris Kool*, a psychedelic comic strip by Philippe Caza, **Actuel**, 1970.
OVERLEAF: Practical jokes, psychedelia style.

KALEIDOSCOPE
GIVES BLACK EYE

49¢

Pass this real Kaleidoscope around the room - everyone who looks gets a **BLACK EYE!** Loads of laughs and fun for everyone.

K69

HILARIOUS SPRINGING SNAKE IN A TRANQUILIZER BOTTLE!

When someone reaches for a DOWN they get UP TIGHT! $69 .... $ —

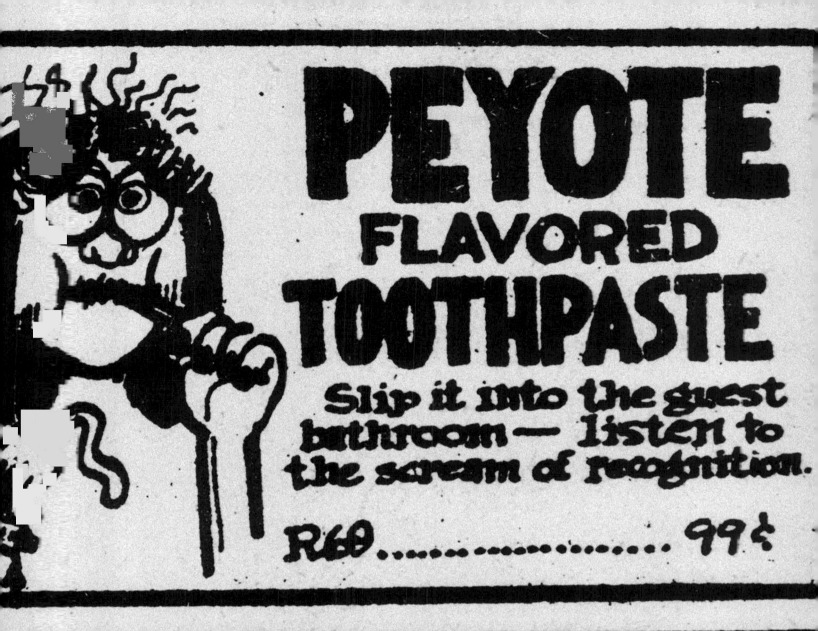

PEYOTE FLAVORED TOOTHPASTE

Slip it into the guest bathroom — listen to the scream of recognition.

R60 .... 99¢

HIDDEN CUSHION
MAKES NOISE LIKE
POLICE SIREN

Slip it under the sofa cushion — When someone sits on it watch 'em flush stashes

P89 .... 75¢

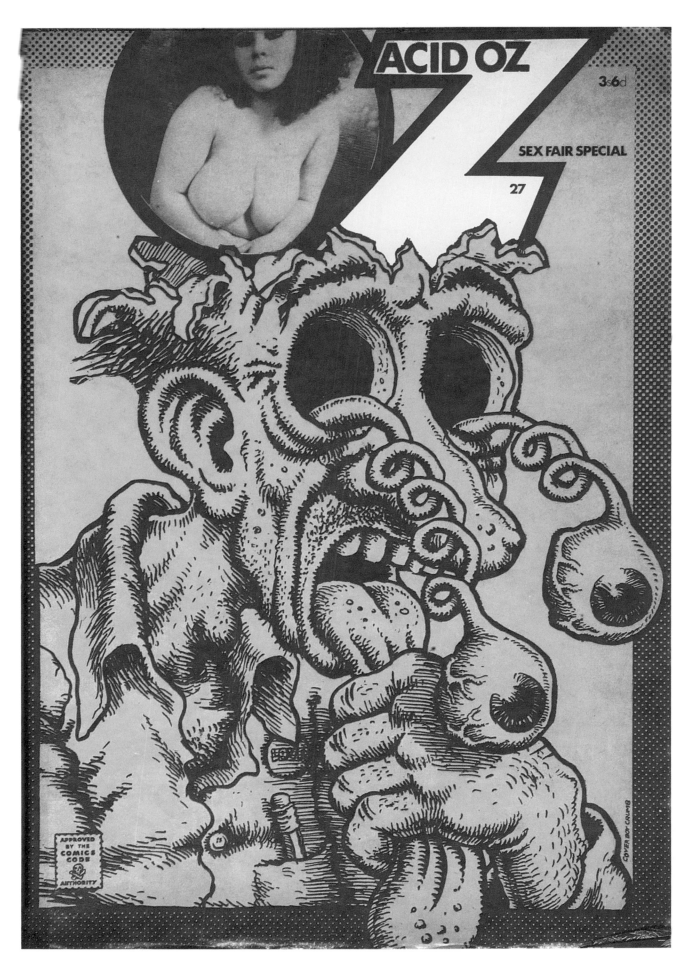

OPPOSITE: LSD was always good for a laugh. **it**, London, 1971.
ABOVE: **Oz**, London, 1970.

ABOVE: **Oz** rallies the troops to legalize pot, 1968.
OPPOSITE: **Pamphlet for the Marijuana Parade, New York, 1970.**

5TH AVE. MARIJUANA PARADE
SAT. MAY 6 11:30 A.M. WASHINGTON SQUARE PARK
MUSIC! SPEAKERS! REFRESHMENTS!
PARADE STARTS: 2:00 P.M. UP 5TH AVE. FLOATS! TRACTORCADE!
PARADE TERMINATES: 2:00 P.M. CENTRAL PARK. MUSIC! COMICS! INSPIRATION!
MAY 6
FREE THE HEADS! JAIL THE FEDS!
SAVE YOUR ROACHES!
REPEAL POTHIBITION
CAREY! PARDON ABBIE!
SOLIDARITY FOR ANARCHISTS
ABOLISH VICTIMLESS CRIMES!
P. Bramley
RE-ASSEMBLY POINTS, SHOULD 5TH AVENUE BE CLOSED BY KOCH-ROT, WILL BE UNITED NATIONS PLAZA AT FIRST AVENUE AND 42ND STREET, AND THE NEW YORK TIMES BUILDING AT 229 WEST 43RD STREET.
FOR MORE INFORMATION CONTACT THE 5TH AVE MARIJUANA PARADE COALITION POB 392 CANAL ST. STATION, NYC, NY 10013 -(212)-533-5028

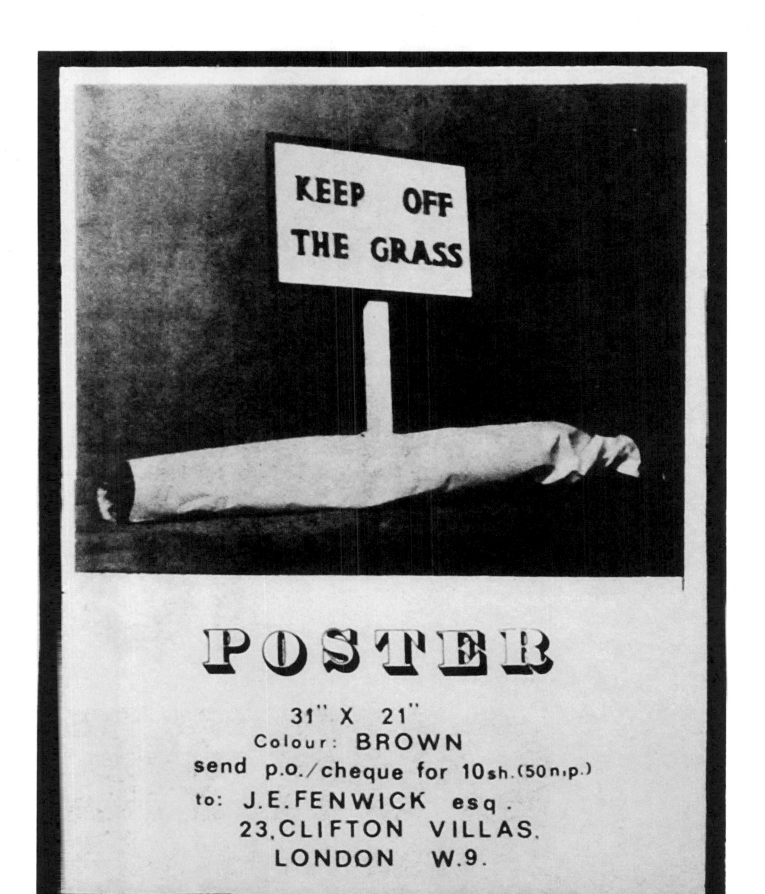

WE AGREE

FREE WEED

Canada, as everyone knows, is about five years ahead of the U.S. in that celebrated cause, the great legal dope race. Now, with a little help from our Canadian friends, that legal grass gap may be tightening up.

The help has come in the person of Michael Sudds, a 23-year-old former computer programmer turned cannabis-crusader, and his fledgling organization, Free Weed. Free Weed is a cooperative actively dedicated to the overthrow of the government of marijuana in Canada and the United States. Although legalization of grass through petitions, demonstrations and public education is the ultimate aim of the organization, a sideliner of their activities is of unique interest: they're offering insurance against dope busts. That's right—insurance, just like the protection you buy against auto accidents, illness, theft or death. Membership in the cooperative carries an assurance of up to $1500 worth of qualified legal counsel for charges of possession, and up to $5000 for sale of grass and it's derivatives. Coverage includes only cannabis-related charges, including hashish, uppers, downers and acid. Hard shit is excluded.

Free Weed is the United States' version of CF & S Contracting Co. Ltd. of Victoria, B.C. Sudds opened the first CF & S office in Victoria in January of this year, and shortly thereafter opened an office in Vancouver. The Vancouver office was raided and an employee beaten, so it was decided to close down the office and conduct all business by mail and telephone, a practice which will continue in the Bay area.

In addition to the insurance coverage, members of Free Weed will receive affidavits of "nonviolation of privacy." These are legally-binding documents testifying that the undersigner is not an undercover agent or police informer. Thus, a member can avoid the usual paranoia when turning-on around strangers, simply by asking them to sign the document. If they sign, the member is protected against a bust; if they won't sign, you just keep your stash stashed.

Membership in the cooperative organization costs $50 for the first six months, and $50 a year thereafter. According to Sudds, the 500 or so paid members north of the border represent all economic and social positions, from students and hippies to lawyers and doctors. A large percentage of the membership has come from middle-

HOW THE LITTLE MERI WARNER PLANT GREW HAPPILY EVER AFTER

Meri Warner was a plant who lived in a pot and spent all of her days trying to grow big and green. Her friend, Or Ganic, lived in the garden nearby. He spent all his time trying to grow big and healthy. Meri and Or had help from Mr. Head, who cared for them and tried to help them to their thing. Mr. Head pulled out other weeds growing around them, gave them water and fertilizers, and turned the record player up LOUD so they could hear their favorite grooving music.

With all of the good and hopeful things, life was still a day-to-day struggle for Meri Warner and Or Ganic to grow green, healthy and HIGH. Much of the fertilizer Mr. Head gave them just sat there and did nothing. Before long the fertilizer began to build up around them, trying to destroy Meri and Or. This made Meri and Or very sick, and it frightened the friendly worms away.

(Now, here comes the pitch.) One day, Mr. Head gave them a little of this new natural soil stuff, called NATCH-RAL, in a lot of water. Meri and Or each got ONE drop a day. They could feel the soil loosen up and the fertilizer starting to go to work again. Before long Meri was feeling it and started to grow an INCH a day. Or got big and full of vitamins. They tripped out together and the friendly worms came back. And if you think that's how the Little Meri Warner Plant Grew Happily Ever After, you're wrong, because one day Mr. Head came and cut them down . . . and it was all NATCH-RAL's fault.

Mr. Head, help Meri and Or grow green, healthy and HIGH. Send $2.69 to P O BOX 6263, Albany, California 94716, and we'll send you a 4-ounce bottle of organic NATCH-RAL.

class housewives. "One housewife," according to Sudds, "asked for 20 applications so she could sign up all the women in her neighborhood."

In the organization's six months of operation in Canada, only three members have been busted and represented by the coop's lawyers. It's a fair assumption that the sort of individual willing and able to put up $50 for bust insurance is pretty cool about weed, anyway.

Sudds claims that in the first week that he's been in the Bay Area, with no publicity except an item in the Chronicle giving his phone number, he's received about 350 inquiries, many people pledging payment upon receipt of a contract.

Though all business will be conducted by phone and mail, the only list of members' names is kept secure in a lawyer's vault. An identification number is assigned to each member to keep his name off police suspect lists.

Sudds plans to further expand the organization as soon as things are rolling well in the Bay Area. Berkeley will be the site of the "head office" for the United States, with advertising from coast to coast. Eventually, he hopes to establish an overseas office in London.

Free Weed has already caught the attention of the news media across America. Time and Newsweek magazines are reportedly running coverage, and Sudds has appeared on TV and radio interview shows.

Police investigations of the organization are a certainty, according to Sudds. "Our lawyers have managed to stall off investigations for another three or four months," he said, "and then we'll be ready to fight fire with fire." The parent organization in Victoria was subjected to investigation but came through with a clean bill. Sudds expects much the same result in the U.S.

Speculating on the future of the legalization problem, Sudds expects that within five years Canada will flash the green light; "Then America will either have to follow suit or close down the border, like during Prohibition. That'll put Free Weed out of business, but then, that's what we're in business for—to go out of business."

Anyone interested in information or membership should call the Berkeley office at 834-1206, or write to Free Weed, P.O. Box 134, Larkspur, California, 94939.

by Jon Stewart

Jill Johnston On Amazons As Warriors

Tantric Runners

Folsom Art Show: Creation In A Cage

Berkeley Barb

Issue 508, May 9 - 15, 1975
204
25¢ BAY AREA, 50¢ ELSEWHERE

WILL WE EVER SMOKE LEGAL DOPE?

85

In the freedom of that power
Of all wisdom and of love
All the shit of worldly centuries
But nourishes the rose
And all good and gracious creatures
Grow great within themselves
And find in the mouth of Lions
The holy Book of Peace.

Psychedelic poster, artist unknown.

GEORGIA STRAIGHT

TYRANT'S FOE... THE PEOPLE'S FRIEND...

56A POWELL STREET
VANCOUVER 4, B.C.
PHONE (604) 688-3686

MEMBER,
ANARCHIST PRESS MOVEMENT (APM)
UNDERGROUND PRESS SYNDICATE (UPS)
LIBERATION NEWS SERVICE (LNS)
PRENSA LATINA (PL)

GEORGIA STRAIGHT is published weekly Wednesday by Georgia Straight Publishing. Second class mail registration no. 0868.

Unclassified Rates: $1.00 for the 1st line, additional line. 50c for a box number.

Display Advertising: $3.00 a column in
Subscriptions: $5.00 per half year subscr
$9.00 per full year subsc

THE GEORGIA STRAIGHT cannot
sible for cash enclosed in the mail
manuscripts and art work which is
will be held for one month ONLY u
full-sized, stamped,
bers on

Power
to the people!

**THE FREE PRESS
GETS MILITANT**

Class consciousness and student revolts
John and Yoko in bed
Diggers and Yippies
protests against the Vietnam war
Chairman Mao and Che Guevara
Bolcheviks versus capitalists
pirate radio and the IRA
Watergate and Nixon

INFORMATION

THE east village OTHER

VOL.6 NO.10   FEB.2,1971   25¢ OUT OF TOWN 35¢

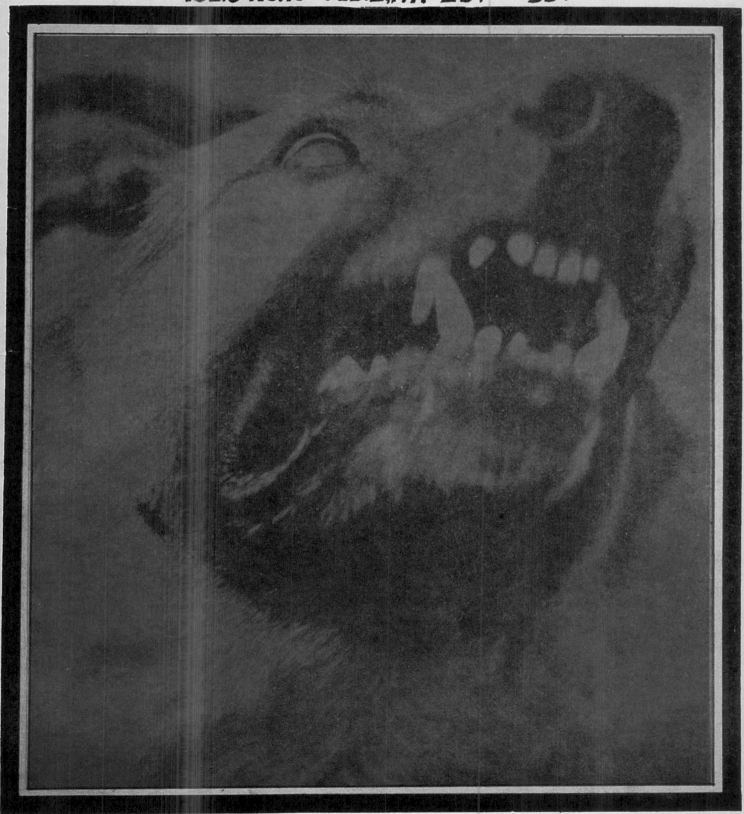

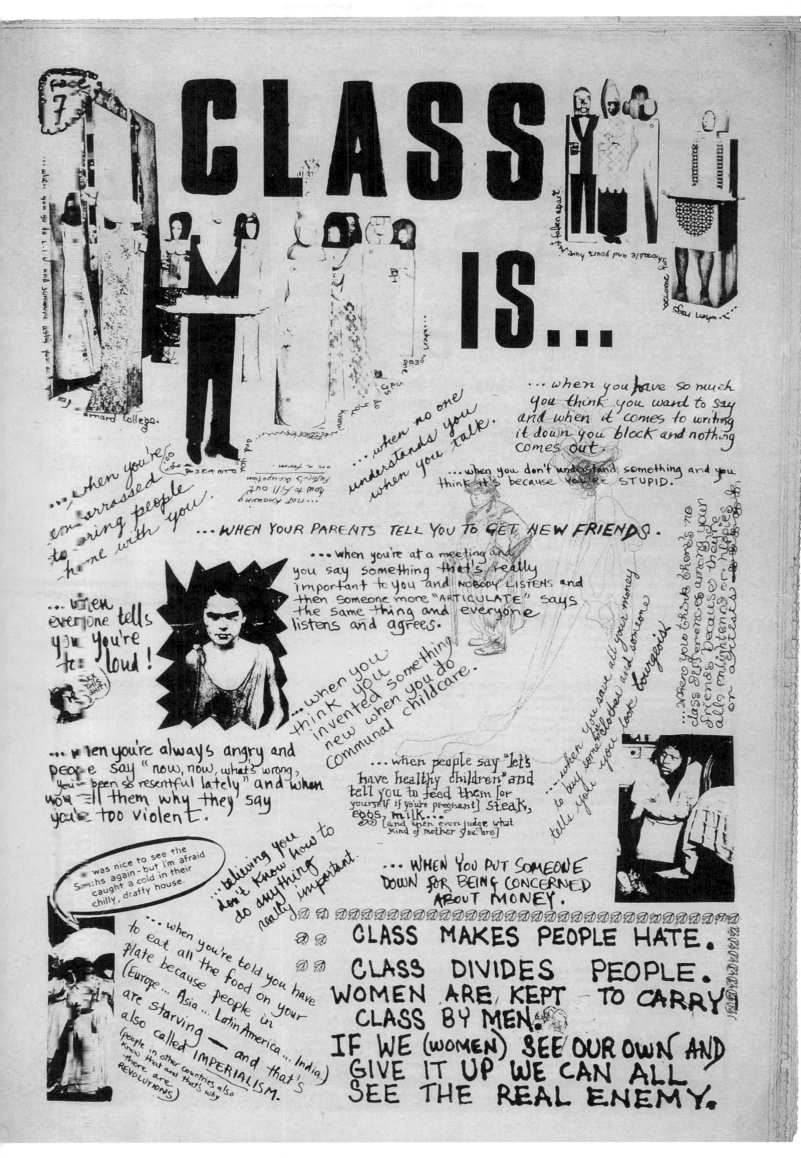

THE BATTLE OF BERKELEY

(See page 6)

RAT

SUBTERRANEAN NEWS

SUMMER DOLDRUMS ISSUE
THE GREAT CHUCK BERRY COMES TO TOWN (BACK)
(FRONT) LENNON YOKO WANG IT UP!

JUNE 12 - 18

n.y.c. 15¢ outside 25¢

PLEASANT DREAMS, JOHN & YOKO

by Paul, Susan, Dick and Tamar
LIBERATION News Service

When John and Yoko tried to enter the United States a few weeks back, they were denied permission because John was an undesirable alien - John had once been busted for having some marijuana around his house in England. Having been busted for dope makes you too undesirable to visit the United States unlike President Thieu of South Vietnam who enters our land, his hands dripping blood.

When John and Yoko were told they couldn't come into the States they side-tripped to the Bahamas where they promised a protest against the United States and war. Like previous John/Yoko protests this one was to emanate from their hotel room -- they would remain in bed for ten days attempting to draw world-wide attention to their thoughts.

Upon arriving in Freeport, the main airport for the British Bahamas, John and Yoko decided those once beautiful, now tourist-infested, islands wouldn't suit their high purpose. The hotels in Freeport charge foreign tourists sucker prices and aren't accessible to the Americans invited to visit John and Yoko during their demonstration.

So Yoko and John caught the first flight out of Freeport headed for Montreal. It was there, at the Queen Elizabeth II Hotel, that we planned to talk with them.

"How?"

"We'll call them on the phone and tell them we're from Liberation News Service and we want to interview them for the underground press in the United States. We have a note for Yoko from John Wilcock saying we're beautiful people they should talk to. Wilcock and Yoko are old friends."

The idea of talking with super Beatle and his beloved got us all hyped up. We decided Susan would do the calling because she was best at talking to the bureaucrats we'd surely have to go through to reach the dynamic duo.

"Is this the Queen Elizabeth Hotel? Can I talk with John Lennon and Yoko Ono?"

"You'll have to talk with the person in room 1748 about that, and that line is busy."

"Can I hold on until the line is free?"

"Alright, I'll keep ringing."

Five minutes later the call went through. The guy who answered was one of those who serves as a buffer between famous people and the outside world.

"Hello, can I talk with John or Yoko?"

"Who is this?"

continued on page 18

93

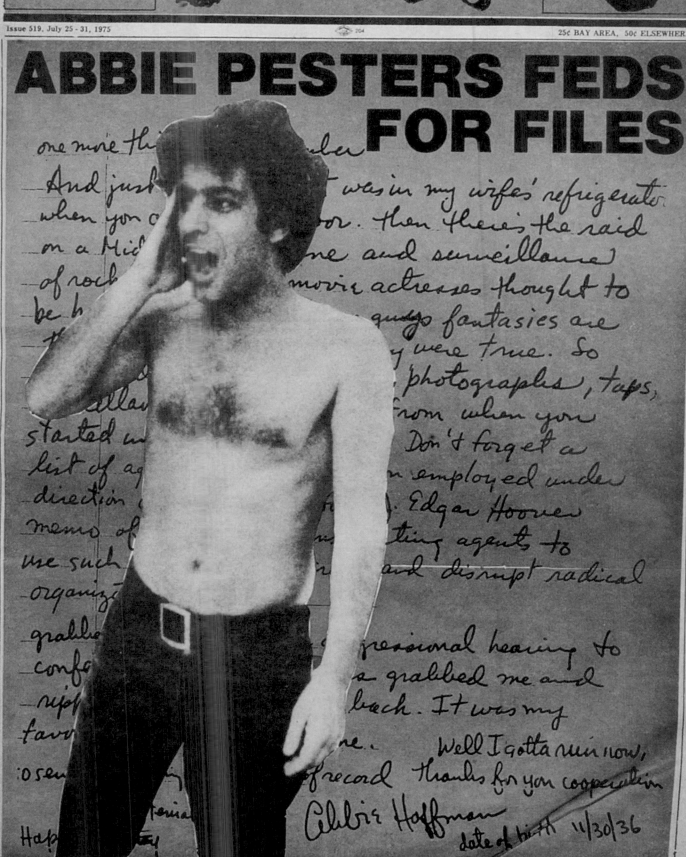

Hayden's Sanitized Senate Race

Acupuncture Now Legal For Holistic Healers

Berkeley Barb

The Maytals

Issue 519, July 25 - 31, 1975   204   25¢ BAY AREA, 50¢ ELSEWHERE

ABBIE PESTERS FEDS FOR FILES

free

THE DIGGER PAPERS

N

E

1% FREE

SOME TO FORGET:

FORGET the war in vietnam. Flowers are lovely.
FORGET America's 3300 military bases. Make music.
FORGET Wichita Vortex Sutra. Words are stronger than flesh.
FORGET planned war with China. Beauty is Carnaby Street.
FORGET the Dominican Republic. Todo Todo Hassan Sabbah.
FORGET police Brutality. The cops are your friends.
FORGET upheaval in negro ghettoes. Spades ain't hip.
FORGET the Rumford Act. Show love.
FORGET the National Guard. Positively Fourth Street.
FORGET inmates on deathrow. It's a long time passing.
FORGET hypocrasy of business. The merchants are your friends.
FORGET U.S. billion dollar investment in South Africa. Money is.
FORGET HUELGA DiGiorgio. We all live in a yellow submarine.
FORGET organized crime. Eternity is long and, sometimes, wide.
FORGET HUAC. The sun's not yellow, it's chicken.
FORGET concentration camps for subversives. It's a bummer.
FORGET FSM, VDC,SDS,SNCC,MARK COMFORT. Big Brother and the Holding Co..
FORGET Mime Troupe, Lenny Bruce, The Beard. Strobe lights are groovy.

YOU'RE FREE TO FORGET. SO FORGET! FOLLOW THE CALM BUSINESS TACTICS
OF THE PSYCHEDELIC SHOP, THE I AND THOU, AND ALL OTHER MARKETEERS OF
EXPANDED CONSCIOUSNESS (MOE'S BOOKSTORE IS IMPORTANT, REALLY!) AND
DIG YOURSELF. TOUCH REALITY ONLY FOR SEX, ONLY TO EAT, AND ONLY TO
JOIN THE ARTIST'S LIBERATION FRONT FOR YOUR OWN SAFETY.

AFTERALL, EXPANDED CONSCIOUSNESS IS A SELFISH HIPPY KISSING THE
SYSTEM'S ASS FOR THE GREATER GLORY OF THE LONELY DROPOUT, ISN'T
THAT RIGHT, UNCLE TIM!

THE DIGGERS.

where is PUBLIC at?
where are PUBLIC streets at?
therefore
an erection in the panhandle.

the PUBLIC parks - here you can pitch a tent anytime.
PUBLIC STreets on riot with truckloads of arms protecting
the private property of super-charging merchants.

the PUBLIC beaches - here you can paddy-cake any old time.

PUBLIC streets where fantasy laws justify the concepts of
LOITERING & VAGRANCY.
the PUBLIC schools - here you can be conditioned to PUBLIC
opinion in order to express yourself in
the PUBLIC consensus.

PUBLIC streets where agents patrol,undercovered in 'hip' costumes.
the PUBLIC transport system - here drivers black and white riders
for free.
PUBLIC streets where parking meters tick off legality.
the PUBLIC hospitals - here you can born, healed, passed away away.
PUBLIC streets where exhausting autos pollute the air and
mutilate the people.
the PUBLIC housing developments—
here you can live a life now done.

PUBLIC streets where lonliness crowds silent, up-tight sidewalks.
the PUBLIC officers - here is the understanding of PUBLIC service.

WHERE IN THE STREET CAN TWO FINGERS TOUCH
WHERE IN THE STREET CAN YOU GET OUT OF NEIGHBORHOODS
WHERE IN THE STREET CAN YOU ESCAPE THE ECONOMIC NET
WHERE IN THE STREET CAN YOU TRIP OUT YOUR DOOR AND SMILE AT SINCERE
WHERE IN THE STREET CAN YOU HITCH A HIKE DOWN THE BLOCK
WHERE IN THE STREET CAN YOU TAKE OFF YOUR SHOES AND SING AND
DANCE WITHOUT DISTURBING THE DEATH CALLED PEACE

in voice THE DIGGERS demand an ERECTION!
THE BALLING BOWL
a FREE PUBLIC structure in the panhandle where individuals can
swim in vinyl pools filled with vaseline, WAIL LOVE to downcast
brows, and carry-on as much as they want until they think it
beautiful to stop.
THE DIGGERS fully understand that the
cost of erection can be added to the PUBLIC debt
and especially appreciate Captain Kiely's
generous offer of men and machines to quicken
the rise of the ERECTION and give meaning to
its eventual climax.

UP THE BALLING BOWL!

THE DIGGERS.

ABOVE: Digger pamphlets put together by Peter Berg,
Emmett Grogan, Peter Coyote and Richard Brautigan.
OPPOSITE: Abbie Hoffman, legendary activist and
co-founder of the Yippies (Youth International Party).
Berkeley Barb, July 1975.

VIETNAM QUIZ

O.K. KIDS, YA GOT 15 MINUTES TO FINISH DIS QUIZ - A HIGH SCORE AND YA COME WITH ME!

1) The Geneva Conventions on Indochina held in 1954 stated that...
a) Ho Chi Minh could have North Vietnam and the United States could have South Vietnam.
b) That the U.S. and it's allies should hold elections in the South to decide what government South Vietnam wants.
c) That the division was only temporary and elections would be held throughout the whole country to reunify Vietnam.
d) That France was to retain Vietnam as a colony.

2) The United States prevented the scheduled 1958 elections...
a) To preserve democracy there.
b) Because the people in Vietnam were not ready to have elections.
c) Because a CIA report to President Eisenhower revealed the at least 80% of the people would have voted for Ho Chi Minh.
d) To see how mad the people would get.

3) The best statement of the Domino Theory is...
a) We have to invade Laos to protect Cambodia.
b) We have to invade Cambodia to protect Vietnam.
c) We have to invade Vietnam to protect Thailand.
d) We have to invade China to protect the U.S.
e) All of the above.

4) The opposing sides in Vietnam are...
a) The forces of good and the forces of evil.
b) Spiro T. Agnew and Abbie Hoffman.
c) The Military-Industrial complex and the people of Vietnam.
d) Mother and apple pie versus godless communism.

5) Ho Chi Minh used portions of the U.S. Declaration of Independence when writing his own countries declaration because...
a) He thought it would trick the U.S. into thinking he wasn't a communist.
b) He wanted to mislead his own people to believe he was pro U.S.
c) He strngly believed in independence for Vietnam and respected the revolutionary deeds of our American Revolution.
d) He couldn't think of anything original.

6) The napalm in use in Vietnam is for...
a) Burning factories and buildings.
b) Burning supplies of food.
c) Burning fields of marijuana.
d) Burning people.

7) Vice- President Ky of the pro U.S. government of South Vietnam stated that his favorite hero of all times was...
a) Mao-tse Tung
b) Jerry Rubin
c) Adolf Hitler
d) Alfred E. Neumann

8) The Vietcong are...
a) Russian infiltrators who fight against the U.S.
b) Chinese infiltrators who fight against the U.S.
c) Vietnamese citizens who fight against the U.S.
d) Cuban infiltrators who fight against the U.S.

9) The National Liberation Front of South Vietnam or the Vietcong has a program calling for...
a) The dictatorship of South Vietnam by Hanoi.
b) Free elections representing all interests, land reforms, and democratic freedoms.
c) The dictatorship of South Vietnam by China.
d) Invasion of the United States by 1972.

10) The Vietnam War...
a) Is helping the rich get richer and the poor get poorer.
b) Is good for the economy.
c) Is helping to fight inflation.
d) Is an inexpensive project.

11) More bombs have been dropped in Vietnam than in...
a) World War I
b) World War II
c) World War I and World War II put together.

12) The Vietnam War was...
a) Declared in 1961.
b) Declared in 1963.
c) Declared in 1965.
d) Never declared.

13) Nixon failed to announce the Cambodian invasion until after it happened because...
a) He wanted to protect the American people from premature protest.
b) He wanted to surprise the Cambodian people.
c) He forgot until the last minute.
d) He was afraid of world-wide disapproval.

14) The U.S. move into Laos was a(n)...
a) Incursion
b) Pre-emptive strike.
c) Protective reaction.
d) Peace feeler.
e) Invasion.

15) In view of the My Lai Massacre, Lt. Calley...
a) Was used by the government to do it's dirty work and then singled out.
b) Should be freed since killing is nothing new.
c) "Only followed orders."

16) The United States is...
a) Is winning quickly in Vietnam.
b) Is winning slowly but surely in Vietnam.
c) Is not trying in Vietnam.
d) Is getting it's ass kicked in Vietnam.

TRUE OR FALSE

17) The Apollo moonshot, by the merest coincide happened simultaneously with the invasion of Lao

18) Many major oil companies from the U.S. have already chosen drilling sites for offshore oil wells in Vietnam, and are eager for the situation there to become 'stabilized'.

ESSAY QUESTIONS

19) In the briefest possible essays, defend two of the following ratioales for invading Laos.
a) If the North Vietnamese get supplies through Laos, then the people will be able to eat. If they eat they will fight Americans and kill GIs.
b) It is the sworn duty of the U.S. to stand by her allies and help them in their hour of need, whether they want it or not.
c) To make sure that Southeast Asia is protected from communist subversion, so that they too can enjoy electric toothbrushes, parking lots, and pollution.
d) Because Vietnam is all used up.

20) In the briefest possible essay, compare and contrast the U.S. invasion of Laos with the following
a) The U.S. invasion of Cambodia (1970).
b) The U.S. invasion of Vietnam (1961).
c) The U.S. invasion of Cuba (1961).
c) The U.S. invasion of the Dominican Republic(
e) The U.S. invasion of Nicaragua (1927).
f) The U.S. invasion of Guatemala (1954).
g) The U.S. invasion of North America (1620).

SCORING... (Answers × 8:

Give yourself five points for each question correctly answered. Any cheating automatically d squalifies you from the quiz. The answers can be found on page . Here is a grade analysis.

0 to 60 points--- You should cancel your subscription to Reader's Digest and subscribe to Nola Express.

60 to 80 ponts--- You're watching too much Walter Cronkite.

80 to 90 points--- You're probably a weekend radical who hits all the demonstrations without knowing half of what they're about.

90 to 100 points--- Lock your doors and destroy this quiz immediately... you know too much.

Vol 3, No , Issue 208, Aug. 8 – 14, 1969
20-2 University Ave., Berkeley, Ca. 94704, 849-1040

PUBLISHED
WEEKLY   204

15¢ BAY AREA   25c ELSEWHERE

CHRIST IN KHAKI

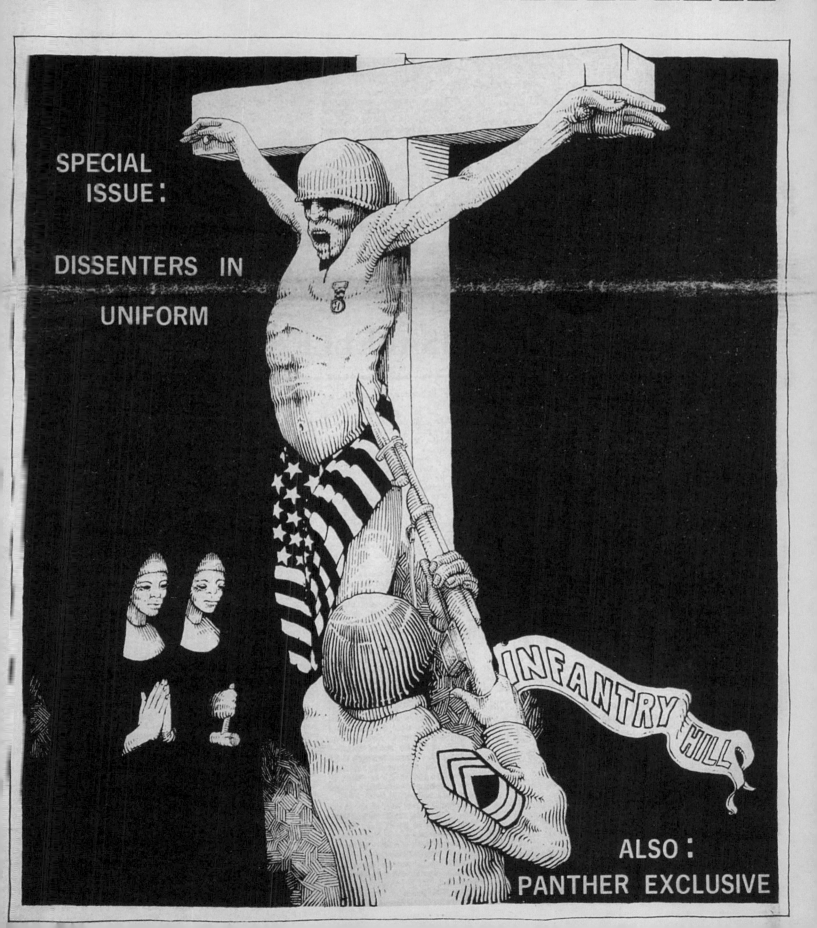

SPECIAL
ISSUE :

DISSENTERS IN

UNIFORM

INFANTRY HILL

ALSO :
PANTHER EXCLUSIVE

SUPPORT OUR BOYS IN VIETNAM

KOREA, GERMANY, JAPAN, ENGLAND, ITALY, CANADA, CUBA (GUANTANAMO), ANTIGUA, ARGENTINA, ARUBA, AUSTRALIA, AUSTRIA, AZORES, BELGIUM, BERMUDA, BOLIVIA, BRAZIL, BURMA, CAMBODIA, CHILE, COLUMBIA, CONGO, CORSICA, COSTA RICA, CRETE, DAHOMEY, DENMARK, DOMINICAN REPUB, ECUADOR, EGYPT, EL SALVADOR, ENIWETOK, GREE, GREENLAND, GUAM, GUATAMALA, HAIT, HONDURAS, HONG, KONG, ICELAND, INDIA, INDONESIA, IRAN, IWO JIMA, LAOS, LIBERIA, LIBYA, MALI, MEXICO, MOROCCO, NETHERLANDS, NEW ZEALAND, NICARAGUA, NIGER, NORWAY, PAKISTAN, ISRAEL, PANAMA, PANAMA, PARAGUAY, PHILLIPINES, PORTUGAL, PUERTO RICO, RYUKUS, SAINT LUCIA, SAIPA, SAUDI ARABIA, SCOTLAND, N. IRELAND, SENEGAL, SEYCHELLES, SPAIN, SURINAM, TAIWAN, THAILAND, TRINIDAD, TURKEY, URUGUAY, VENEZUELA, MARSHALL, MARIANAS, BONINS, VOLCANOS, ALGERIA, GIBRALTER, MALT, AFGHANISTAN, ETHIOPIA, FINLAND, IRAQ, IRELAND, LUXEMBOURG, MALAYA, LEBANON, ANTIGUA & &, DETROIT, CHICAGO, OAKLAND, S.F. BERKELEY & CZECHOSLOVAKIA * (TROOPS O OUR HERO RUSSIAN ALL

SERVING PROUDLY

U.S. ARMY

10p

ink

The Other Newspaper September 1971

david cooper: alternative psychiatry. jim haynes: alternative sex . vince hines :alternative to racism. mike roth :alternative aggression. robin blackburn +mick farren:alternative politics

PREVIOUS PAGES OPPOSITE AND ABOVE:
Campaigning against the Vietnam war.

99

RAT

SUBTERRANEAN NEWS

LIBERATED
DOCUMENTS
PAGE 8

may 3-16, 1968
n.y.c. 15¢ outside 25¢

HEIL COLUMBIA

Rat

issue # 17

DEC 17 – JAN 6

25¢ IN NYC

35¢ OUTSIDE NYC

NEW MORNING — CHANGING WEATHER

Rat was born from the student protests of 1968 at Columbia University. Eighteen months later, in late 1969, **Rat** got radical and supported the Weathermen, who advocated armed guerrilla action.

101

Published by the Red Mountain Tribe, Inc.   January 29-February 5, 1971   Vol. 2   Vol. III/Number 28/Issue 80   15¢ Bay Area/30¢ elsewhere

BERKELEY TRIBE

Nixon Asks Revolution, Power for the People

I WAS A HONKY LOVER AND LIVED

See page 5

FIGHTING THE BLACKLASH

VOL. 1 NO. 11 ISSUE 396 MARCH 16–22, 1973
342 UNIVERSITY AVE., BERKELEY, CA. 94701 849-1040

PUBLISHED EVERY FRIDAY — Berkeley BARB 1973

25¢ OUTSIDE OF BAY AREA 15¢ BAY AREA

ABOVE AND OPPOSITE: Two rival Berkeley papers, the **Barb** and the **Tribe**, go head to head on the issues that matter. For the full story see page 237.

PROLETAIRES DE TOUS LES PAYS, NATIONS ET PEUPLES OPPRIMES, UNISSEZ-VOUS !

la cause du peuple

1 F
Boite Postale 130, Paris-20°
C.C.P. : N° 3048991 - LA SOURCE

JOURNAL COMMUNISTE
REVOLUTIONNAIRE PROLETARIEN

2° ANNEE
MERCREDI 10 DECEMBRE 1969

1

NOUS SOMMES LES NOUVEAUX PARTISANS

Les patrons lockoutent, licencient des milliers d'ouvriers repérés avec l'aide de leurs chiens policiers dans les ateliers et pour finir appellent les C.R.S. A Sochaux, à St-Etienne, l'E.D.F. et ailleurs. Cernés par la haine des travailleurs, les patrons provoquent. Et leurs larbins dans l'Etat, font de la provocation la règle du gouvernement, des mouchards et des gendarmes les héros du régime. La misère à la ville et à la campagne, la dictature dans l'usine et dans la rue, c'est la nouvelle société imaginée par la racaille gaulliste.

Pour intimider les travailleurs, il faut les provoquer ; pour ne pas laisser un pouce de terrain à la révolte, les forces de répression doivent occuper tout le terrain. Face à cette occupation, les collabos courbent l'échine. Les syndicalistes cassent la grève à l'E.D.F. parce que Chaban appuyé par ses C.D.R. a haussé le ton ; ils signent un accord à Manufrance qui enlève aux ouvriers la liberté d'agir dans les ateliers sans leur accord. La racaille provoque, les collabos capitulent.

Mais des résistants, il y en a. Partout dans le peuple, les ouvriers brisent les cadences, bloquent la production, séquestrent les patrons. Les paysans pénètrent dans les préfectures et emmènent les préfets ou les ministres dans les fermes. Un mot d'ordre rallie toutes les couches populaires opprimées : séquestrons les patrons-despotes, les fonctionnaires corrompus, les profiteurs ! Rendons coup pour coup ! Pourquoi craindre les exploiteurs ? Nous sommes l'écrasante majorité : ouvriers, employés, techniciens, petits paysans et commerçants, étudiants, lycéens. Pourquoi respecter les exploiteurs ? Ce sont les fauteurs de misère. Tant qu'ils seront libres, nous, nous ne le serons pas. Contre eux, un cri qui fait balle :
NOUS SOMMES LES NOUVEAUX PARTISANS !

OPPOSITE: 'We Are The New Partisans.' **La Cause
du Peuple**, Paris, December 1969.
ABOVE **Actuel**, Paris, April 1971.
Maoists versus freaks, freaks versus Maoists.
Actuel's 'pleasure revolution', led by Gilbert
Shelton's *Furry Freak Brothers*, was an irritating
thorn in the side for the proletarian Left.

The Digger

Issue No. 18 30 Cents June 23—July 14

Ford workers jack~up ❧ Blueprint for Survival

NIXON, BIG BUSINESS,
THE MAFIA &
THE CIA

WATERGATE
LIFT~OUT DOSSIER

OPPOSITE: **The Digger**, Sydney, July 1973.
ABOVE: **it**, London, September 1972. Nixon and the Mafia – and Watergate wasn't far away.
OVERLEAF: Nixon's cronies exposed by the underground press. **Berkeley Barb**, March 1974.

5

11

Watergaters STURGIS & Cuban expatriate BERNARD BARKER.

12 D

B

C

A

12

FRANK STURGIS

(YIPST

108

7

8

6

E. HOWARD HUNT

9

IXON'S HIRED

10B

10A
15

HITMEN

of PIGS

IS

ERGATE

13

14

n' kn

LUSIVE!)

ROMAN POLANSKI'S PRICK IN PURE GOLD

IT/150   March 22—April 5 1973   Price 15p.

x 'Last Tango'—The Unbuttered Facts x
x Mike Zwerin on the French Common Cause x

PIRATES!—
WHEN TERROR
STALKED
THE NORTH SEA...

BLOODY SUNDAY
IRELAND
TWELVE MONTHS ON

IT/147 23 February 1973 Price 15p.

THE INSTANT IMMORTALITY RACKET

NASTY TALES TRIAL
THE INSIDE DOPE

L'APPEL DU 18 JOINT

soulas

Moi, JE NE SIGNE PLUS RIEN !

Voici donc l'appel du 18 Joint. Une nouvelle da□ historique peut-être, en tous cas, la première initiative dans not□ cher pays pour dépénaliser le cannabis et chercher à démythifier le □neux « problème de la drogue ».

Un manifeste signé par plus de 150 personn□ des journalistes d'opinions diverses, des médecins, des avocats, □s musiciens, des cinéastes, des acteurs, des écrivains, des dessinateu□ des gens connus pour n'être pas des dégénérés notoires comme devr□□ l'être les ignobles « drogués » dont parle une certaine presse ; □né par des gens inconnus, aussi, comme le sont les milliers d'amateu□ de drogues douces en France. Un texte simple, qui rappelle que la m□rijuana n'entraîne aucune accoutumance physique, et que des centain□ □ jeunes fumeurs d'herbe sont poursuivis chaque année. Un texte □ les signataires reconnaissent publiquement avoir commis l'acte « □ntaux » de fumer ou de déguster une plante que des millions de perso□ consomment de par le monde...

Les traditio□nels hallucinés du Parisien □béré et d'ailleurs y verront un signe inéluctable de notre décadence, d□□□es préféreront sans doute le silence, pourtant, ce texte existe □□rmais et nous espérons qu'il sera signé par des milliers de perso□□. anonymes ou non, afin de rendre caduque une pénalisation arbitra□□.

Toutes les signatures sont les bienvenues : App□ du 18 joint, C/O Libération, 27 rue de Lorraine, 75019 Paris.

Les premiers signataires

Abrahams Jean-Jacques, Annabel, Areski, Dr. Atlan □ □Alessandrini Paul, Alessandrini Marjorie, Arietta Adolfo, Anquetil G□s, Backman René, Bourgeade Pierre, Béranger François, Berger □□ule, Bizot Jean-François, Baratier Jacques, Bastide Jean-Pierre, Bo□□le Romain, Bardet Vincent, Bodevent Jean-Louis, Barouh Pierre, Bo□ □cques-Laurent, Bok Philippe (médeci□), Colombel Jeannette, □□□ Patricia, Chesneaux Jean, Copi, Clémenti Pierre, Castagnet Pa□ □ □opferman Emile, Carpentier Jean (médeci□), Cahiers du Cinéma, Ca□ □ Louis-Jean, Cullaz Maurice, Deleuze Gilles, Duits Charles, Dollé Je□□Paul, Dupré Jean-Louis, Dubois Bernard, Davezies René, Devy Mich□ □achy Marc, Dautin Yvon, Delessert Philippe, Dosse Roger, Druillet P□□ppe, Dietlin Eric, Dubenton A□ne, Erlinguer Serge (médecin), Fro□ □□ Gérard, Font Patrick, Ferré René, de Fréminville Bernard (mé□□□□) Fluence, Fourastié Philippe, Glucksmann André, Grasset Jean-Ba□□ □te Geismar Alain, Guattari Felix, Godli□, Gébé, Gir Mœbius, H□□□□ Jim, Held Jean-Francis, Houdart Blandine, Huppert Isabelle, Isser□□□ Dominique, Ithurriaque Jean (médecin), Jaubert Alain, Jacquot □□□□, Kalfon Jean-Pierre, Kouchner Bern□rd, Karsenty S□□□, Kan Alain, Levy-Leblond Jean-Marc, Levy-Leblond Elis□□ (médecin), Le Forestier Maxime, Landau Maria (médecin), Letté Je□□ □□ul, L□yotard Jean-François, Laurien Elodie, Lacroix Hugo, Levaillant □□□□ Lagrange Valérie, Laperrousaz Jérôme, Laffont Bernadette, Leclerc□□□□ (avocat), Mandryka Daniel, Marcellin Marc'O, Matricon, Merc□d□□ □□en, Matzis Costas, Meunier Jean-Louis, Magny Colette, Muchnik □□□□, Morello Dominique, Maulineux Maud, Mercanton Isabelle, □□□ Edgar, Manceaux Michèle Mémmi Michael, Merleau-Ponty (a□□□□) Negroni François, Najman C., Nicoulaud Gilles, Oswald P.J., □□□□□ Hélène, Ogier Bulle, Orla, Pinhas Richard, Pleyney Marcellin, Pr□□□□ Philippe, Pasquet Sylvaine, Rauch Alain, Revault d'Allonnes, Re□□□□□, Renault Philippe, Rouzaud Jean, Ribbes Jean-Paul, Rochefort Ch□□□□ne, Roche Denis, Raguenès Jean, Righini Marielle, Rosso Serge□□□en, Richard Jean-Vincent, Solle□ Philippe, Saint-James Daniel, Sard□□ Severo, Sery Patrick, Samuel Laurent, Savary Jérôme, Simmonet Do□□□ique, Szejer Myriam (méd.), T□vernier B., Timsit (avocat) Topor, □□□as Thérame Victoria, Verlhomme Hugo, Vannoni Patrice, Varela J□□ □an Eersel Patrice, Vasca Jean, Verdier Jean Pau□, Val Philippe, Yel□□ Jean-Benoît, Zouzou, France Lea, Sami Ayari Fran□□is Chatelet.

Cigarettes, pastis, aspirine, café, gros rouge, calmants, font partie de notre vie quotidienne. En revanche, un simple « joint » de *cannabis* (sous ses différentes formes : marijuana, haschich, kif, huile) peut vous conduire en prison ou chez un psychiatre.

Des dizaines de documents officiels (notamment les rapports La Guardia aux Etats-Unis, Wootton en Grande-Bretagne, le Dain au Canada) ont démontré que le cannabis n'engendre aucune dépendance physique, contrairement aux drogues dites « dures », telles que l'héroïne, mais aussi au tabac ou à l'alcool, et n'a aucun effet nocif comparable (« *Pas même une bronchite, sauf chez les grands fumeurs* », a écrit aux Etats-Unis le directeur de l'Institut national contre l'abus des drogues). Le contenu de ces documents n'a jamais été porté à la connaissance du public français, on a préféré laisser la grande presse mener des campagnes d'intoxication fondées sur des mensonges ineptes.

Dans de nombreux pays déjà - Etats-Unis (Californie, Oregon, Alaska), Pays-Bas, Canada..., la législation sur le cannabis a été considérablement adoucie. En France, on continue d'entretenir la confusion entre drogues dures et drogues douces, gros trafiquants, petits intermédiaires et simples usagers. Cela permet de maintenir et de renforcer une répression de plus en plus lourde : depuis 1969, la police peut perquisitionner chez n'importe qui, sans mandat, à toute heure du jour ou de la nuit, sous prétexte de drogue. Cela permet des arrestations massives de jeunes et des quadrillages policiers. Cela sert à justifier la détention de centaines de personnes, petits revendeurs ou fumeurs de cannabis, quand tout le monde sait que des gros bonnets de l'héroïne sont en liberté. Ces emprisonnements, bien sûr, sont sélectifs et frappen en priorité la jeunesse, surtout la jeunesse ouvrière et les immigrés, particulièrement dans les régions.

Or, des milliers et des milliers de personnes fument du cannabis aujourd'hui en France, dans les journaux, les lycées, les facultés, les bureaux, les usines, les ministères, les casernes, les concerts, les congrès politiques, chez elles, dans la rue. Tout le monde le sait. C'est pour lever ce silence hypocrite que nous déclarons publiquement avoir déjà fumé du cannabis en diverses occasions et avoir, éventuellement, l'intention de récidiver. Nous considérons comme inadmissible toute forme de répression individuelle, soumise à l'arbitraire policier et entendons soutenir activement tous ceux qui en seraient victimes. Nous demandons que soient prises les mesures suivantes :

— Dépénalisation totale du cannabis, de son usage, sa possession, sa culture (autoproduction) ou son introduction sur le territoire français en quantités de consommation courante.

— Ouverture de centres d'information sur les substances psychotropes, en ordre alphabétique : alcool, cannabis, cocaïne, héroïne, LSD, médicaments, tabac, etc.

Nous n'avons que faire de la légalisation de la marijuana, ni de sa commercialisation. Si des trusts à joints s'en emparent, c'est une question de société. Ce texte n'est pas un appel à la consommation. Il vise seulement à mettre fin à une situation absurde.

PREVIOUS PAGES: **it**, on pirate radio and the Bloody Sunday massacre.
OPPOSITE: **Libération** launches its campaign to legalize pot. Paris, 1976.
ABOVE: Mao and the end of the Cultural Revolution. **Seed**, Chicago, 1972.

ABOVE: Drawing by Jean-Marc Reiser: 'Vote for me and I'll sort out your shit.'
Actuel, Paris, February 1972.
OPPOSITE: 'These kids don't have any respect for anything any more.' A pie in
the face for Che. Originally from **Oz**, reprinted in **Mainmise**, Montreal, 1972.

Ah! ces jeunes, ils ne respectent vraiment plus rien.

is published twice-monthly (except July, Augu... January when it is published monthly) by the ...sters League in cooperation with the New ...orkshop in Nonviolence. Subscriptions are $5.00 ...ear. Second class postage paid at New York, N.Y. 1... ...ndividual writers are responsible for opinions exp... and accuracy of facts given. Sorry—manuscripts ca... returned unless accompanied by a self-addressed... envelope. Printed in U.S.A., WIN is a membe... Underground Press Syndicate and Liberati... Service.

International Times is a member of the Under... ground Press Syndicate. Other papers in the syndica... include the East Village Other, Los Angeles Fr... Press, Peace News, Berkeley Barb, The Paper, ... Fifth Estate.

Down with male domination!

**THE FREE PRESS,
THE WOMEN'S MOVEMENT
AND GAY LIBERATION**

Communist lesbians
feminist takeover at Rat
the Society for Cutting Up Men
legalized abortion
drag queens and gay pride
and the shrinks start to rake in a fortune

OPPOSITE: The feminists take over **Rat**, New York, October 1969.
ABOVE: **Actuel**, Paris, January 1971: 'Down with male society!'

ABOVE: 'Phallic Stampede' on the cover of **Actuel**, 1972. The MLF were the French Women's Liberation Movement; the Fhar were the Gay Liberation Front.

OPPOSITE: 'The family is pollution', **Tout**, Paris, June 1971. The mayor of the French town of Tours, Jean Royer, filed an official complaint against the editor-in-chief, Jean-Paul Sartre, for his supposed promotion of homosexuality.

OVERLEAF, LEFT: A manifesto for the MLF, from **Le Torchon Brûle**, Paris, 1972.
OVERLEAF, RIGHT: **Other Scenes** celebrates International Women's Day, March 1970.

TOUT!

CE QUE NOUS VOULONS : TOUT

QUINZDMADAIRE

1F

LA FAMILLE C'EST LA POLLUTION

GRAINE DE RO

Prenez de tout cœur
Ces Graines de Roses
Toutes fraîches écloses
Pour votre Bonheur

Recommandé

Le groupe M.L.F

Le groupe M.L.F de Rouen s'est formé à l'origine, à partir de la lecture de l'article sur les femmes paru dans l'Idiot International, paru en 70. Puis, des copines de Paris sont venues nous présenter le film sur la grève des femmes de Troyes, le groupe s'est alors réellement constitué. Première nécessité ressentie par les filles : se parler. C'est la période "réunions-déballage" Heureusement on avait une chouette copine, Yannick, qui avait l'art de parler de ses problèmes et qui nous a toutes beaucoup aidées à parler, à dire pourquoi on était là, tout ce qu'on avait sur la patate. En même temps on ressentait le besoin de populariser notre mouvement, de faire des "actions". Intervention à la fête des mères, ça tombait bien, en même temps que la fête Jeanne d'Arc ! On a distribué des tracts (fêtées un jour, exploitées toute l'année), l'accueil des rouennais a été très mitigé. On

en a profité pour faire une petite intrusion très mal vue, à la remise des décora- tions aux mères- ritantes. Il y a eu aussi une grosse af- faire sur Rouen : "L' infanticide de Oissel". Un couple a essayé d'aller jeter un nou- veau-né dans la Seine. Le M.L.F a posé les problèmes de la contraception, de l'avortement, des crèches. Le couple é- tait prêt à accepter notre aide juridique, mais on a été court- circuitées par les avocats nommés d'of- fice. Avril 72 : élec- tions municipales : on en profite pour faire des "bombages" en villes sur le thè- me : avortement, con- traception libres et gratuits. Le film "Coup pour Coup" sort. Le M.L.F. pré- sente le film, mais on avait mal calculé no- tre coup ; la salle était remplie de gauchistes de tout poil venus voir si les filles du M.L.F se foutaient à poil et utiliser la tribune offerte pour s'entredéchirer sur le rôle des syndicats... (Ils annoncèrent à la fin que les bourses de l'un de leurs camarades é- taient suspendues. Nous voulûmes savoir où, mais nous n'eûmes pas de réponse). Juin 72, c'est la grève à Thionville, on organise des col- lectes, on met l'accent sur le fait que c'est une grève de femmes. On monte un sketch sur l'avortement qu'on joue dans les rues. Ça marche, c'est au moment de l'affaire de Marie Claire. (voir photo du groupe rue du Gros-Horloge). On continue à se réunir régulièrement en week-end, en A.G, en commissions. On rencontre le Plan- ning Familial sur l'avortement, on est allées en vacances et maintenant on fait le journal....

Ce qui ne va pas....

- Nos actions restent ponctuelles, fonction de l'événement.
- Nos actions marquent notre existence, mais ne nous lient pas aux autres femmes.
- Forte participation aux actions, mais a- près chaque action l'unité du groupe est menacée.
- Manque d'analyse des actions.
- On craint les contacts parce qu'on ne sait pas quoi faire des filles qui voudraient nous rejoindre.
- Il y a diverses tendances dans le groupe, mais toutes ne s'expriment pas.
- On n'arrive pas à définir ce qu'on veut : quelles femmes doivent se libérer et par quels moyens ?
- Sur quoi on veut agir : sur les femmes elles- mêmes ou sur les structures ?
- Les filles ex-militantes sont mal perçues par les autres : problème des leaders.
- Des filles viennent aux réunions mais ne s'impliquent pas.
- Participation irrégulière aux réunions (un jour 50, un jour 5)

- On décide toutes ensembles d'une action de longue haleine et on se retrouve quelques unes à la faire.
- On désire trop la cohésion du grou- pe, il vaudrait peut-être mieux se séparer pour former des groupes ayant des objectifs communs.
- On cherche un local....

Paris, Lyon, Bordeaux, Nice etc... avez vous les mêmes problèmes que nous ?

On aimerait bien voir la vie des groupes dans le torchon.

3

funny ideas ideas by funny women
by sunny sunny women
by funny ideas
sunny

Woman's Day!

fabulous women — women

The little secrets from fabulous women

Franziska's Erdbeercreme: ½ pound strawberries, cut into small pieces. Cook one (4 servings) envelope of vanille pudding with half the amount of milk indicated. Carefully mix the pudding, strawberries and lots of whipped cream.

I like ice cream on a stick!

Dessert Delight: Gelatine in ⅔ cup water. Add 2/3 cup boiling water. ¾ cup, 1 cup milk and 1½ teaspoon extract. Chill in icetray and cut into cubes, serve with mandarin oranges.

Kathy's Charm: dissolve 1 bag 1/3 cup cold water plus almond icetray 1/3 cup sugar and with.

why not just eat a piece of cheese, a slice of Italian bread and a ripe peach or try a fresh fig with a piece of ricotta salata?

I like fresh blueberries, lightly sweetened with cold milk, served in a flat wide bowl, with buttered pumpernickel!

I like guava paste with cream cheese and saltine crackers

Did you ever try to cook pumpkin, cut into ½ inch cubes, with sugar and vinegar for a long time, until the pumpkin color get brown and the whole stuff like syrup? Good with meat.

LEARY'S LOVER VOWS--
'We'll Fast To Death'

Berkeley Barb

VOL. 17 NO. 10 ISSUE 395 MARCH 9-15, 1973
2042 UNIVERSITY AVE., BERKELEY, CA. 94701 849-0 0
PUBLISHED EVERY FRIDAY ©Berkeley BARB 1973
204
25¢ OUTSIDE OF BAY AREA 15¢ BAY AREA

SEED

CHICAGO VOL 6 NO 8 35¢

LITTLE GIRL OF ALL THE DAUGHTERS YOU WERE BORN A WOMAN NOT A SLAVE

WORDS LAURA NYRO
MUSIC KARMA GRAPHICS

OPPOSITE: A woman's place, past and present versions. **Berkeley Barb**, March 1973.
ABOVE AND OVERLEAF: feminism or the cover of **Seed** and on a poster for International Women's Day, 8 March 1970.

125

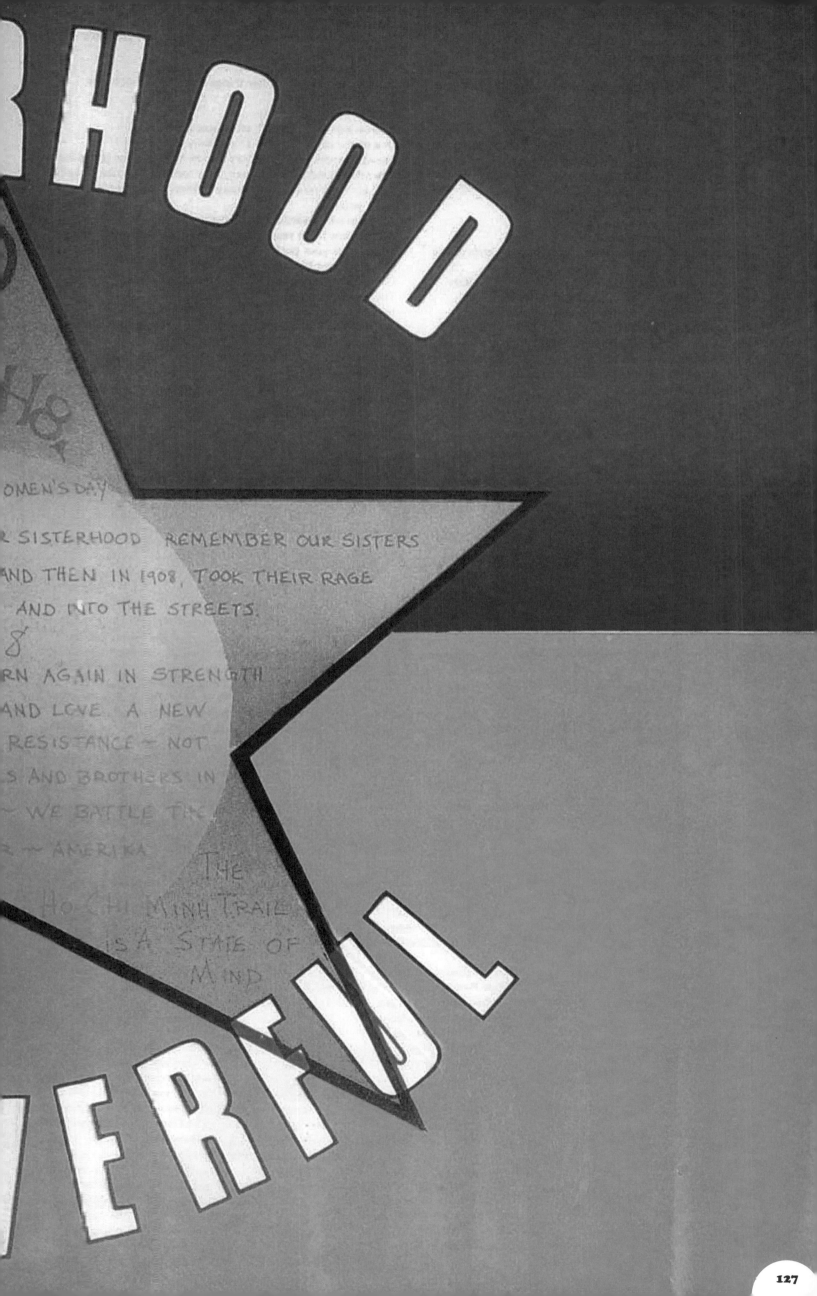

RHOOD

OMEN'S DAY

SISTERHOOD   REMEMBER OUR SISTERS
AND THEN IN 1908, TOOK THEIR RAGE
AND INTO THE STREETS.

RN AGAIN IN STRENGTH
AND LOVE. A NEW
RESISTANCE — NOT
AND BROTHERS IN
WE BATTLE TH
AMERIKA
THE
HO CHI MINH TRAIL
IS A STATE OF
MIND

EBVL

LA DANSE DU SPERME

Seul nénuphar charrié sans dommage dans le flot bourbeux de cette presse du cul que nous vomissent Amsterdam, Copenhague ou Nouillorque, Suck éclate de tendresse, de sérieux et d'humour : la pornographie y trouve ses marquises et le noble postérieur humain ses assises. Les créateurs, Bill Levy, Jim Haynes, Willem de Ridder et notre bonne Germaine Greer (qui galipette dans le dernier numéro en nous dévoilant ce superbe et baveux panorama qui n'appartient qu'à elle) ne sortent pas de la poubelle à ragnagna de ces mercantis crapuleux qui vous engangent de la rente sur le désir frustré. Ils ont fondé It et Oz et se sont couverts de blessures au plus fort de la bataille underground de Londres. Mobilisés depuis 1969 sur la libération sexuelle, ils partent du principe que tous les médias sont bons quand il s'agit de baisser la culotte aux préjugés. Amsterdam leur doit ses deux festivals du film pornographique, les fameux Wet Dream Festival dont le second s'achève sur le pont d'un bateau dément, orgone à moteur qui court les canaux de la ville.

Ils viennent de lancer, ces sournois, un roman-photo pornographique, drôle et superbement mis en page, The Virgin Sperm Dancer : un type devient nana pour vingt-quatre heures et assume sur ses amants tous ses phantasmes passés. Les auteurs, qui sont aussi acteurs, n'ont pas travaillé dans la morosité et nous préparent d'autres livraisons de cet ordre. Jim Haynes, qui nous gratifiait l'an dernier de ses chroniques facétieuses, est venu émettre quelques joies joyeuses jusque dans nos bas-fonds.

Jim Haynes : La pornographie est trop souvent froide et laide. Le sexe n'y est qu'objet de profit. Comme nous avons horreur de critiquer et de devenir grincheux, nous avons décidé de produire un érotisme tendre, joyeux et sensible.

Actuel : A ce propos, l'éditeur Eric Losfeld vient d'être condam-

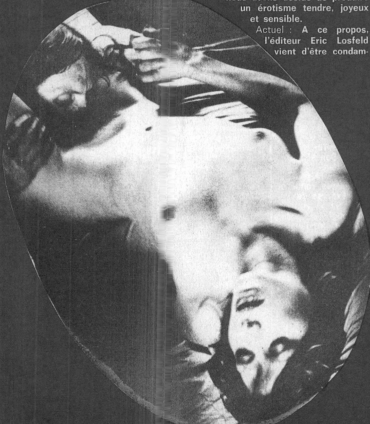

né pour la énième fois, outrage aux bonnes mœurs, paraît-il. Huit mille francs d'amende pour un bouquin qu'il avait déjà édité il y a plus de dix ans sous un autre nom. Pas mal, non ? Il n'y a vraiment pas de quoi fouetter un cul ! Les magistrats, pour le condamner ont établi une subtile distinction entre l'odieuse pornographie et l'érotisme de bon ton...

Jim Haynes : Pouark ! Ce classement est complètement idiot. La pornographie des uns est l'érotisme des autres.

Actuel : Comment avez-vous démarré Suck ?

Jim Haynes : Nous utilisons la sexualité comme médium, et pas un journal n'en parlait. Un lundi après-midi de 1969, à Londres, nous nous sommes réunis, Germaine Greer, Bill et moi-même. Il y avait également notre copain Heatcote William, mais il a passé tout le temps de la réunion à faire l'amour dans la chambre à côté... Heureux augure ! Bref, nous étions, et nous sommes toujours, persuadés que la révolution sexuelle est la clef de toutes les autres : si l'on s'ouvre de ce côté, on s'ouvre partout, à tout. De toute façon, on ne possède que son corps.

Actuel : On peut aussi se faire mal.

Jim Haynes : C'est une affaire de conscience. Si tu aimes quelqu'un, contente-toi de sa propre satisfaction, peu importe comment il ou elle y parvient. L'amour passe par le bonheur de l'autre, c'est une politique...

Actuel : Pourquoi es-tu parti faire Suck à Amsterdam ?

Jim Haynes : Avec Copenhague, peut-être, c'est la ville la plus libre du monde. Et puis j'aime bien Willem de Ridder, l'un des fondateurs d'Aloha, un grand maquettiste. Je pensais : à Amsterdam on va être tranquille. Dans le premier numéro on indiquait une boîte postale à Londres. Scotland Yard l'a fermée. Les flics anglais se sont pointés à Amsterdam voir la police hollandaise. Quand ils ont demandé notre interdiction, les Hollandais leur ont ri au nez. Suck est légal.

Actuel : A quel moment la libération sexuelle s'est-elle organisée en mouvement ?

Jim Haynes : Vers 1965, avec la fondation de la Sexual Freedom à Berkeley, le « révérend » Jefferson Fuck Poland qui en est à l'origine (un type extrêmement chaleureux qui se fait maintenant appeler Jefferson Fuck tout court) organisait des soirées incroyables, des manifestations étonnantes, puissantes. Je ne suis pourtant pas une orgiaque de tous les jours. Je crois qu'il faut bâtir des relations humaines à long terme avec les gens, sans se braquer sur le contrôle et l'acquisition. J'ai une amie qui flippe quand on parle d'orgie mais prend son pied quand on évoque une cérémonie amoureuse... Je trouve très important de connaître le corps de ses amis.

Actuel : La libération sexuelle ne te semble-t-elle pas d'une qualité différente chez le freak qui essaie de l'assumer en famille et chez le bourgeois qui la consomme comme un loisir canaille ?

Jim Haynes : Possible. Mais j'ai remarqué que tous les gens nus se ressemblent, qu'ils soient fascistes, communistes ou anarchistes... Intéressant, non ? J'ajoute

que je n'aime pas ce que je nomme le « syndrome de la performance ». L'orgasme n'est pas le seul objectif à atteindre, le corps tout entier est érotique. On peut faire l'amour en se tenant la main, passer la nuit ensemble sans s'affronter sexuellement.

Actuel : Près de Los Angeles, dans Topanga canyon, j'ai assisté à un séminaire de psychothérapie sexuelle. On y pratiquait la nude therapy, enfermés à vingt, nus, toute une semaine, dans une piscine, sans contact avec l'extérieur. La bouffe passait par une fenêtre. Des cris rauques résonnaient sous la voûte comme ces orgasmes de W.R., les mystères de l'organisme.

Jim Haynes : Et pourquoi pas ? Un grand nombre de névroses et de déséquilibrés émotionnels viennent d'un manque d'affection : donc, aimez plusieurs personnes ! N'en aimer qu'une, c'est n'en pas profiter, n'en rien retirer...

Actuel : Après la Sexual freedom league, quoi d'important ?

Jim Haynes : Crumb et les comix, le women's lib, tiraillé à ce sujet entre deux attitudes : un puritanisme réactionnaire ou le « baiser plus et mieux » de Germaine Greer. Il serait temps que les femmes n'attendent plus la sonnerie du téléphone et qu'elles sortent chercher ce qui leur convient. Qu'elles partent à l'abordage, qu'elles se remuent ! L'autre soir dans un restaurant, une femme m'a dit : « Tu me plais ». Formidable ! Très important ! Mais la plupart des types ne supportent pas, ils flippent quand les rôles s'inversent... A Suck, nous ne croyons pas à la perversion. Un mot comme « homosexuel » nous irrite : ce n'est qu'un classement, la seule distinction possible est entre le sexe accepté et le sexe refusé. Les clubs sexuels vont à l'encontre de la véritable libération. Les homosexuels se battent la plupart du temps pour leur chapelle. Qu'ils se battent pour les autres formes de libération sexuelle au lieu de revendiquer pour eux l'ensemble du combat. Un grand combat reste : la libération

sexuelle ... s enfants. Attendons. J'ai déjà ... contré des gosses de freaks ... nants, ouvers et délurés. N ... hibés, ni pervers, ni réprimés

Actuel : ... France, vois-tu une évolution ?

Jim Haynes : Je suis un incurable optimiste. Bien sûr, l'heritage de Madame de Gaulle est lourd : elle a rep ... gé la France dans le passé ave ... ses voilettes pudiques sur le ... dre décolleté. Mais Paris est ... e ville sensuelle, on y marge L ... et beaucoup, on y baise ... lisse... On y est ... giquement ... ypocrite, comme en Angleterre ... l'on tolère le sexe artisti ... et coûteux pour les gens r ... hes. Au delà des quartiers libres, ... banlieue, c'est la tasse. O.K. ... banlieue d'Amsterdam n'es ... s rigolarde non plus. La grande ... le permet l'anonymat et dilue ... pression sociale qui se ress ... dans les petits groupes.

Actuel : ... a parlé de bestialité. Ça ne ... gêne pas ?

Jim Haynes : Ce n'est pas mon problème, mais tout le monde a besoin d'amour. Il y a des gens qui ne t ... ent pour les aimer que des c ... ens, des chats, des perroquets ... u des cochons en tire-bouch ...

Actuel : ... es deux Wet Dream festival ... en prépares un autre ?

Jim Haynes : Je préfererais organiser des « Love célébration » dans u ... grand château, ou sur un bateau ... dant une semaine. Des re ... de toutes sortes, bien th ... J'aimerais ouvrir un bordel ... t tous les visiteurs seraient le ... prostitués... quarante personn ... par jour, un banquet, un sauna, ... a belle musique...

Actuel : ... as-tu jamais été chaste ?

Jim Haynes : Non, je ne crois pas aux mythes ... mantiques.

Actuel : E ... xpérience à laquelle te con ... t Germaine Greer l'année der ... e...

Jim Haynes : Me faire enculer ?... Je me suis ... cordé un délai jusqu'à la fin ... 1973.

ABOVE: **The Wet Dream Festival**, Europe's first erotic film festival, took sexual liberation to its limits. **Actuel**, November 1972.
OVERLEAF: **Sexual Liberation** for sale, or just a manifestation of male chauvinism?

Beserkeley Records: How They Blew It

Berkeley Barb

Babe Ruth

Issue 555, April 2 - 8, 1976   Copyright: Berkeley Barb 1976   204   25¢ BAY AREA, 50¢ ELSEWHERE

SEXISM ON TRIAL

Exclusive Interview With S.Korean Opposition Leader

The International Tribunal on Crimes Against Women: A Special Report

Why KPIX Won't Let You See 'Helter Skelter'
Page 10

Local Agribusiness Conspiracy Unfolds
Page 5

Big Time Sports: It's No Game
Page 13

Paul Krassner On Media Misinformation
Page 6

Culture Schlock In Sunny Florida
Page 12

New Offering From Sci—Fi Master John Brunner
Page 12

Volume 13, No. 7 (604) Feb. 13-19, 1976

LOS ANGELES
FREE PRESS

Jailed Pot Possessors May Be Out of the Joint Soon

The Harrises' Unedited Statement on the FBI

The CIA's Top Gun (cont.)

Jack Anderson: Hoover's Good Side

Plus: Krassner, Bukowski & Expanded Guide to Local Events

Jerry Rubin Discovers:
THE FEM

JAN · 76

ALE IN ME

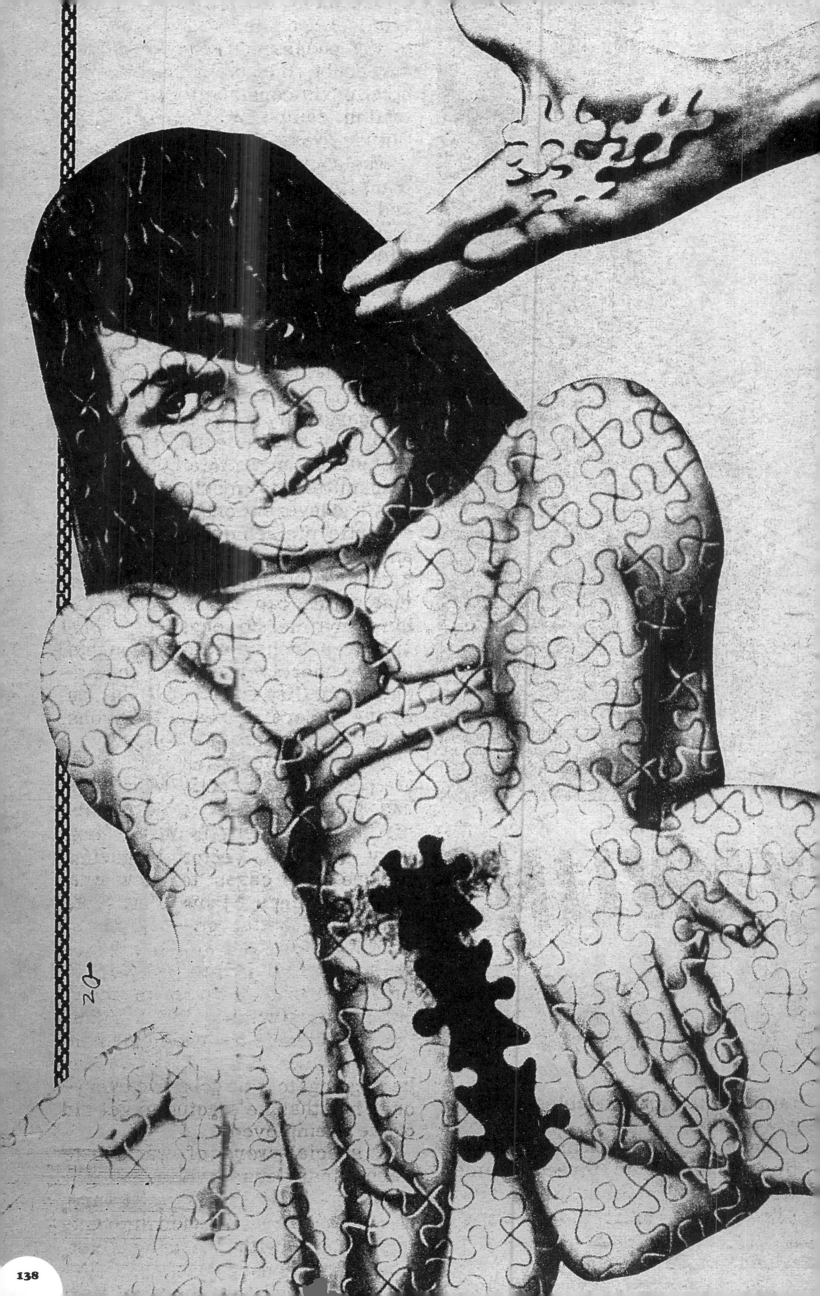

PREVIOUS PAGES, LEFT: **Hundert Blumen,** an eminent German member of
the Underground Press Syndicate. Berlin, 1973.

PREVIOUS PAGES, RIGHT: The Mona Lisa shows her fangs.

OPPOSITE: The abortion puzzle, as illustrated in the **Berkeley Barb,** 1973.
Abortion is still a hotly contested issue in the USA today.

ABOVE: "No more of this!" **Actuel** supported the legalization of abortion
in France, 1973.

FLY

DANCE Aug. 8 SAT

with
BRUTE FORCE
CHILDREN of GOD
COMMUNICATIONS
WORKSHOP
BEV & LORRAINE
OCEAN

JAM
with
INSECT TRUST
JIMMY the FLEA
& OTHERS

benefit for
Alternate U.
at Hotel Diplomat
108 W. 43st.
Sat. Aug. 8 - $2.50

New York after-dark is a kaleidoscope of colour

Judson Mobile Health
Unit has moved
Stanton & Pitt Sts.
1pm - 9pm
Mon-Sat -
call 208-19

Special exhibit at the
American Museum of
Natural History
thru Aug - call TR3-1300
ecch
THE EFFECT OF
POLLUTION
ON NEARBY FISH

Benefit concert and film
aug. 18 tues. Lute Songs of the Renaissance - Janet Steele & Lucy Cross
with a screening of Midge Mackenzie's 7 & 10 pm
"Bushes #1" "Women Talking"
Washington Square Church - 135 W 4
proceeds to Women's Liberation CINEMA ($12)

SISTERS & BROTHERS OF THE 3RD WORLD HOMOSEXUAL COLONY
IN BABYLON (AMERIKKKA):
an ad hoc committee has been formed concerning our oppression, and actions to be taken to guarantee our participation and survival in the revolutionary future.
an important meeting will take place on Friday, August 14th, 8pm, at 124 West 23rd St. 3rd floor.
all gay people of color are urgently invited to attend.
LAGIMA TOSHINDE MBILASHAKA!!
SEIZE THE TIME!! ALL POWER TO THE PEOPLE !!!
VENCEREMOS !!!

The city that made it big. In sights and ... cit emegt

This film is rated
BLECCH
-RAT
(No stars for sexist movies)

MUSIC
FREE Rock Concert
in Tompkins Sq. Park
Ave. B & 7th St.
eLephant's memory
Wed Aug 12 - 8pm

GAY DANSE-A-FAIR
Every Fri during August 9pm
Weinstein Hall Sub-Cellar at NYU
University Pl & 8th St
Handcraft & Photo exhibits
→ Christopher St. Liberation Day Comm

VOICES OF EAST HARLEM
Aug. 9 - 6pm - Kaiser Park, Coney Island
Call 593-2876 for info

GOOD
Paradox food from
your friendly vendor
at 8th St & University Pl.
weekday afternoons.

FOOD
FREE
PERFORMANCES:
Dirty Ferdie Comes Clean - Aug 15
The Terrible Angels (Venezuela) - Aug 19
Cinnamon (Childrens Play) - Aug 29 - 3pm
Recuerdos de Tulipo (...) Aug 29
Henry St. Settlement - 766-1414

NEW FEDERAL THEATER →
the third world revolutionists
DODO - 2 plays
Thur Aug 13-16 8:30p
202 Henry St. WO 7-1100

N.Y. Theater of the Ameri...
2nd summer ...
fest. ...
- Aug 15 - ... pm
... Spanish
... Greatest
23.

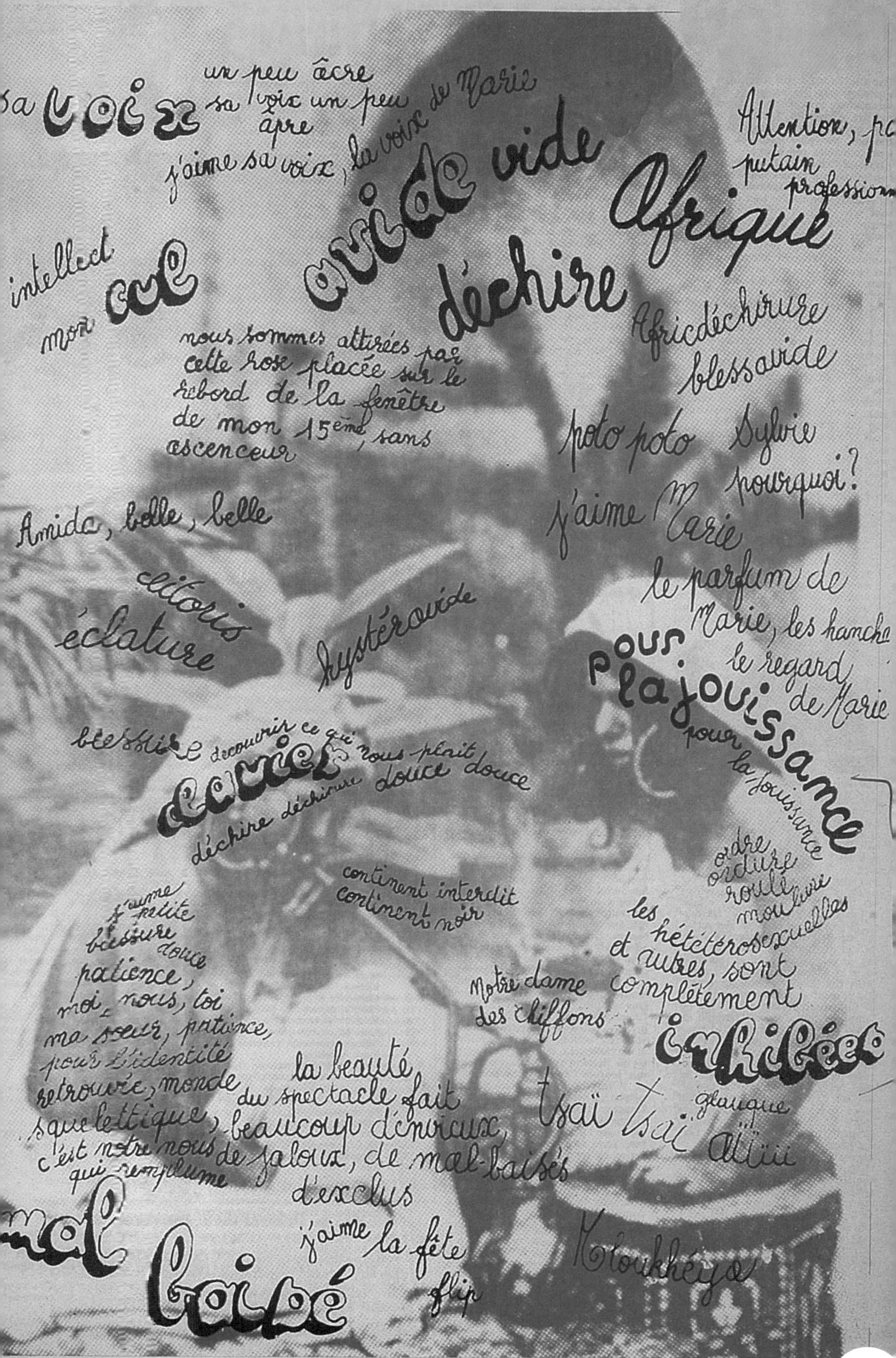

sa **voix** un peu âcre
sa voix un peu âpre
j'aime sa voix, la voix de Marie

avide vide

Attention, pa
putain
profession

Afrique

intellect

mon **cœur**

déchire

Africdéchirure
blessavide

nous sommes attirées par
cette rose placée sur le
rebord de la fenêtre
de mon 15ème, sans
ascenceur

poto poto Sylvie
pourquoi ?

j'aime Marie

Amida, belle, belle

le parfum de
Marie, les hanche
le regard
de Marie

clitoris
éclature

hystéroïde

pour.
pla jouissance
pour la jouissance

blessure **écrire** découvrir ce qui nous plait
déchire déchirure douce douce

ordre
ordure
rouille
mouille
les hétérosexuelles
et autres, sont
complétement

j'aime
petite
blessure
douce
patience,
moi, nous, toi,
ma soeur, patience,
pour l'identité
retrouvée, monde
squelettique,
c'est notre nous
qui remplume

continent interdit
continent noir

Notre dame
des chiffons

inhibées

la beauté
du spectacle fait
beaucoup d'envieux,
de jaloux, de mal-baisés
d'exclus

tsaï tsaï glauque
Aïïï

mal

baisé

j'aime la fête
flip

Kioukhéya

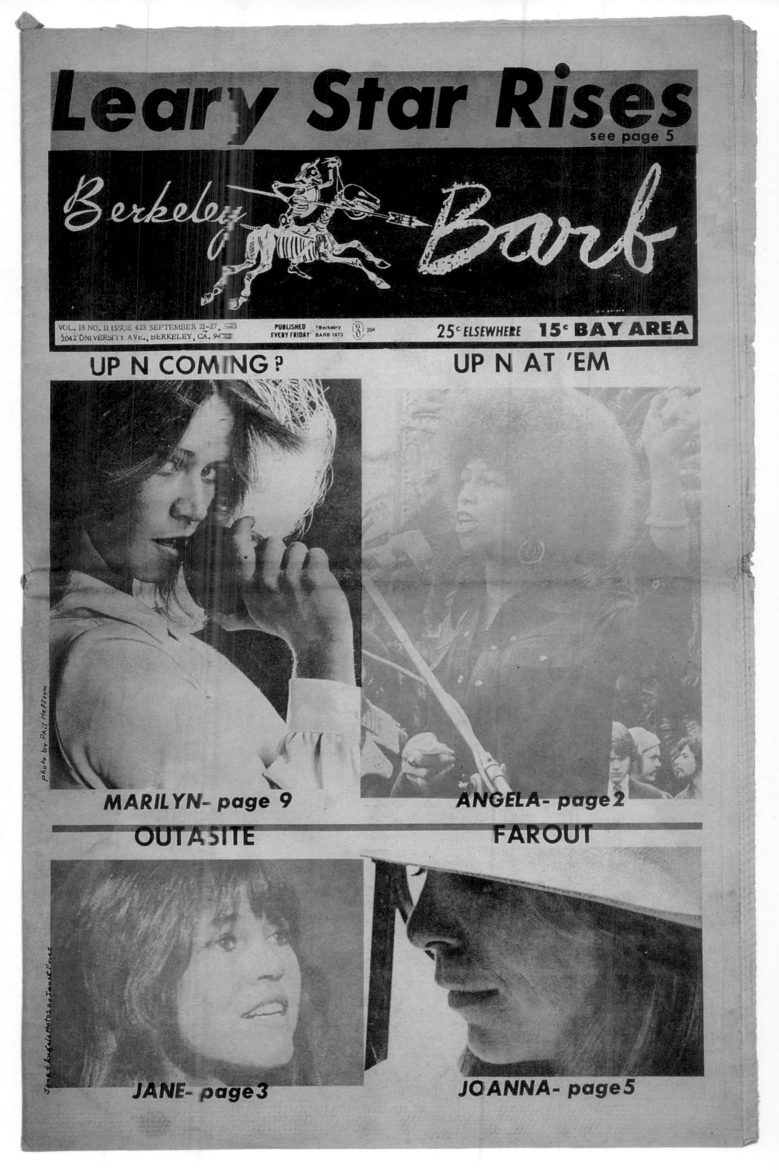

Leary Star Rises

see page 5

Berkeley Barb

VOL. 18 NO. 11 ISSUE 423 SEPTEMBER 21-27, 1973
2042 UNIVERSITY AVE., BERKELEY, CA. 94...

PUBLISHED EVERY FRIDAY ©Berkeley BARB 1973

25¢ ELSEWHERE 15¢ BAY AREA

UP N COMING?

UP N AT 'EM

photo by Phil Heffern

MARILYN- page 9

ANGELA- page 2

OUTASITE

FAROUT

JANE- page 3

JOANNA- page 5

PREVIOUS PAGES, LEFT: **Events for everyone – Rat**, New York, 1970.
PREVIOUS PAGES, RIGHT: **Free-form poetry – Hobo-Québec**, Montreal, 1971.
ABOVE: **Women on top – choose your own icon. Berkeley Barb**, September 1973.
OPPOSITE: **Glad to be gay in the Free**, August 1970.

SAY IT OUT LOUD:

I'M GAY & I'M PROUD

GAY LIBERATION SUPPLEMENT

Of The Los Angeles Free Press   Section **2**   Friday, August 14, 1970

"We've Come A Long Way, Baby" —GLF/LA

TOUJOURS GAY--
PARADE POINTS WAY!

VOL. 17 NO. 26 ISSUE 411 JUNE 29-JULY 5, 1973
2042 UNIVERSITY AVE., BERKELEY, CA 94701
PUBLISHED EVERY FRIDAY ⓒBerkeley BARB 1973
25¢ OUTSIDE OF BAY AREA 15¢ BAY AREA

ALSO INSIDE:
GINSBERG on WATERGATE and LEARY
-- pages 10, 11

WATCH OUT FOR NIXON'S MINDFUCKER

ABOVE: San Francisco's first Gay Freedom Day parade. **Berkeley Barb**, June 1973.
OPPOSITE: Poster from **Rat**, New York, 197_.

144

Gay Community

Celebration of Love and Life

Berkeley Barb

25¢ BAY AREA - ELSEWHERE 50¢

Issue 620, July 1 - 7, 1977 ISSN: 0005-9161 Copyright: Berkeley Barb 1977

UD BEACH
GAY PARADE
...A Photo Spectacular!!!

Trouble For Huey!
Battle For KPFA!

Tenure For Edwards!
Suicide For Fun?

ôte ta perruque, jean-raoul, on t'a reconnu

Les New York Dolls montrent leurs culs poilus en tirant sur les cordes de leurs Gibsons. Alice Cooper provoque Sacher Masoch qui ne répond pas. David Bowie essaie vainement de tirer de la semence d'une guitare basse. La dialectique de la provocation et du dollar se développe en spirales d'Archimède. Pourtant, les émules de 1925, les nostalgiques du boulevard du Crépuscule et les décadents au petit pied et au gros portefeuille ne sont que pâles plagiaires, malgré leur talent de musiciens et de show-men.
A New York, depuis quinze ans, les « drag queen » font bien mieux et en jettent un peu plus. Le théâtre de travestis, qui libère un des derniers ressorts du tabou, celui de l'homosexualité, a revitalisé le scandale. La nudité affable, la sexualité tremblotante, le hurlement tragique ou la politique braillarde, d'un coup et pour un soir semblent affadis. Les Cockettes elles-mêmes ont raté leur entrée à New York. Ils sont apparus comme de tristes émules et ont abandonné dans le « village » leur fraction la plus nickelée, le bel Hibiscus en tête. Galonné comme Malboro, celui-ci emmène les Angels of Light au front de la décomposition et du sarcasme nostalgique. Les jeudi, vendredi et samedi soir, à minuit, au bout de Jame Street dans le fond délabré de Grennwich Village, ils s'exposent gratuitement, noblesse et mécénat obligent, collectionnant tous les chics du moment. Marlène s'avance d'un pas chaloupé, les soldats du Vietnam tirent sur une dernière pipe, la poudre d'argent flotte, le strass volette, falbalas, brandebourgs et aiguillettes, souquenilles d'or, passements et passepoils, ils sont dû soudoyer la costumière de l'Opéra de Baltimore. On rit de les voir si belles et la salle est bourrée, le public d'une présentation de Dior quand Rubirosa, Patino et Trujillo ne craignaient encore rien et saupoudraient leurs concubines de renard bleu.
Cela même n'est que frivolité. Dans le souterrain, les vrais travestis affichent un talent somptueux et ironique. Cascades de miroirs où l'on se perd, ces ricanements sur soi-même à faire pâlir Kierkegaard. Depuis longtemps, chacun s'est forgé un personnage puisé dans la collection des images pieuses d'Hollywood, Maria Montez, Alexis de Lago, Marylin à cinq exemplaires, Jackie Curtis qui sait se faire toutes les têtes. Ce demi-monde a ses stars. Cette année, elles ont pour nom Candy Darling qui nie son passé d'homme et perce à Broadway et Holly Woodlawn, l'héroïne de Trash qui a ressorti ses costumes d'adolescent. Ce monde s'exhibe avec un panache que ne risquent pas l'Alcazar et la Grande Eugène. In the search of the cobra jewels est la dernière pièce du club des travestis écrite par Harvey Finstein, l'Oscar Wilde de cette Arcadie qui n'a rien de spartiate. On ébranle les colonnes de temples longtemps délaissés. Le Dieu Pan frappe, le monde maudit s'assume, grotesque, vivant, drôle, parfois pathétique, fièrement pathologique, l'exhibitionnisme devient un évangile. Babylone, ici, montre ses parties honteuses, les plus révélatrices et les plus vivantes. A l'ombre des grandes tours, Messaline et Jarry ont trouvé de dignes émules. Ils occupent le devant de la scène, la princesse Lee Radziwill les fraye, et héberge Mick Jagger, sa sœur Jackie Onassis s'en inquiète — un peu seulement — car tout cela est tellement « Schwartzo ». Ce spectaculaire est ancré dans l'angoisse déracinée d'une société qui a manqué le coche de sa révolution. L'underground orne les parties huppées alors que les gens chics s'encanaillent dans un chassé-croisé d'ennui somptueux. Voilà la scène : c'est la fin d'un acte. Ce paravent éblouissant masque la mort d'une éthique. Les gens de talent y fleurissent et y meurent, petits rats plus ou moins piégés de tous ces fromages. Les photos sont de Gilles Larrain, deux mille photos de travestis, un livre à venir. Consultez sinon le prochain numéro de Zoom. La plus belle série, dont une photo éclate sur la prochaine double page : le travesti le plus méconnu de New York, qui se prend pour la Pavlova et ne se dépare jamais, Taylor Meade, acteur remarquable, grand augure de ces dégoulinades, poète, quatre-vingts films underground, longtemps attaché à Warhol mais incorruptible de l'underground artiste, l'un des premiers homosexuels à avoir relevé la tête — en ricanant comme Hyma — vingt fois agressé et le corps tailladé par des gouapes. Il a connu toutes les scènes, baladant son air de douairière ironique d'un vernissage chic au plus noir des bas-fonds. Il raconte.

57

OPPOSITE: No comment, but note the date: 1977.
Liberation comes late to the beaches of California.
ABOVE: Taylor Mead, pioneering drag artist, as seen in **Actuel**, Paris, 1973.

À quand remonte l'apparition des « drag shows » dans l'underground et ce goût pour le « camp », l'ornement et le décadent ?
Les travestis affluent depuis toujours à New York où la tolérance est, en tous sens, à la mesure du gigantisme. Le goût de la folie, la culture et la défonce, les grands délires des grandes rebellions et l'affirmation du Gay Lib n'ont fait qu'accentuer la tendance déjà sensible dans une partie du cinéma underground, marquée par l'Opéra de Jean Cocteau. Flaming Creatures, le film de Jack Smith, en est le signe magnifique. Quant à moi, je n'avais rien compris puisque j'ai refusé de jouer dedans, en pensant que cela ne serait que basse pornographie, alors que Jack Smith a tourné la première épopée travestie. Je regrette d'avoir mis si longtemps à oser me travestir. Les folies m'ont assumé, et nous ont libérés. Les travestis de New York ont ouvert une porte de secours à l'homosexuel du Middle West qui présente une nette tendance suicidaire.
Pourquoi New York est-elle une ville plus libérale ?
Lindsay, le maire, est un libéral qui a bénéficié lors de son élection du suffrage de dizaines de milliers d'homosexuels. Il le sait. Et les homosexuels brimés finissent par aboutir à New York. A Los Angeles par exemple, ils sont fichés et certains doivent présenter une carte à la moindre acquisition. Dans l'Iowa, pire encore : on les fauchait il y a seulement quinze ans. De toute façon, l'homosexualité fait courir de graves dangers. On en tue cinq ou six par semaine rien qu'à New York, un quart des meurtres peut-être. Les homosexuels ont encore peur de se présenter en tant que tels dans un commissariat et de déposer plainte. Ceux-là sont la proie rêvée des petits truands.
Et le Gay Libération ?
Il s'est battu sur quelques points concrets, a démarré il y a trois ans sur la fermeture autoritaire de certains bars par la police, s'est énormément gonflé en deux ans, bouleversant l'attitude du public en se manifestant sans complexes avec des militants qui ne présentaient pas l'apparence stéréotypée de la « tante ». Mais il a pris peu à peu un côté puritain : comme souvent les groupes politiques, il a enfoui l'humour sous les manifestes.
J'ai une amie », Wayne County, qui chante dans un groupe de rock travesti. Ce faisant, elle manipule un vagin en caoutchouc et le stimule pour rire. Le directeur d'une université de New York a coupé le courant pendant leur dernier show et les types du Gay Liberation se sont rués à les attaquer en les accusant « d'insulter à la cause homosexuelle ». A se prendre trop au sérieux le Gay Lib se ridiculise : les militants avaient déposé des amendements auprès du conseil municipal de New York pour obtenir une modification de certains règlements et se sont rendus à la séance pour appuyer leurs projets : comme certains conseillers municipaux osaient sourire à leur vue, ils se sont bêtement énervés et se sont mis à hurler : « Comment ! vous osez sourire ! » Le projet n'est pas passé.
Si le milieu homosexuel est dangereux, l'underground semble l'être aussi ?
La scène en général l'est, dans la mesure où elle brasse en marge des milliers d'individus névrosés, psychopathes, déséquilibrés qui y trouvent la seule survie possible. Le mélange donne le humus dont se repaissent écrivains, poètes et cinéastes. Mais plus tu vas à l'aventure, plus la jungle t'entoure. Mon premier réalisateur, underground bien sûr, avait d'inquiétantes absences dans le regard : il voulait absolument m'enfermer dans une malle et, je le crains, l'y laisser moisir un moment pour réussir son joli plan. Il y a déjà eu beaucoup de morts. Trois des actrices du film Cléopâtre, de Michel Auder, sont décédées. La dernière, Andrea, la jeune actrice défoncée des films Heat et Trash, de Warhol, s'est suicidée cet été. Elle était merveilleuse. Quand nous avions de l'argent, nous louions une limousine et nous allions faire un peu de scandale dans un quelconque vernissage. On dit que Warhol lui avait refusé dix dollars le matin même... Tout l'underground sait qu'Andy promet plein de trucs et ne tient guère. A ce niveau de célé-

brité, on se sent peut-être obligé de dire oui à tout le monde, mais à manipuler des gens malheureux pour mieux tourner leurs états d'âme, on risque des explosions. Ce qui se produisit deux fois : un jeune mec tira sur Andy et y a six ans et je détournai le coup de feu en me jetant sur son bras. En 1968, Valérie Solanas, auteur de Scum, vexée qu'Andy n'ait pas produit sa pièce Up my ass, pansit le blessa gravement de deux balles de revolver. Andy exploite beaucoup et brime tout autant les riches que les pauvres. Une de ses superstars, Edie Sedgwick, une héritière de grande race, s'est suicidée de dépit quand il a renouvelé ses superstars et que, du jour au lendemain, il ne lui a plus parlé.
A-t-il gagné beaucoup d'argent avec ses films ?

Évidemment. Ils sont tournés en trois jours, improvisés, portés par les sentiments et les névroses des acteurs. Holly Woodlawn par exemple. Andy n'en voulait pas à la télévision où elle avait, disait-on, volé une machine à écrire. Puis un jour, il a lu les mémoires d'Holly dans un cahier d'écolier... C'est fait. Il existe une subtile hiérarchie parmi les superstars : aucune promotion pour la plupart — au contraire d'Hollywood, et un coup pourtant. Personne les chanceux : Candy Darling ou Holly. Ou le petit faveri Joe Dallesandro, qu'Andy, généreux et voulait entretient ainsi que la famille, jusqu'au petit frère qu'il vient d'envoyer au collège. Les autres stars touchent cent, deux cents ou trois cents dollars pour leur participation au film. Pour Nude restaurant, la première année d'Andy, j'ai

touché vingt dollars, cent francs, pour interpréter le rôle principal. Après quoi des films comme Flesh ou Trash qui ont coûté respectivement vingt et dix millions, rapportent des milliards...
Personne ne te poursuit ?
Peut-être le ferais-je un jour. A mon avis, il n'a pas fait nos trois meilleurs films : San Diego Surf, avec Viva et Joe Dalessandro, The Detective avec l'énorme Bridget Polk dans le rôle du détective et L'imitation de Jésus-Christ, avec Patrick, le James Dean de l'underground. Pas plus que l'ineffable Tarzan dont j'incarne la bouffonnerie. Je me suis brouillé avec lui après l'ultime maquignonnage auquel il s'est livré au printemps dernier, avec les marchands d'art : il a organisé une vente de ses toiles et les a rachetées lui-mêmes pour faire monter les cours, 300 000 F le tableau. Les toiles d'Andy sont peut-être étonnantes, mais c'est de la mauvaise peinture qui ne devrait pas mieux se vendre qu'Oldenburg ou Rauschenberg. J'ai dénoncé cette manipulation, au grand émoi du monde artistique. Je n'ai en rien à faire de bousculer la vingtaine de profiteurs et la quinzaine de milliardaires qui contrôlent la spéculation. Malgré tout, on adore encore Andy. Le personnage reste tellement génial dans une scène absurde et malade. Et puis, les bons souvenirs, lorsqu'on tournait tout le temps et n'importe quoi, décontracté et stoned... ça rend bien naturel. On devrait faire fumer un peu les grands acteurs d'Hollywood : ça leur éviterait bien des grimaces stéréotypées. Alors qu'en général les acteurs fument dans la vie et s'abstiennent avant le tournage.
D'où vient l'argent ? Le cinéma underground a-t-il toujours eu des mécènes et des relations avec la haute société ?
Beaucoup d'artistes viennent de la grande bourgeoisie. Ils y gardent des contacts. J'ai personnellement préssé plusieurs milliardaires à Art... ils sont assez peu nombreux, toutefois, à passer la scène. Au premier chef, on trouve Jérôme Hill, qui n'est pas seulement un mécène. J'aime bien son film Portraits, le seul film autobiographique de milliardaire

(qu'on a vu à Paris en novembre, au studio Acacias). Son grand-père était l'un des magnats des chemins de fer. Pour une part, tout le cinéma underground new-yorkais lui doit d'exister. L'un des grands films de l'underground, Hallelujah the hills, des frères Mekas, s'appelait Hallelujah the woods avant que Jérome Hill n'en dépanne la production. Hallelujah the hills illustre bien les relations du cinéma underground et du milieu chic : l'acteur principal Peter Beard est le meilleur ami de Jackie Kennedy, une sorte de précepteur de ses enfants. Un mec haut en couleurs qui a voulu créer un parc national de grands fauves au Kenya et a manqué de s'y faire tuer, l'homme qui a installé les Stones chez Lee Radziwill et dont Jackie a dit : « Son rêve : inviter Charles Manson pour un week-end... »
Quand tu réfléchis à ces quinze années passées dans le cinéma underground, qu'en retiens-tu ?
D'abord le souvenir de mes premiers films en 1960, à San Francisco, alors que la rénovation urbaine et les flics avaient raison des derniers beatniks du quartier de North Beach. On les a dispersés pour les supprimer et ils ont ainsi essaimé : qui l'eût cru ? Flower thief, le voleur de fleurs, qu'on tournait alors, est peut-être mon film préféré. A l'époque les cinéastes underground s'intéressaient surtout à l'homme, ses manies et ses déviances. Ils sont engagés à fond aujourd'hui dans l'expérimentation électroniques, la recherche colorée ou la vidéo.
C'est pourquoi je tourne moins, et souvent des films vidéo. Auparavant, j'avais tourné avec Markopoulos Iliac Passion un pensum pompeux et chiant. L'underground est resté trop underground. Nous avons confié nos films à Jonas Mekas, qui nous avait fait connaître par sa chronique du Village Voice. Il les a enterrés dans sa lugubre cinémathèque, dont chaque fauteuil est isolé pour bien s'assurer qu'on ne parle pas à son voisin. Mekas est un élitiste qui croit que quelques centaines de privilégiés peuvent, seuls, apprécier l'Art. Quant à lui, il a tendance à préférer le chiant...
Cours-tu encore les vernissages et les manifestations d'avant-garde ?

On m'invite peu, parce que je me manifeste toujours à contretemps. Au concert de Stockhausen, je me suis senti très libéré par la musique et j'ai dansé en lançant des avions en papier : l'avant-garde se tirait la tronche. J'ai failli me brouiller avec le Living theatre à Cassis il y a cinq ans, lorsqu'ils jouaient Mysteries and other Pieces. Julian Beck restait assis une heure durant à marmonner sans relâche : « Nous devons arrêter la guerre du Vietnam ». Cela devenait à la longue tragiquement solennel, au point de me taper sur les nerfs. Je me suis levé et j'ai crié : « Vive Johnson ! Vive la peste, vive la mort, à bas les intellectuels ! » Je hais les procédés. Un Marseillais m'a traité de « cul de poisson ». Le public était très choqué. Une heure après, je dansais avec le Living dans les rues pendant le happening de Lebel, qui avait distribué des flûtes à tout le monde. Un gros nuage bleu flottait sur la mer et c'était bien ainsi.

The History Of Drag

Dave Patrick

by Bob Schildgen

On Halloween, in San Francisco, when thousands of normally normal folks will actually run around in costumes normally reserved for the opposite sex, they will be part of a mass sex identity change which is normally taboo even in such an abnormally transexual city.

Halloween, the great witching time when the souls of the dead come forth, is also a sacred time here when everyone is permitted to drag right into strange worlds in which they would not normally find themselves.

The smugness of this city, the pride which many of its straight residents take in their tolerance of sexual non-conformity, would lead you to believe that it's the first place in the world that allowed such far-ranging transvestism.

Yet nothing could be farther from the truth. The Great Sexual Masquerade is as old as history. Transvestism has been around since Eve and Adam McAdam donned the undifferentiated fig leaves, and it will undoubtedly survive all cultural transformations.

The shamen in some "primitive" societies, whose androgynous nature allowed them great freedom in matters of clothing, were revered for their spiritual powers. Tiresias, the ancient Greek supershaman, was actually changed from a man to a woman by divine power.

The ancient Greeks had many kinaidos, men who went around in frankly feminine garb and makeup. The ancient Hebrews even had transvestite temple priests, the kadesh, who lived in the world of both female and male, while the dragqueen "contrary societies" among certain Native Americans are well known to first-year anthropology students.

And the Elizabethan theatre, which allowed only male actors, even in the most feminine roles, may have been the most artistic and enduring drag-festival of them all. Shakespeare himself is reputed to have played many a feminine role, and there are rumors in some scholarly circles that the famed dark lady of his sonnets was actually an attractive young black or Moorish actor.

The most amazing transvestite in European history was, of course, a Frenchman—Chevalier d'Eon de Beaumont. Born in 1728 he made his first mark on European diplomacy when he was sent with French diplomats to patch up relations

with the Russian Empress Elizabeth. He managed to smooth things over by gaining intimacy with Elizabeth's ladies-in-waiting as a lady-in-waiting himself.

Although he was an accomplished swordsman, and a successful dragoon in the Seven Years' War, his appearance, mannerisms, and lack of heterosexual affairs led his enemies to accuse him of being female, especially when he was living in London. In the early 1770s, the English papers ran many caricatures of him as half-man, half-woman.

He became a famous figure there, and thousands of pounds were publicly bet on the question of his sex. Always a publicity-hungry man, he rather enjoyed the controversy, to the point that he was even accused of promoting the gambling for his own profit.

Finally, as if in a gesture of ridicule aimed at both English and French societies, he announced that he was a woman.

From that point he dressed as a female and enjoyed the title of baroness.

Although d'Eon Beaumont had many political and financial difficulties in his long and immensely interesting life, he was considerably more fortunate than the transvestite Roman emperor, Heliogabalus, who ruled for a few years around 220 A.D. Trained as a transvestite priest in a Syrian cult, Heliogabalus was not at ease with himself or his position as emperor.

Unlike these who will revel in drag on Halloween, a change in clothing was not enough to satisfy his need to change sexual identity. Since the gods weren't obliging enough to transform him, as they did Tiresias, he took it on himself. The historian Dio Cassius says that Heliogabulus, "Planned, indeed, to cut off his genitals altogether, but the desire was prompted solely by his effeminacy. The circumcision which he actually carried out was a part of the priestly requirements of Elagabalus, and he accordingly mutilated many of his companions in like manner."

According to Cassio, this emperor as cruel to himself as to others, did not stop at circumcision, but became perhaps the first known human being to request a sex-change operation. Cassio says that, "Heliogabulus carried his lewdness to such a point that he asked the physicians to contrive a woman's vagina in his body by means of an incision, promising them large sums for doing so."

Whether the operation was actually carried out is a mystery. It was probably superseded by his death in one of those inevitable late Roman assassinations.

The history of theories of drag is almost as complicated as the history of drag itself. For secure straights who are enjoying the festivities of transexuality, I must quote the early, and somewhat severe Wilhelm Stekel, who speculated that "The latent homosexual becomes a transvestite only on account of his guilty conscience."

Nietzsche's observation is probably a lot more comforting to us all. He says "Everyone carries within himself a pattern of womanhood derived from his mother; that determines whether he should respect or depreciate women.

So, whether your sexual quest is to be like or unlike your mother, to improve on or parody her, you should still enjoy the masquerade, and become the mask as much as you want. As I said, E. and A. McAdam didn't know the difference. When they found out, they covered it up. Since then, the coverings have gone through many magic transformations, and there's no reason why people can't drape in the alternate identity of their choice, at least on the Eve of All Saints.

Celebrating The Gay Festivals

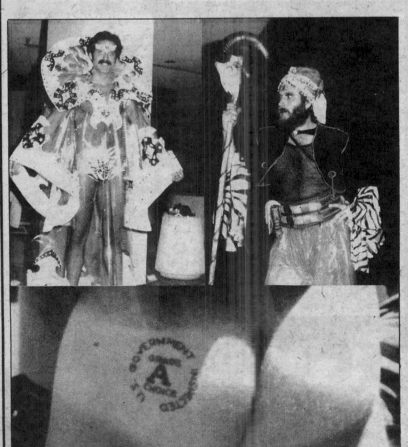

When six blocks along Polk Street are closed down this Sunday for Halloween festivities, the costumes could even outdo those pictured above from last year's Beaux Art Ball and from the last two Gay Freedom Day parades.

Goldie Glitters New Ash Smash

PAULA PUCKER

(extracted from a reflection by Martin Worman)

There is the Palace. There is Cindirella. There is Goldie Glitters. There is time and we are in it.

Goldie plays Cincirella at midnight October 2, 7 and Halloween, the 31st. Her co-stars include Scrumbly, Pristin Condition Fau-a Pucker, Jon Elowers, Riggie and others who were on or around stage for those golden, glittering Cockette days.

This show is not like the old ones. Goldie insists. There is money. There is one designer. There is one director. They are from Los Angeles. There is the Palace. That's in San Francisco.

"Where else," I asked, smoking a huge Acapulco Gold joint in the back seat of a '54 Rolls limo, "where else but in San Francisco could a boy from Paterson, New Jersey, escort a queen to the Palace?" It was summer 1970. I was Goldie's favorite chorus boy. My first appearance in a Cochette show, Hollywood Babylon. The extravaganza the Cockettes "surfaced" with.

Two weeks before I'd been brought to rehearsal and this very all, very thin presence on stage was complaining "I need men in my number." I was at the top of the aisle looking for a place to be invisible and so I joints. "There's a man," she pointed a two-inch black fingernail toward the back of the theatre. The few heads in the front rows turned. So did mine. "Where?" I asked. "Do you want to be in my scene?" She asked my name and proceeded not to remember it for months.

Not even the night the Dream

Cowboy opened the door of the Rolls for us and we stepped onto the red carpet under the Palace marquee. Goldie was being gabby reporter in black chiffon with a studio-rented escort in a borrowed tux. She greeted the stars and flubbed introductions, never letting go of my arm. "It's a great night for Hollywood. It's a great night for America," I bubbled stonesmiling, paying no attention to her ravings and lots of attention to dark, curly-haired Richard who was escorting Kreemah. "It's just like Hollywood," Goldie said as we lounged at the candy counter in the lobby, "the stars are left alone as the studs cruise each other."

No one knows Hollywood like Goldie. No one knows how to be a star like Goldie. She came up from Venice in early September to announce a Halloween show at the Palace in which she was going to play Cinderella. There was no money, no story, no theatre, no music, no director, but there was Goldie and "my designer from LA. He does fabulous things. What more do you need?"

Goldie moved back to Los Angeles in November after nearly three years of Cockette fame. She spent ten quiet months on the grey Venice beach making only occasional trips to the jewelled city of so many triumphs. She embroidered her bluejeans. A rest from rhinestones. But there is glamour. There is the Palace. There is your own show.

Patrick Marca Registrada is the designer for Goldie's Cinderella. Registrada and Gary Bates whom Goldie selected as director, came from a traditional theatre xackground stronger than any the "former Cockettes" have encoun-

tered. Bates, currently completing his Masters in Dance at U.C.L.A., is choreographing the show as well. They enlisted the help of a UC Irvine classmate of Registrada's Timothy Troy, to arrange and com-

pose some incidental music, including a wedding march for bells and tympani based on the mathematical configurations of Goldie's horoscope.

The three cretons of the show

are cerebral. Giving a vocabulary to the neververbalized Cockette aesthetic. Never verbalized by Cockettes, that is; especially Cockettes like Goldie — but she's ready for it now.

EAST-COAST OWNED

KRE-BERKELEY STILL OUT

by David Armstrong

The strike of seven broadcasters and a supporting group of reporters at Berkeley radio station KRE has entered its second week, with little immediate likelihood of an amicable settlement.

At stake in the dispute, which is pending before the National Labor Relations Board, is the employees' choice of unions, the size of starting salaries, and the adop-

tion of health and welfare pension benefits. Another cause of discontent, although not a specific target of strike demands, is the out-of-state ownership of a station that many employees want to make more repsonsive to community issues and concerns.

KRE was unionized until early last year by the International Brotherhood of Electrical Workers. When that contract expired, employees decided to affiliate with

the American Federation of Television and Radio Artists (AFTRA), generally considered the more progressive of the two unions.

That's when the trouble began. The employees' requests for AFTRA affiliation, with its starting weekly salary of $242.50 and generous pension benefits, was countered by a contract offer from the station's management that was somewhat less generous. The two sides negotiated for over a year until finally, the employees, who have been without union affiliation of any kind in the meantime, walked out.

Striking disc jockeys and newsmen have since been joined on the picket lines by representatives of the Central Labor Council, who sanctioned the strike. They have also been bolstered by the presence of striking stringers (freelance reporters), who have put a freeze on many of the station's news sources in solidarity with the strike.

Management has struck back with some actions of their own, including the hiring of non-union scab labor, primarily from the University of California, at far below union scale. The station has

also apparently decided that now is the time to begin actively recruiting minority employees -- a practice that, according to striking News Director Kent Waterman, KRE has not been noted for in the past.

"As far as I know," Waterman told BARB, "KRE has never had a minority person on full union salary before." Strikers view this as a move to both polish the station's image, and to drive a wedge between community groups and the striking employees. Individual strikers also report tempting offers from management to return to the fold, offers which they have seen fit to refuse.

Another cause of employee discontent is the lack of local control over the station. KRE is the only California holding of Horizon Communications, Inc., an East Coast-based group that includes retired broadcasting biggie Chet Huntley, who owns 25% of the station.

"These guys all live on the East Coast," said Waterman in a telephone interview, "except for Huntley, and he lives in Montana. It strikes me as a tragedy that Berkeley, which is one of the most

progressive communities in the country and has one of the finest universities in the country, has to settle for ownership that is 3,000 miles away.

"We've been trying over the past months to build up our coverage of community news. Yet the station is owned by men who can't possibly know or care much about this community."

Waterman speculated that KRE will be up for sale when its FCC license expires this Nov. 30. If so, he reasons, the station's present management may be delaying acceptance of the proposed AFTRA contract so its future owners will not be bound by a labor contract they had no hand in negotiating.

Not so, replies Station Manager Ollie Hayden. "I don't own the station, but as far as I know," he told BARB, "KRE is not for sale. In any case, a station that is being struck is not an attractive buy for prospective owners."

In the meantime, the strike continues. Strikers and supporters will continue picketing, as well as leafleting East Bay businesses that continue to support their advertising.

ON STRIKE

FRAGILE

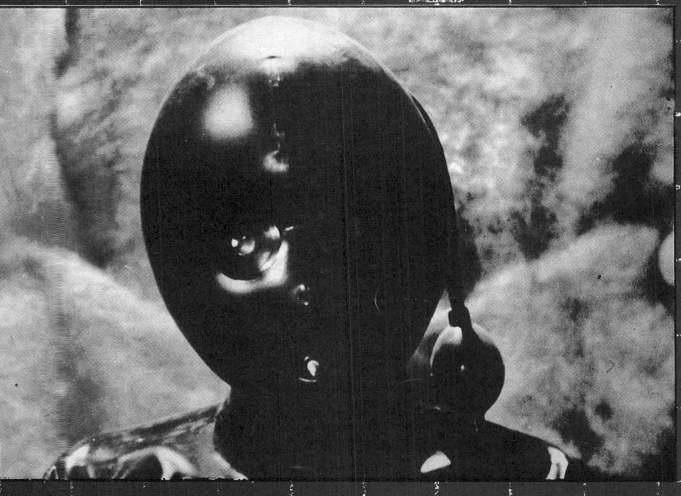

THE GREAT ROCK 'N' ROLL SWINDLE

SPÉCIAL

LESBIAN FEMINISM ISN'T A WHITE MALE TRIP

by Jill Johnston

THE CAPTURE OF SUSAN Saxe in Philadelphia March 27 gave rise to a predictable collusion of media interests with the continuing backlash against feminism and the fear, tolerance, misunderstanding and ignorance of lesbianism in the country at large as well as within the movement and the conflicts among lesbian feminists themselves.

If it weren't Saxe it would've been somebody else. After the SLA shootout in Los Angeles last year there were scattered items in the media alluding to Mizmoon and her friends as "lesbians" and more recently in reference to the search for Patty Hears. . . ."lesbian communes" in Colorado and elsewhere as alleged hideouts of the fugitives.

The capture of Saxe provided the opportunity authorities (media, etc.) to identify by inference criminal violence against the state with the feminist movement. Saxe herself implicated the movement or swept it along with her as she issued a dramatic statement shortly after her apprehension reading that she intended to "fight on now in every way as a lesbian, feminist, and an amazon."

April 5 I picked up Newsweek on a plane out of Albuquerque and found what I was looking for right after the Faisal coverage. "The arrest (of Saxe) followed a widespread and sometimes high pressure FBI hunt for Saxe and (Katherine) Power, among lesbian and radical feminist groups in Connecticut, Kentucky and elsewhere. Similar groups have been connected in recent years with the underground flights of such wanted woman as Angela Davis, Bernadine Dohrn and Patty Hearst. . .despite her arrest.

Saxe vowed to 'keep fighting as a lesbian, as a feminist, and as an amazon.'

"If they picked up Mark Rudd and he said he vowed to keep on fighting as a heterosexual I guess I'd wonder who these heterosexuals were. I'd think they were pretty dangerous if this dude had been on the ten most wanted list for robbery and assault and murder by association. If I were heterosexual myself I'd wonder what we were supposed to do to keep up the good fight."

Sexual Identity

My point is that in 1970 when Saxe allegedly held up this bank in Boston with Katherine Power and three males who were ex-convicts, one of whom shot and killed a policeman, it's highly improbable that sexual identity as a political issue figured in the action. By sexual identity I mean the priority any woman places on her being politically and spiritually as a woman, either as a woman who continues to relate sexually to males or as a woman who relates sexually to other women.

Saxe and Power were Brandeis students who were involved in the student strike center and the national strike information center and various antiwar activities. It's unclear from all the statements whether they were lovers at the time. It's also unclear what the nature of their feminism was if any.

Lovers or not, there's no essential connection between sexual activity and political persuasion on the one hand, or between the latter and feminism, since many political women have subsumed their identity as female under a variety of left or radical causes.

I'd be very surprised to hear that two radical/feminists were out robbing a bank with three heavy straight dudes in 1970. The radicalesbians I knew in New York at that time identified with every oppressed class and they were pretty angry at the government and they believed in its overthrow and in socialism etc. etc. but they had already severed connections with the White male left and were seriously questioning what remained of their association with Blacks and with gay males.

The most basic concern of radical lesbians then was lesbian identity and the drive out of the closet and tentative rapprochements with third world women and tactical confrontations with straight fem-

ists. The latter were themselves engaged in an agony of separation from left causes that were increasingly viewed as male or male dominated. The coalition attempts in '69 and '70 to form a mass movement were thwarted by this growing recognition of feminists associated with the left, that forming alliances with males or political action, subverted feminist interests and priorities.

By the late '60s there were three types of political women: those associated exclusively with the left, those identified exclusively as feminist and/or lesbians, and those who related across the boards as feminists, socialists, pacifists, and everything.

I was one who never related to male politics of any sort and for whom feminism was a shocking political awakening. I came to feminism for that matter from the more exclusive place of a minority identification as a lesbian. I didn't know I was a woman any more than my straight sisters did. The primary struggle was to dissociate ourselves from male definitions.

When I heard that women were blowing things up with men I thought they were men or male styled guerrillas.

A Liability?

There are thousands of lesbians in this country and possibly a mere handful of them who ever participated in violent action at any time with angry males. That women like Saxe and Power and Oughton and Dohrn and Boudin and Alpert became political feminists and/or lesbians out of the male left and in reaction to it has now become an interesting liability to the movement. Certainly the credibility of lesbians is at stake, but the credibility of lesbians has never been established anyway.

The perfect vacuum has been maintained

for the opportune moment to direct negative attention to the movement through its radicalesbian elements, which by this time are pervasive.

From the point of view of the media, the shots of Valerie Solanas in 1968 were those of a privately disturbed person; the alleged robbery and assault by Saxe and Power in 1970 becomes that of political fanatics like the Panthers stalking the streets of Oakland; the isolated women here and there who've befriended them as fugitives become "lesbian communes" with overtones of violent revolution.

The lesbian/feminist movement is much subtler and more subversive than the male models of historical change. The women I know at least are not so dumb as to think there's anything worth taking over. Women with SDS and Weatherpeople were participating in male ideas of change through new and enlightened leadership. As for reform within the structure itself, we root for our Bellas and our Chisholms, but we know that true revolution is a glacial process of unknown cell structures that will evolve out of shared bits of profoundly internalized consciousness.

This consciousness, which is at first realized through the painful acknowledgement of hierarchical oppression, is transformed by degrees into the birth of the self and the celebration of spontaneous behavior appropriate to the individual and her perception of the constantly changing environment and social conditions.

Everywhere I go in the united snakes of amerika I sense this incredible internal struggle and it has no political name. It's the feminism you'd never read about in the papers.

The Saxe behind the headlines or the life between a robbery and a capture is one of these women. The Saxe who issued a dramatic statement in the wake of her arrest is a desperate person appealing to a support group; the violent

male left.

Her appeal strains the facilities and sentiments of sisters who extend warmth and support for every woman, especially those driven under any circumstances to extreme actions and who at the same time deny identification with actions committed by individuals under the banner of the male left or any violence committed in the name of lesbian/feminism.

There is in other words no organized lesbian feminist action against the state or individuals. Even the rape squads maintain primary attention to the victims of rape and to methods of deflection or prevention.

Deception

Saxe's statement included a question about her danger: "They called me a dangerous woman. Dangerous to whom? to my people? to the sisters I love?" -- and the answer could be yes. The sisters don't rob banks with ex-male convicts except as private individuals. The association of the "sisterhood" with 1970 bank robberies is a telescopic deception used (by the media) to discredit a movement without credit and without responsibility for individuals who committed crimes in the context of the patriarchal contest between fathers (right) and sons (left).

The sons themselves are now dispersed and disarmed without the intimate support of their sisters who defected to feminism.

The revolution in Ireland wouldn't exist without the sisters. The new and unprecedented revolution in the world is the bloodless revolution of the sisters.

Many sisters no longer wish to help the sons undo the fathers who in turn oppress the sisters. The sisters who banded with the sons in this last effort against the fathers are now stranded in their troubles by the sons who have no political platform or cohesion or resources or interest in a movement they abandoned and are thrown onto the compassion of the sisters whose only struggle is for self-realization and ultimately for a global corrective to the dangerous escalation of human masculinity.

The lesbians who hail Saxe and Power as romantic projections of our helplessness are confirming the developed stereotype of lesbians as Bonnies without Clydes. All creative unconventional women have been lesbians and even Willa Cather is on a postage stamp. The conventional women still relate to the oppressors by opposing them. This cooperation with the sons is as ancient as the origin of the patriarchy.

Cooperation in this sense is a fruitless opposition. Cooperation in this present hassle for instance is to believe in the FBI. The FBI wants fugitives who robbed banks and were accessories or agents of murder. They're not "infiltrating" any movement, there isn't anything to infiltrate, they're going about their business and harassing a lot of innocent people while they do it and contributing to the general atmosphere of fear, intolerance, misunderstanding, and ignorance of a movement that has a profound commitment to the spiritual resurrection of women.

The collusion of the media in the negative innuendos surrounding lesbian/feminism is merely one more serious indication of the unwillingness of the arms of established interest to regard the efforts of oppressed peoples (women, lesbians, etc.) as vital correctives acting in the global public concern for survival and celebration.

The male left is dead and so are the women who did it with them.

The Saxe who was picked up March 27 can't be the same woman who robbed a bank in September 1970. The opportunity to articulate this distinction will possibly be made available to her. I don't know any woman who hasn't thought of robbing a bank for instance is to some bad dude but I don't know any woman who would implicate the whole movement in a per-

See page 20

"FIRST, A GREETING TO ALL MY SISTERS. COURAGE, ESPECIALLY TO ALL OF MY SISTERS UNDERGROUND IN AMERICA. STAY FREE, STAY STRONG. I INTEND TO FIGHT ON IN EVERY WAY AS A LESBIAN, A FEMINIST AND A AMAZON. THE LOVE I SHARE WITH MY SISTERS IS A FAR MORE FORMIDABLE WEAPON THAN THE POLICE STATE CAN BRING AGAINST US. KEEP GROWING, KEEP STRONG. I AM A FREE WOMAN, AND I CAN KEEP STRONG. PASS THE WORD. I AM UNAFRAID."

— SUSAN SAXE

SUPPORT PROTECT OUR SISTERS & BROTHERS UNDERGROUND

SISTER PICK ME UP

SISTERS, CUT THIS OUT AND USE FOR HITCHHIKING

letter to lyn

I.
the door stained red with wine
glass shattered in the corner
outside the air is cold
the neighbors very far away
all the way
across the street
no where to go.
shocking to tell the truth
        tell the truth
        tell the truth

II.
I see soul pair eyes
hidden in blue shadow
eurlashes deny the real
nail/ acceptable above the brow
not below the knee
        i see your eyes, sister
        i see your soul
you call your breasts wrinkled lemons,
hide them under ½ inch foam, learn
to like your thighs only to hear
you have ugly feet.
how long will we listen to men
who tell us they love us?
who call us frigid or maniac & turn away?
how long will we stand as dolls on a shelf
        buy me   buy me
        one house & i'm yours.

        i'm mine, sister.
        how about you?

        —alta

Tribe/21

Has Fame Gone To Her Head?

Cut out the circles ... spin the rings ...
and discover the silliest, bravest
and the most beautiful gesture of 1972.

Illustrated by Mike Moore.
Photograph by Keith Morris

157

Demidjuk, George Melly, David N...

Melly. OZ is a member of UPS

Det. Inspector Fred (wouldn't it b...

nderground Press Syndicate) and s...

ccasional subscriber to LNS

Artists photographers cartoonists a...

illustrators should submit contribu...

Jim Anderson c/o OZ Offices.

NTDOWN IS A PAPERBACK MAGAZINE ASSEMBLED BY TH...
NTDOWNMAG AND IS PLANNED FOR PUBLICATION FIVE T...
UNTDOWN IS AN ASSOCIATE MEMBER OF THE UNDERGR...

Black power

THE FREE PRESS FIGHTS FOR EQUAL RIGHTS

Assassination of Malcolm X
bloody riots in Watts and Detroit
the FBI shoot to kill
prison revolts across the US
Black Panthers show might is right
Bob Dylan sings about George Jackson
the authorities clamp down hard
the underground press is bugged

LEFT: The FBI is run by hypocritical crook J. Edgar Hoover.
OPPOSITE: **Fifth Estate**, in 1969, introduces the Puerto Rican equivalent of the Panthers, the Young Lords.

NEWSPAPER OF DETROIT
n. 9 - 22, 1969
ol. 3, No. 18 (70

THE FIFTH ESTATE

15¢
20¢ outside Detroit

THE YOUTH MADE THE REVOLUTION & THE YOUTH WILL KEEP IT,

THE YOUTH WILL CONTINUE TO MAKE THE REVOLUTION THROUGHOUT THE WORLD!

as women—as this system has told us we were; because we are thrown in jail, beaten over the head, just as much as the men are. Ericka Huggins was the first one that had to deal with all this, that had to endure all this madness, and so the women in the community are relating to this very much.

So I think that these people, these women, are going to stop acting like the lesser half and are going to start acting like the other half and pick up arms and have to defend themselves just like the men do"

Artie Seale

KIDNAPPED

International Black Appeal

THE CONDITIONS OF BLACK AND POOR IN THIS COUNTRY IS GETTING WORSE. UNEMPLOYMENT IS SHOOTING UP AND THOSE THAT ARE WORKING ARE WORKING FOR LOW WAGES.. THERE ISN'T ANY HOUSING TO BE HAD AND THE EUROPEAN MANIAC IS FLOODING THE BLACK COMMUNITY WITH DRUGS!

THE UNITED FOUNDATION AND ITS TORCH DRIVE HAVE THEIR OWN PROBLEM IN LESSENING, LET ALON REMOVING, THE ROTTE CONDITIONS OF OUR BROTHERS AND SISTER

CONSEQUENTLY, SOME GROUPS HAVE TRIED SELF HELP IDEAS ONLY TO SEE THEM FLOP FOR LACK OF BREAD. IN OTHER WORDS, THE UNITED FOUNDATION AND OTHER KLANISH AGENCIES HAVE FAILED TO RECOGNIZE OR EVEN LEND A HAND TO OUR EFFORTS!

PLUS THE REVOLUTIONS IN WATTS, NEW-ARK AND DETROIT AND OTHER REVOLTS BY BLACK COLONIES IN THE U.S. HAVE SUMMARIZED THE NEED FOR SELF-HELP BLACK & POOR PEOPLE TO COME UP WITH A PROGR THAT WILL BE LESS LIKELY TO FOLD UP AND STEAL OUR MONEY

THE PURPOSE OF THE INTERNATIONAL BLACK APPEAL IS TO RECEIVE & MAINTAIN A FUND FOR USE EXCLUSIVELY FOR CHARITABLE, RELIGIOUS, EDUCATIONAL & SCIENTIFIC ENDEAVORS EITHER DIRECTLY BY CONTRIBUTIONS TO ORGANIZATIONS

EMERGENCY FOOD & HEALTH CENTE LABOR STRIKE & DEFENSE FUNDS LEGAL DEFENSE SERVICES WHAT THE FEDERAL GOVT. WON'T DO... WE WILL!

C'était un jeune Noir à la mode. Il y a quelques années, Emory Douglas tenait une boutique de bonbons africains. Il est aujourd'hui ministre de la Culture du B.P.P. Il a conçu l'ensemble du matériel de propagande des Panthères On lui doit les admirables posters que nous présentons.

OPPOSITE: Posters and pamphlets raise awareness of black issues.
ABOVE: Emory Douglas's poster designs for the Black Panthers, as published in **Actuel**, June 1970.

October 29-November 11, 1970   Vol. 5, No. 13 (117)

25¢

COPS & PANTHERS
See Page 3

photo/John Collier

FASCISM NEXT DOOR - See PAGE 8

photo/ Alan Mass

ABOVE: Cops versus Panthers on the streets of Detroit.
OPPOSITE: A stylized portrait of Huey Newton, founder of the Black Panthers.

Volume Three Issue Thirty-Three

Copyright/Atlanta Cooperative News Project/1970

Monday, August 17, 1970

The GREAT speckled BIRd

20¢

25¢ outside Atlanta

you can't jail

the revolution!

I have been for a long time interested
in the matriarchial societies of the
past

But I am even more interested in the
one of today — that is the society of
Black women.

Some Black women feel it is not fair
to the Black men of today to want to
proclaim our Liberation

We still feel sorry for him — as a mother
feels about a crippled child

It is still present in our minds the white
man's emasculation of his manhood

And like a child learning to walk — he is
just not gaining his self-respect.

But listen Black Sisters we held
Black men up for over 300 hundred years

No matter how heavy the Burden
   WE HELD HIM UP

And kept the children coming and
growing
   WE HELD HIM UP

And kept the clothes washed and house
cleaned
   WE HELD HIM UP

We worked for the white man and helped
pay the bills
   WE HELD HIM UP

And while holding him up we kept Faith
and Loved him

I am not saying it wasn't our job —
It was — there was no one else to
do it.

I am saying it is time for us the
Black women in this country to stand
up from under and out from behind
the Black man.

There has always been a hill or
point of conflict to conquer in any
man's war

And the Black women has helped her man
take HILL 749 —

with her Love and Strength — she put Power
in his hands and Pride in his heart.

And because the time was Right — he
took that hill.

How PROUD we are of him.

He's in a standing position now — and the
next hill — well success is assured.

He is a man now — a Black and
Beautiful man
   more Power to Him.

But we the Black women of this
country have been the tools of
men long enough — and it's time
they laid these time worn tools
down.

Every so called great man
of this country has come under
the Black women's hands

We raised the white man — changed his
diapers and washed his naked dirt

And from our breast flowed all the
wisdom of the ages — and he used
this wisdom to destroy our Black
men and our babies.

Now it's time for us to stand up
from under and out from behind
the man oppression.

   POWER TO THE BLACK SISTERS
   OF THIS COUNTRY

You the white woman must also face the
fact that you are not Free

You too have been the tool of the
white man

Unlike the Black woman you were put
on a Pedestal and Paraded and Praised
as a senseless object of beauty.

He made you believe you were not
capable of doing anything for yourselves.

His politics and livelihood is based on
making you more Fuckable to him.

You his senseless — Blond haired — Blue
Eyed — white gloved —
   LADY

The white man created the term LADY to
give himself a sense of identity because
he could not deal with your woman
hood.

And in all of his dictionaries
LADY has never and can never be
adequately defined. ("An Attribute of
Abstraction" — Websters)

On the other hand the Black woman
never knew how to or had time to become
a LADY.

She was too busy keeping the country
clean
   washing for it
     scrubbing for it — and
Oh yes, changing its shit. —
     keeping it Nice for
      Company.

And when the Company came she went
back to her place.

And you the white LADY came in and
took the praise for her Genius

And you were ever praised for your
excellent training of her.

And all the while the white man looked
on at his trained LADY

Parading you as he would a prize
thoroughbred — But of less Value

For when the company left he snatched
your babies from your arms and gave them
to the Black woman

HE SAID — she knew better how to care
   for them
You were not allowed to nurse or dress
your own babies

HE SAID — It would expand your (bosom)
   and that's not seeming for
   A LADY

He reminded you often of your duties
as a LADY — to look pretty and be
at his disposal when he wanted you

Not need — Just want.

And to satisfy your longing
for womanhood he gave you the term
(LADY) And pinned it on your bosom
with frills and fancy lace

And you too were forced for hundreds of
years to swallow this shit

Even when it gagged you at the thought
of another dose

But you were LADIES and it wouldn't
be seeming to spit it out

It is time for you to let the white
man know that you'll no longer be
the object of his sexual sickness

AND YOU TOO MUST DEMAND YOUR
FREEDOM BY STANDING UP FROM UNDER
AND OUT FROM BEHIND THE WHITE MAN's
OPPRESSION.

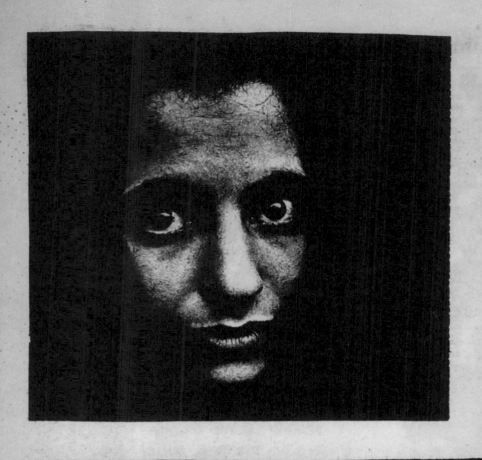

i cant stand the silence
and in contained anger
i wait
for the man who can measure up to my fury
and inside my vacuum of emptiness
i scream
WE WANT POWER
TO CONTROL OUR BODIES, MINDS AND LIVES
TO SET OUR SOULS FREE
TO CREATE WHAT NEVER WAS

i feel feverish and restless
capable and paralyzed
bewitched by the meaning of womanhood
frightened to let myself surface fully
and i cry
WE WANT TIME
TO STUMBLE AND FALL
TO RISE BY OUR OWN FORCE
AND WHEN WE FAIL
OUR SISTERS WILL JUSTIFY US
all my life
i have been limited
by forces i had no control over
now i want to go beyond all boundaries
infinitly limitless
and i shout
WE WANT MADNESS
TO MAKE CHANGE
TO EXPRESS THE DEEP SOURCES OF ECSTASY
IN OUR SOULS
TO FEEL THE MAGIC OF IMMORTALITY

smooth and soothing is the night
but i am possessed by unknown violence
it hurts to be and breathe and live
WE WANT STRENGTH
TO SURVIVE THE PAIN
TO DESTROY WHAT CAUSED OUR SOULS TO FEAR

i am calling on you my sisters
to save the earth from man's insanity
how long shall we bleed?
man's destructive imagination
has chained us and raped us and killed us and burnt us
he has misused our bodies
made our minds whither
and our souls dry out
he has left us naked, shivering, humiliated, cheated and lied to
he has drained our wells of life, energy and wisdom
and in no womans land
where the sin died thousands of years ago
we ask
WHERE IS CONFIDENCE?
WHERE IS FAITH?
WHERE IS TRUTH?

i must go to war
in the streets
in the sunlight
in the homes
by the rivers
in the back allies
beyond the skies
in the night
its been too long
and time has come
i must go to war
and dying or winning
i will sing
WE WANT FREEDOM
TO REACH OUT FOR OUR SISTERS
IN LOVE AND TRUST
IN LOVE AND UNITY
TO REACH OUT FOR ALL PEOPLE OF THE UNIVERSE
IN LOVE AND SOLIDARITY
AND ONLY SO WILL WE TOGETHER
DESTROY THE EVIL FORCE THAT KEPT US APART
THAT DENIED US THE RIGHT TO BE HUMAN
AND WE WILL STOP SHADOWBOXING WITH DEATH
AND TRULY BUILD WHAT NEVER WAS

FOR PRESIDENT OF
THE UNITED STATES OF AMERICA

YOUR VOTE IS LEGAL SACRED AND PRIVATE

NOV. 5, 1968

IN YOUR PRECINCT

VOTE

VOTE ONE

VOTE

NOV. 5, 1968

WRITE IN

Dick Gregory
PRESIDENT

GREGORY
ONE VOTE
CAN NOT BE BOUGHT SOLD OR TRADED

WRITE IN   VOTE

Mark Lane
VICE PRESIDENT

When I am elected president

by Dick Gregory

"Because I have an awareness of and a sensitivity to human needs and problems, because I am a statesman more concerned with solutions to human problems than personal obligation to political colleagues, and because I am hopeful that the democratic process will prevail, I have declared myself a write-in candidate for President of the United States."

● Leadership that ignores 30 million black Americans as full participating citizens in this democracy, that maintains segregated reservations of poverty and disease for Indian-Americans, that keeps Mexican-Americans toiling in the fields, that harbors Puerto Rican-Americans in rat-infested ghettos, that sends thousands of young men to a country 12,000 miles away to kill, that fails to take away control of the cities from the crime syndicate, and then demands law and order from the poor and powerless is the leadership that will no longer be tolerated or permitted in America.

There must be a rebirth of American democracy — for the child of 1776 is dead. Freedom has been strangled by lawmakers who refuse to respect the Bill of Rights. Equality was mortgaged at a price too high and the payments in years of patience, suffering, endurance, and hope are now in default because black people and other minorities recognize that they have been cheated; therefore they demand a full share of American Constitutional rights now! A rebirth of American democracy must come in a revolutionary manner and no slower — there must be a quick change to bring rights to the minorities, food for the starving, jobs for the poor, sanitary and safe housing to replace ghettos, to end an unexplained war, to regain world respect for the United States, and to assure human dignity for all Americans.

Moral pollution is the number one problem facing this country today. When the nation's leaders preoccupy themselves with political compromises, vague promises, and distortions of the meaning of their action in order to appeal to voters rather than identify and solve human problems, we find ourselves in a moral crisis. Moral pollution allows congressmen to steal from the taxpayers and punish only the black of their group. Moral pollution permits a nation to wage war in the name of democracy but requires the poor and the black citizens to be nonviolent in obtaining their rights in a democracy. Moral pollution means our leaders cry out for law and order, but limit it to "crime in the street," which is America's new way of saying "nigger."

While I support measures to be taken by all citizens for an orderly and safe nation, I refuse to concentrate on black crime and ignore white crime. I refuse to accept the premise that the cities must be armed like fortresses against tax-paying, freedom fighting demonstrators. The crime syndicate does more harm to American cities in one day through dope pushing, murders, extortion, high interest loans, prostitution, gambling, and pay-offs to politicians and officials than one summer of looting and arson in the ghettos.

Therefore, I am proposing the creation of a special unit in the Justice Department to vigorously prosecute the activities of the syndicate in the United States. And to create better police community relations, I propose federal legislation requiring a minimum starting salary of $10,000 per year for policemen as a step in establishing a new image for them. I propose a unified nationwide training program for policemen. The more knowledge the policeman has, the less he will have to rely upon his nightstick or his gun.

I propose giving the policman two guns: a revolver and a tranquilizer gun. Anytime a policeman used his revolver, he would be subjected to thorough examination. I can see no excuse for a drunk or a child being shot to death if a cop is carrying a tranquilizer gun. I propose a program whereby policemen would be urged to "Support Your Local Community," thereby changing the policeman's image from that of an overseer of wrongs to an advocate of rights. The policemen must become vitally involved with every aspect of the community to which they are assigned.

I am not just against the war in Vietnam — *I am against war!* The political, social, and economic consequences of this war are disastrous to every hope, ideal, and possibility that is American. The money which is needed desperately to end pollution of human life is being spent on high explosives, napalm, and military ventures. Instead of being taught to live, our youth are being taught to kill; and rather than earn the respect of all the world, we court the scorn and hatred of the untold millions of the world's less fortunate populations.

The United States has no legal or moral right in Vietnam. There has been no congressional declaration of war. The United States' actions violate the Geneva Accords which she pledged to observe. The United States' actions violate the United Nations' Charter inasmuch as South Vietnam is not a member of the United Nations. I propose the immediate end of United States hostilities in Vietnam. The bombing must stop, there must be recognition of the territorial realities in Vietnam, and the National Liberation Front must be recognized.

I am sick and tired of having to apologize for the acceptance of public aid by needy people. It is in the public interest, especially under the capitalist system to raise the living standard of the lowest to a position where it can afford to enter the marketplace. It was on this principle that the United States rebuilt Germany and Japan and established the Marshall Plan. Farmers regularly receive federal subsistance. The airlines are financed by federal subsidy. The railroads continue to exist because of federal grants. Great oil companies receive enormous tax allowances; and, yet, somehow poor families without employment must apologize for receiving public aid.

At least three-fourths of this nation's black population inhabit the major cities. Their rate of unemployment is double that of whites. I propose the creation of jobs by the construction of industrial complexes. These industrial complexes would provide the work market for the unemployed in underdeveloped areas of the nation and the deteriorated urban ghettos. Also, they would make possible employment for those unemployed urban dwellers who would choose to move out of the city. These industrial complexes would serve as the focus for newly developing communities and rehabilitated communities that have homes, schools, industry, recreational facilities, adequate jobs and other necessary institutions for a total wholesome environment.

● Ten million Americans are suffering from malnutrition and hunger. Study after study have shown children born with incurable brain and body damage because the mother did not have proper food during pregnancy; children growing up without milk, or bread, or meat in their daily diets — in America. Official government response to hunger and starvation has been a food stamp program administered by state and local officials who determine who the poor are and how much aid will be given them. Thus, thousands of Americans, millions of Americans are dependent for their lives on the political decision of local officals. There is no reason at all why food cannot be freely and quickly given to the poor to distribute among their hungry numbers during emergencies and/or on a routine schedule.

● The present draft age is 18 years old. Thousands of our young men are being sent to Vietnam to fight and thousands are returning home injured, lame, facing limb amputation, and dead. Yet these very same young men who are sent all over the world to wage war and make responsible decisions regarding life and death are not given the right to exercise the vote to influence the political policy that continues the war. I propose that if America can decide that you are old enough to die for your country, then you are old enough to vote for your leaders and American domestic and foreign policy. Thus, the voting age minimum should be set in all states at 18 years old immediately.

● To fight for the rights of one minority in this country to the exclusion of another is not my idea of fighting for human rights under our Constitution. To free the black man while keeping the Indian up on the reservation is a step backward in the struggle for equality for all Americans. There must be immediate recognition of the Indians as American citizens, thus entitled to all rights and privileges granted by the Constitution and laws of this country.

It is ironic indeed that the most American of the Americans are not full citizens of this country. Maintaining federal segregation of the Indians on the reservations where the highest degree of tuberculosis exists and the highest number of suicides are committed each year among the youth than anywhere in this country is a disgrace of international proportions. We must act and act quickly to bring that Indian down off the reservation and integrate him into this society.

● In the interests of brotherhood and humanity we must always have foreign aid. There are desperate needs all over the world. We are capable of sharing our national resources to end hunger, disease, poverty, and ignorance; yet, we must make sure that our help is designed to meet real needs of people in foreign lands rather than impose on them our own military obsession. As President of the United States, I would propose that 98 per cent of all foreign aid money be spent for health, education, food production and technical advance. I would seek to build stronger nations in terms of healthy and stronger people, rather than focusing on military strength. The dominant theme of this nation's foreign policy must be human compassion instead of military obsession.

● It is my hope that the youth of America will be the antidote to moral pollution and will bring this nation back to its senses. The youth represent the greatest moral potential in the history of this country and they are out there trying to create a better environment for all Americans. I recommend to the youth who are concerned about what to do for human suffering to go to that poor white hillbilly and help him organize and obtain relief from suffering in this society. Do not be fooled into thinking that all poor white folks live in Appalachia. Poor white folks live in every large urban area in America.

« Il compito più difficile viene dopo che hai preso il potere quando devi affrontare il problema di costruire un nuovo mondo ».

ANGELA DAVIS

« RIVOLUZIONE NON È SOLO LOTTA ARMATA »
« RIVOLUZIONE È ANCHE SINONIMO DI LIBERAZIONE »

Questo ha dichiarato fra l'altro, alla stampa Angela Davis, filosofa marxista e militante del Black Panthers Party, arrestata martedì 16 ottobre dopo due mesi di clandestinità. Il tribunale di New York ha posto una cauzione di 25.000 dollari per il suo rilascio, definendola «criminale pericolosissimo» (ora fra le dieci persone maggiormente ricercate dall'FBI.

Anche per Angela Davis, come per Huey Newton, per Eldridge Cleaver e per Rap Brown, il tentativo di liquidazione fisica non passa attraverso assassinio freddo, come per molti quadri intermedi o militanti di base del BPP, ma si serve di accuse penali gravissime.

L'imputazione di omicidio e rapimento che grava su Angela, è solo l'ultima di una serie di azioni legali ed incostituzionali che mirano a toglire dalla scena culturale e politica questa militante che fondava il suo prestigio su una eccezionale preparazione filosofica e teorica. Marcuse parla di lei come della « migliore allieva » in quarant'anni di insegnamento — e quando Angela inizia l'attività didattica nel settembre del '69 all'università di California (Los Angeles), le sue lezioni sono affollatissime. La battaglia con il rettore dell'ateneo inizia immediatamente: si tenta di allontanarla dall'insegnamento con ogni mezzo; le sue lezioni vengono registrate e sottoposte all'esame di un comitato che indaga sui contenuti e sui metodi didattici.

L'alta qualità del suo insegnamento non può essere contestata, ma nel giugno del '70 Angela, accusata di attività sovversiva e rivoluzionarie viene radiata dall'università, mentre all'interno della facoltà nasce spontaneo un movimento di solidarietà che le permette di continuare ad insegnare grazie alle colletto di professori e studenti.

In questo periodo di tumultuose polemiche con le autorità universitarie, Angela si occupa attivamente della difesa di un gruppo di detenuti negri delle prigione di Soledad, accusati di aver ucciso una guardia carceraria. È uno dei molti processi in cui la magistratura americana, razzista e classista, può permettersi di privare gli imputati di ogni diritto costituzionale: farse di una giustizia criminale che mette a tacere i testimoni scomodi, costruisce prove false; si vale di manipolazioni procedurali.

Nell'agosto di quest'anno i « Soledad Brothers » tornano alla ribalta: Jackson, che sconta in carcere da dieci anni un furto già confessato da altri, viene liberato da un'azione di «commandos» mentre sede insieme ad un compagno come testimone in una causa che non lo riguarda. Il giudice e due giurati sono presi come ostaggi per assicurare la fuga dalla corte: dopo una sparatoria con la polizia tanto avvolta nel mistero quanto sospetta, Jackson, altri due negri e il giudice rimangono uccisi. Secondo le autorità i rapitori in fuga avrebbero sparato al giudice provocando l'intervento della polizia.

Dopo qualche giorno all'America indignata viene offerta una sensazionale notizia: l'arma usata dai commandos appartiene alla Davis ed è la filosofa stessa che ha affittato il camioncino usato nell'azione.

Un'altra militante rivoluzionaria è ridotta all'impotenza da un procedimento penale; mentre i « liberals » d'America gridano ad un'ennesima montatura politico-giudiziaria, i gruppi più radicali rivoluzionari non si preoccupano di stabilire la colpevolezza e l'innocenza condividendo appieno le azioni ed il pensiero di Angela Davis: - Certo chi parla di rovesciare il governo, di distruggere il capitalismo si scontra con la possibilità di perdere la vita. Ma questo non vi deve fermare perché non dovete considerare la vita, la vita individuale come un valore così importante... Io ho dato la mia vita alla lotta. Se perderò la vita nella lotta, bene, questo è quello che dovevo fare. -

CREDIT **Other Scenes**, November 1968. Dick Gregory stood as the Peace and Freedom Party candidate for the US presidential elections. ABOVE Angela Davis, Black Power heroine and international icon, seen here in the Italian paper **Re Nudo**, Milan, November 1970.

169

FREE ANGELA

**SOUL AND SOLEDAD
ANGELA DAVIS**

ACTUAL
60 RUE DE RICHELIEU
PARIS 25. FRANCE

BULK RATE
U.S. Postage
PAID
San Diego, Calif.
Permit No. 662

with this subscription

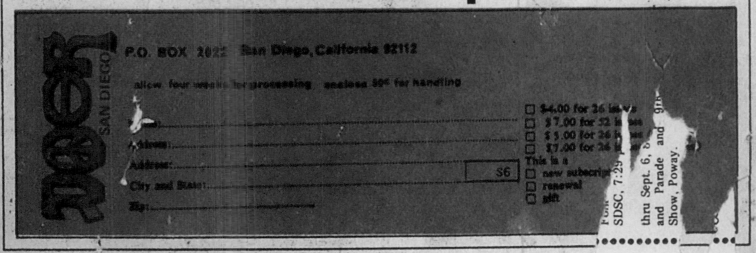

P.O. BOX 2022   San Diego, California 92112

allow four weeks for processing   enclose 50¢ for handling

Name: _____

Address: _____

Address: _____ $6

City and State: _____

Zip: _____

☐ $4.00 for 26 issues
☐ $7.00 for 52 issues
☐ $5.00 for 26 issues
☐ $7.00 for 26 issues
This is a
☐ new subscription
☐ renewal
☐ gift

SDSC, 7:29
thru Sept. 6,
and Parade and
Show, Poway.

Angela Davis was jailed for allegedly participating in a kidnapping plot to free George Jackson.
Bob Dylan wrote a song in Jackson's memory: 'Authorities, they hated him / Because he was just too real.'

Women's Issue

Inside:
Calendar of Events
Movie Guide
FREE Classifieds

DOOR
SAN DIEGO

Vol. 3 Issue 7 Sept. 1-14

25¢ 35 CENTS OUTSIDE SAN DIEGO COUNTY

GEORGE JACKSON IS DEAD

George Jackson
Sept. 23, '41 - Aug. 21 '71

George Jackson was murdered.

He predicted that he would be murdered in his book, *Soledad Brothers, The Prison Letters of George Jackson*. The prison officials and guards have viciously fulfilled his prediction.

The official line is that Stephen Bingham, a lawyer, smuggled Jackson a pistol in a tape recorder. The gun supposedly used a nine millimeter pistol, would not easily fit into many tape recorders; and those that would accommodate it would be subject to a thorough search. According to John Thorne, George's lawyer, anyone going to see someone from the adjustment center is given a very thorough search that would miss nothing the size of this gun. If the impossible did happen, and it got through the search, it would have had to have been in a place that would require some time and privacy for George to get it out of the tape recorder.

Warden Nelson stated that prisoners with visitors are under "sporadic surveillance" and thus could have passed the gun. Thorne stated that when he visited George they were watched "at all times" by prison guards.

George Jackson was the leader of a revolutionary movement inside the prison walls and thus subject to maximum surveillance at all times. Bingham's parents state that their son was wholly committed to non-violence and wouldn't

Continued on Page 12

RE NUDO

25 gennaio · 25 febbraio 1972 · n. 10 · anno III · Lire 200

■ **JOHN SINCLAIR: «ROCK E GUERRA DI POPOLO CONTRO LA MUSICA E LA CLASSE DEI PADRONI»**

■ **ALLEN GINSBERG CONTRO PORCI, AMFETAMINE E SISTEMA**

■ **I COMPAGNI DI RE NUDO SI PREPARANO ALLA PRATICA SOCIALE:**

A MILANO E TORINO NASCONO

LE PANTERE BIANCHE ■

ABOVE: The White Panther Party were a political collective, founded in support of the aims of the Black Panthers.
OPPOSITE: The Art Ensemble of Chicago were leading exponents of free jazz.

POLICE
RIP-OFF

BLUES &
JAZZ

ANN
ARBOR
Sun
RAINBOW
COMMUNITY
NEWS SERVICE

10¢

PEOPLE'S
BALL-
ROOM
TO OPEN

Issue 38   Published by the Rainbow People's Party   August 18-Sept.1,1972

GREAT BLACK
MUSIC

ART
ENSEMBLE
OF
CHICAGO

173

NORTH: THE KID

SOUTH JERSEY: THE BLA

Protect the planet!

THE FREE PRESS SUPPORTS GREEN POLITICS

The free press is first to discuss the greenhouse effect the oil crisis water pollution the dangers of junk food Native American rights the future of the earth

THE east village **OTHER**

VOL. 4, NO. 33   METROPOLITAN 15¢   JULY 16, 1969

ABOVE: When astronauts landed on the moon, the human race got a whole new perspective on the earth.
OPPOSITE: On 21 April 1971, 20 million Americans went out into the streets to celebrate the second-ever Earth Day. Thirty-five years later, the future of the planet still hangs in the balance.

STEM LOUTER KABOUTER

AMSTERDAM: LES SCHTROUMPFS DE LA REVOLUTION

ABOVE: In 1971, the Kabouters became the first green representatives on Amsterdam city council.
OPPOSITE: **Oz**, London, 1971. A sexed-up view of ecology that's hard to resist.

Post-
Scarcity
Anarchism

ABOVE: 'Yuk!' The underground press was into ecology before
anyone else had heard the word. *Actuel*, Paris, 1971.
OPPOSITE: Poster from **Other Scenes**, New York, 1971.
OVERLEAF: Centre-page poster from **Seed**, 1971.

THE CARS BR

OUT

OUT

DRIVE

AND

THE POISONING of our WATER SUPPLY

lower river has been virtually eliminated.

The Environmental Protection Agency has found that the threshhold odor number of the river water doubles on the average once it passes the Baton Rouge industrial complex. This higher odor number is sustained and reinforced by other odorous wastes as the water flows to New Orleans. From time to time, "slugs" of highly odorous water were noted and threshhold odor numbers 3 to 5 times the average were sometimes detected. The characteristic odor of the river also changes from that of "musty" to one of "oily-petro-chemical" as the water moves down river. Large scale sampling methods used in conjunction with complex analytical techniques have resulted in the identification of 32 individual organic compounds in the New Orleans finished water supply. Some such as nitrobenzene and isocyanic acid are toxic; many of the others such as chloroethyl ether, camphor and styrene are highly odorous, and needless to say all are undesirable in a potable water supply.

In conclusion, therefore, the most obvious problem resulting from the discharge of petrochemical and refining wastes to the Mississippi River are taste and odor in the drinking water supplies and the contamination of the food fish caught in the lower Mississippi River. Beyond this immediate problem, however, is the concern over the possible health hazards of these chemicals to the people consuming the processed water.

Some environmentalists have expressed an additional concern over the ultimate fate of the refractory chemicals in the estuarine and marine environment in the Gulf of Mexico. Once these materials reach the waters of the Gulf it is inevitable that some of them will enter the food chain of which man is often the last link.

- From a report submitted to the Senate Subcommittee on Air and Water Pollution, James J Friloux is deputy chief of the Lower Mississippi River Field Station of the Environmental Protection Agency.

In looking at a chemical profile of the Mississippi River from River mile 505 (Arkansas-Louisiana state line) to below New Orleans, it is obvious that there is a gradual increase in selected undesirable chemical qualities of the river. All of these chemical increases represent a deterioration of the quality of drinking water utilized by the Lower Mississippi area inhabitants.

The total dissolved solids discharged into the river by industry between St Francisville and Luling Ferry has increased from about 4,000 tons per day in 1958 to about 20,000 tons per day in 1969. In addition, about 4000 tons per day are discharged to the river

between Luling Ferry and Port Sulfur. Industrial demands for Mississippi River water have increased significantly in the past ten years. Total water withdrawn from the river by industry and thermo-electric plants between Baton Rouge and Port Sulfur has increased from about two billion gallons per day in 1950 to about 5 billion gallons per day in 1969. Thermo-electric plants utilized an estimated two billion gallons per day in 1969 while industry utilized the remaining 3 billion gallons. In addition, approximately 175 million gallons per day of ground water are used. All but an estimated 280 million gallons per day is discharged back to the river.

- From a staff briefing report on Kaiser Effluents Discharged at Baton Rouge and Gramercy, La. Prepared by the Environmental Protection Agency. The report was prepared between August and November 1971. It is 43 pages. This excerpt is from the section titled Hydrology of the Mississippi River.

> "We have now to do with another race. They were few and weak when our grandfathers first met them, but they are now many and powerful....They have made many laws, and these the rich may break but the poor may not. They take money from the poor and weak to support the rich ..."
> —Tatanka Yotanka (Sitting Bull), Hunkpapa Sioux, 1834–1890 —

Darlene Fife

Chevron Oil Co. has filed 7 applications with the New Orleans office of the US Corp of Engineers for the discharge of brine water. Although Mr. Lafleur says "the application approved for Chevron Oil Co was for the discharge of only produced salt water and residual traces of oil from their production facilities" six of the Chevron applications list heavy metals as part of the discharge - cadmium, chromium, copper, iron, lead, manganese, mercury and zinc.

The application referred to in Mr. Lafleur's letter is for discharge into Bayou Lafourche. The discharge includes all of the above metals and ranges from a low of 5 ounces of mercury per day to a high of 110 pounds of iron per day.

Another of Chevron's applications is for discharge into Bayou Barataria. The range is from 2 ounces of mercury per day to 32 pounds of iron per day. The quantity of mercury may seem small but it is cumulative. And it doesn't go away. Swedish scientists studying the pollution of their lakes by mercury say the pollution will last from 10 to 100 years. On the effects of mercury the US Public Health Service says "clinical evidence indicates irreversible effects to the liver and kidneys as well as to the central nervous system from the ingestion of mercurials in small quantities." Because of this, the position of the Federal Water Quality Administration is that "no man made mercury discharges to public waters are permissable." One should be careful not to assume that the position of the FWQA has any enforcement value. The applications by Chevron, for example, are not for a hypothetical future. The applications are simply a request for a license, presumable a piece of paper signed and notarized, to continue what is already being done.

Bayou Lafourche empties into the Gulf of Mexico. Barataria Bay, we are told, was in the past a great place for fishing.

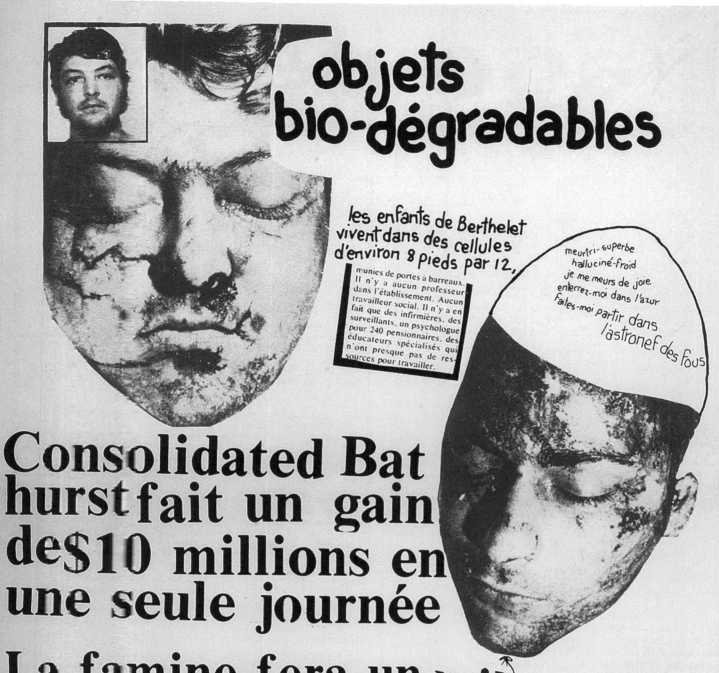

objets bio-dégradables

les enfants de Berthelet vivent dans des cellules d'environ 8 pieds par 12,

munies de portes à barreaux. Il n'y a aucun professeur dans l'établissement. Aucun travailleur social. Il n'y a en fait que des infirmières, des surveillants, un psychologue pour 240 pensionnaires, des éducateurs spécialisés qui n'ont presque pas de ressources pour travailler.

meurtri-superbe
halluciné-froid
je me meurs de joie
enterrez-moi dans l'azur
faites-moi partir dans l'astronef des fous

Consolidated Bat hurst fait un gain de $10 millions en une seule journée

La famine fera un million de morts au Bangla-Desh

le ciel des fixes injecté dans le tube vertébral je m'enfonce dans la pourriture terrestre pour en extraire l'insécable particule de chair-esprit d'où se déclenche toute mutation en corps glorieux

Burton avoue

LONDRES (Reuter — Richard Burton a déclaré samedi soir au cours d'une interview à la BBC. qu'il y a un an il essayait de boire jusqu'à la mort en absorbant jusqu'à trois bouteilles de boissons alcooliques par jour. La raison? L'acteur ne pouvait "endurer la beauté et la richesse de ce monde." Richard Burton a ajouté qu'un médecin de Californie l'avait averti que s'il continuait de certain il ne lui resterait que deux semaines à vivre. L'acteur a décidé par la suite de reculer devant le précipice". Et il peut maintenant "endurer cette richesse du monde".

peu importe la laideur des taudis dans lesquels les gens vivent si on peut les rendre béats d'admiration en face d'oeuvres d'art qu'ils ne comprennent pas

sous paul chamberland

REMEMBER

1890- -1973

WOUNDED KNEE!

Berkeley *Barb*

Issue 501 March 21 - 27, 1975   25c Bay Area 50c Elsewhere

Plot To Destroy American Indian Movement

by Cheryl McCall

History has an uncanny way of repeating itself, often viciously and capriciously -- and in the last ten years of social unrest in America, almost predictably.

What follows here is the unfolding of the latest developments of what more than appears to be a conspiracy to destroy the American Indian Movement (AIM), much in the same manner that government forces have used since people first began organizing to better their lots, dating back to the early 1900's and Eugene Debs.

The orders to stop AIM date back to 1973 and a direct order issued by Richard Nixon and executed by the Pentagon and the FBI in secrecy, as this story will document. This is not leftist paranoia, this is real! Almost from the moment of its birth, AIM has been the target of a concerted effort by the United States Government to either abort it, kill it or otherwise render it harmless. Read for yourself.

"Although the white man may be the most destructive element that the tribes have encountered in their long history, he is not considered by Indians as a permanent fixture on the continent."

Dee Brown, author of
Bury My Heart At Wounded Knee

It was Thursday, March 27, and Tom Poorbear was driving along the highway at a moderate speed towards Rushmore, Nebraska in a late model, white van, conspicuous only from behind. Where the spare tire normally would be mounted on the rear doors, instead was a full-color painting of an Indian. The vehicle, if one were looking for it, stuck out like the proverbial sore thumb.

But Tom wasn't thinking about the van; he'd driven it many times on errands for the American Indian Movement and had other things on his mind. Just the day before, six of his friends had been beaten, kicked and stomped at gunpoint at Wounded Knee on the Pine Ridge reservation in South Dakota. He thought about them.

Bernard Escamilla, another Wounded Knee defendant awaiting trial; Bernard's lawyer, William Rossmore of Connecticut; Roger Finzel of Washington, D.C., a National Lawyers' Guild attorney; Eda Gordon, a Guild legal worker from Baltimore; Cathy James, a legal worker from the AIM defense committee; and Martha Copelman, a Wounded Knee attorney from New Jersey. Roger, Eda, Rossmore and Escamilla had ended up in the Rapid City hospital.

The story he'd been told sounded like a nightmare. The six people had spent two hours on the Pine Ridge reservation Wednesday, investigating the circumstances of the alleged crimes with which Escamilla was charged. Satisfied with what they had accomplished, they drove to the tiny reservation airstrip where they had left their small rented airplane.

When they arrived, they found the plane completely riddled with bullet holes and in no condition to be flown. With years of conditioning about the daily violence on the reservation, the six ran to their car and began to drive away from the airstrip.

see page 2

DEVOLVING EUROPE
NATIONS EMERGING FROM STATES

Many of these nations have active home rule movements; all have a local historical reality. They all want more recognition and support for their unique cultures and will get it.

Red	Blue	Green	Gold	Maroon	Black	White

A futuristic vision of Europe as a land of devolved nations. **CoEvolution Quarterly**, 1972.

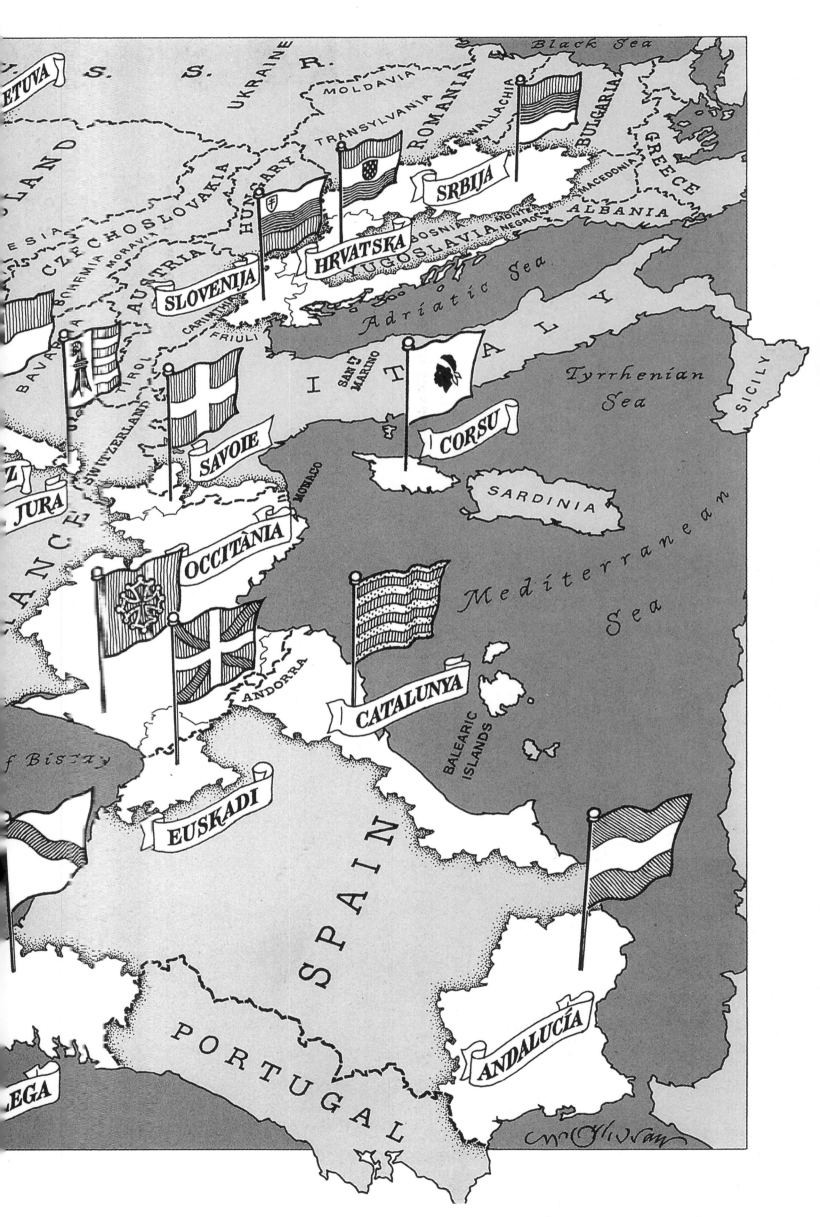

La Conscience de l'Occident a toujours été éprise de Liberté: l'esprit humain est né libre, ou, tout au moins, né pour être libre; mais partout l'esprit humain est enchaîné et il est rendu maintenant au bout de sa corde.

Surreal visions of the future from **Mainmise**, Montreal, 1971.

Les conditions présentes de vie en Amérique en sont une de solitude publique et mortelle. Nous avons réussi à construire une tour de Babel technologique autour de nous et nous sommes occupés, littéralement, à rejoindre le Ciel pour échapper à la Terre. Une nouvelle et géante surpopulation dépend d'une colossale superstructure métallique pour nourrir et transporter tous les humains. Le nombre incalculable de machines qui nous entourent conditionnent nos pensées, nos sentiments, nos impressions sensorielles et renforcent notre esclavage mental à l'univers matériel dans lequel nous avons tant investi.

233

CRÈVE, SALOPE!

ORGASME des lycéens révoltés

Le POP!

1,50 FRANK - 6 av. du Dr A. NETTER PARIS 12e

MEMBRE U.P.S.
AD: OELIF
ERIC JEANMONOD
6 RUE DES PAVILLONS
1205 GENÈVE
SUISSE

R29 arrive! (expression libre, gravure, cadran, pastiche, situ, de Potion, flambistique, et BANDES DESSINÉES SURRÉARÉALISTES. Impression offset. 48 pages 21x29. Abonnement 6 numéros 19,80 F. écrivez tous à RETLERS du 91e SIECLE 44, rue ALPHONSE TERRAY, F. 38 GRENOBLE.

PARTISANEN-PRESSE.
UPM

La "PARTISANEN PRESSE" (UPN) est l'organisation de la presse libre de langue allemande -échange de journaux, copyright commun, échange d'infos, défense commune face à la répression, ...etc..... Leur but: arriver à à une meilleure communication; à une meilleure coopération. Le siège de L'UPN se trouve à Nurnberg (PANGGG, 85 Kopernikusstr. 85 Nurnberg).

pänggg
HIGH-FISH. 30401 GROSS ELLERSHAUSEN . MITTELSTR 48 BEFREIUNG. 433 MÜLHEIM WINKHAUSERWEG 64. -LOVE A. BERLIN 42. LEIPNITZ-STR. 68

EN MEMOIRE DE HOTCHA (PO. BOX 304, CH- 8025 ZURICH §?§?§?§?§!.)

Ce fut le premier ou l'un des premiers journaux libres suisses -et européens en général-, nous disons ce fut, car HOTCHA -Urban Gweber et sa tribu- ont décidé de s'arrêter après trois ans et demi d'activité: 56 numéros depuis mai 68 (tiens tiens!§?) En effet ils aiment les changements -remise en question des habitudes- qui selviennent selon eux qu'à travers les changements."""==="+xxx+%~~°"....?::::::::::::§!!!!!!?ò&&&&& Mais la tribu est toujours là et l'on peut être sûr de la retrouver. La poudre laisse toujours des traces.......?......§... HOTCHA c'était aussi l'organe de liaison des canards marginaux européens (la branche européenne de l'Undergrooonddpress Syndicate: UPS, BOX 26 / Village Station, NEW YORK / N.Y. 10014). Par l'arrêt des activités d'Urban et de sa tribu, la section européenne de l'UPS a été transférée à Londres: BIT / E. UPS, 141 Westbourne Park Road, LONDON, W I). BIT est également une organisation communautaire qui s'occupe de la centralisation des infos marginales et de leur distribution hebdomadaire par un cahier ronéotypé (The New-info Street).....§&&&& **HOTCHA** a également publié **TARENTULA de DYLAN**, et un bouquin (textes, dessins, collages + poster) extraordinaire d'Urban GWEBER: Poëtenz (en vente à la LIBRAIRIE-BAZAR coopérative I rue des Veaux, 67 STRASBOURG????).

Planet news.

NOUVELLES DE L'UNDERGROUND CANADIEN

Mainmise est un canard très chouette qui vient d'avoir un an. Il est important d'en parler car il représente un fort courant marginal dans la société québécoise. Accessible car il est écrit en français, Mainmise est de plus, très intéressant quant au fond : il présente sur 220 pages (faut le faire) des analyses et des expériences alternatives différentes des autres free-press, comme le droit à l'orgasme, le complot du LSD, les joyeux utopistes, etc...

Voici un extrait du dernier éditorial : "Nous avons le LSD moins mystique que celui de notre cher Leary, la japonaiserie moins rapide que celle de notre vieux et cher Watts. Nous sommes moins jolis que nos ancêtres de Carnaby Street et moins fleuris que nos ancêtres de Haight Ashbury. Nous sommes un peu sales mais tout simplement parce que c'est un peu salissant le combat".
MAINMISE 351 rue EMERY, MONTREAL 129.
Abonnement 12 numéros : 12 dollars.

ANATHÈME (Bandes dessinées) PARIS ZINC 6 Avenue du Docteur Arnold-Netter 75 PARIS 12e LOESH 3 Rue du Bassin 43 EGUILLES FRENDS 305 Portobello Road LONDON/W 40 SPRUIT Ercola 32 Grote Hondstr.t.2000 ANVERS REAL FREE PRESS Rondstraat 34 AMSTERDAM LE FAUX VÉREUX, Nîmes (en vente à la "Librairie Bazar.")

"La KATMANDOU est vraiment démente, CHRISTIE en est folle, et moi je me sens hippie quand je la porte. Elle est très longue et frisée de partout, elle fait vraiment partie de moi-même. L'intérieur est élastique comme les trois modèles que je te présente aujourd'hui."

LE 5 NOV. de 21h de 22h sur 258m O.M. k 97ML EMISSION PIRATE POP FOLK FREE

PRESS PARALLELE

24-25 juin PARIS

Il y a une multitude de canards, de feuilles de choux qui paraissent chaque mois; certains le temps c un ou deux numéros; des beaux, des pas beaux, des cons, des pas cons, des en profondeur, des en surface, des merdiques, des géniaux, des rien du tout...Mais, toute cette NOUVELLE PRESSE MARGINALE, expression d' un besoin de Vivre intense, est le reflet, de par sa sincérité, sa spontanéité, d'un important mouvement révolutionnaire face au système. Un mouvement réellement révolutionnaire, et non l'alternative d'une autre autorité Seulement, cette spontanéité, cette méfiance face à l'organisation hiérarchisée, entraine l'isolement de chaque groupuscule et diminue donc l'impact de cette presse parallèle(par l'absence d'un réseau de distribution important), l'espoir de coordonner nos efforts. Le cPOP avait décidé d'organiser les 24 et 25 juin"les journées de la Free Press".Ca nous a d'abord permis de nous rercontrer, de nous connaître, et puis de réunir nos efforts. Mais, pour qu'un vrai réseau d'information(étendu sur toute la France) puisse être établi, il est indispensable d'avoir des correspondants dans chaque coin(au moins un par grande ville Ce qui est vrai pour l'information l'est également pour la diffusion;un certain pourcentage rembourserait les diffuseurs de leurs frais.Si vous êtes décidés pour créer ce réseau,ecrivez-nous VROUTSCH.7a,quai de la Bruche.67.STRASBOURG)

HOTCHA!

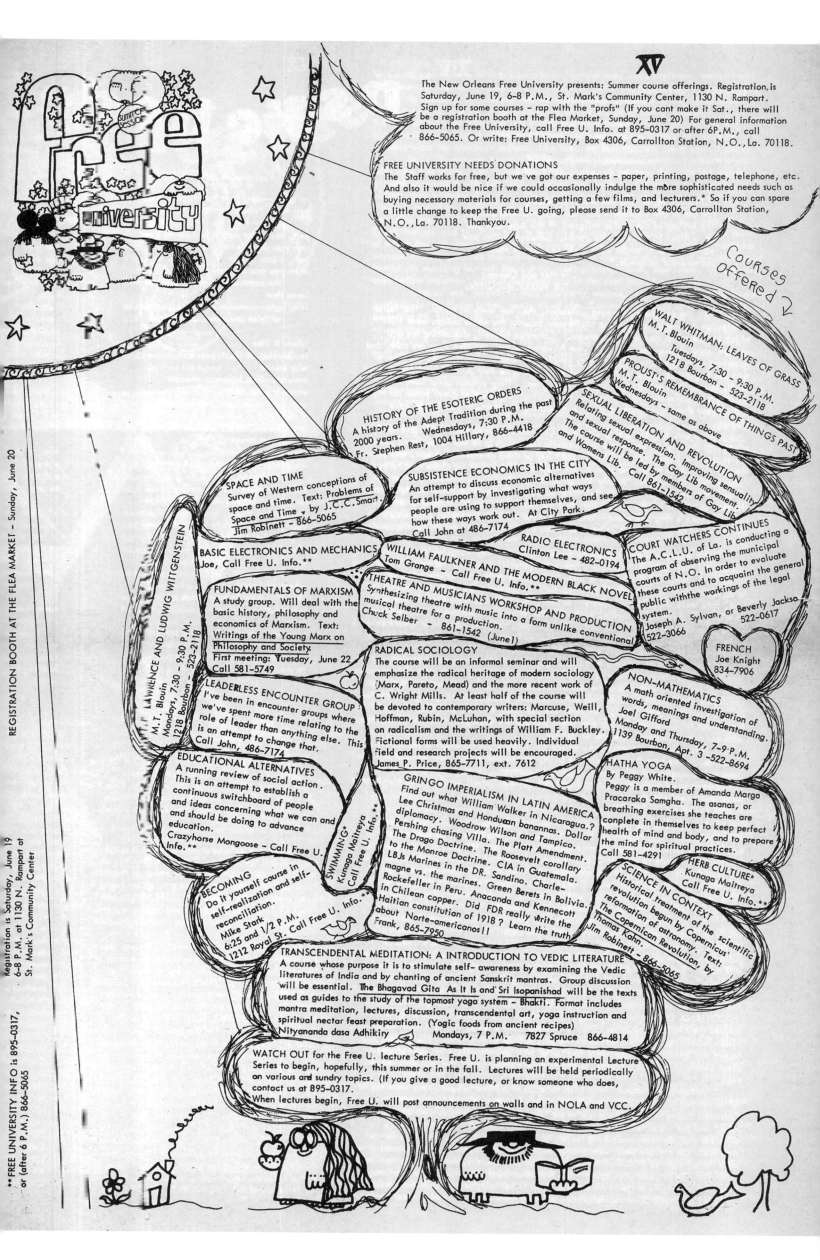

The New Orleans Free University presents: Summer course offerings. Registration is Saturday, June 19, 6-8 P.M., St. Mark's Community Center, 1130 N. Rampart. Sign up for some courses - rap with the "profs" (If you cant make it Sat., there will be a registration booth at the Flea Market, Sunday, June 20) For general information about the Free University, call Free U. Info. at 895-0317 or after 6 P.M., call 866-5065. Or write: Free University, Box 4306, Carrollton Station, N.O., La. 70118.

FREE UNIVERSITY NEEDS DONATIONS
The Staff works for free, but we've got our expenses - paper, printing, postage, telephone, etc. And also it would be nice if we could occasionally indulge the more sophisticated needs such as buying necessary materials for courses, getting a few films, and lecturers.* So if you can spare a little change to keep the Free U. going, please send it to Box 4306, Carrollton Station, N.O., La. 70118. Thankyou.

Courses Offered ↓

WALT WHITMAN: LEAVES OF GRASS
M. T. Blouin
Tuesdays, 7:30 - 9:30 P.M.
1218 Bourbon - 523-2118

PROUST'S REMEMBRANCE OF THINGS PAST
M. T. Blouin
Wednesdays - same as above

HISTORY OF THE ESOTERIC ORDERS
A history of the Adept Tradition during the past 2000 years. Wednesdays, 7:30 P.M.
Fr. Stephen Rest, 1004 Hillary, 866-4418

SEXUAL LIBERATION AND REVOLUTION
Relating sexual expression. Improving sensuality and sexual response. The course will be led by members of Gay Lib and Womens Lib. Call 861-1542.
The course is a part of the Gay Lib movement.

SPACE AND TIME
Survey of Western conceptions of space and time. Text: Problems of Space and Time, by J.C.C. Smart.
Jim Robinett - 866-5065

SUBSISTENCE ECONOMICS IN THE CITY
An attempt to discuss economic alternatives for self-support by investigating what ways people are using to support themselves, and see how these ways work out. At City Park.
Call John at 486-7174

RADIO ELECTRONICS
Clinton Lee - 482-0194

COURT WATCHERS CONTINUES
The A.C.L.U. of La. is conducting a program of observing the municipal courts of N.O. In order to evaluate these courts and to acquaint the general public with the workings of the legal system.
Joseph A. Sylvan, or Beverly Jackson
522-3066   522-0617

BASIC ELECTRONICS AND MECHANICS
Joe, Call Free U. Info.**

WILLIAM FAULKNER AND THE MODERN BLACK NOVEL
Tom Grange - Call Free U. Info.**

FUNDAMENTALS OF MARXISM
A study group. Will deal with the basic history, philosophy and economics of Marxism. Text: Writings of the Young Marx on Philosophy and Society.
First meeting: Tuesday, June 22
Call 581-5749

THEATRE AND MUSICIANS WORKSHOP AND PRODUCTION
Synthesizing theatre with music into a form unlike conventional musical theatre for a production.
Chuck Selber - 861-1542   (June 1)

FRENCH
Joe Knight
834-7906

RADICAL SOCIOLOGY
The course will be an informal seminar and will emphasize the radical heritage of modern sociology (Marx, Pareto, Mead) and the more recent work of C. Wright Mills. At least half of the course will be devoted to contemporary writers: Marcuse, Weill, Hoffman, Rubin, McLuhan, with special section on radicalism and the writings of William F. Buckley. Fictional forms will be used heavily. Individual field and research projects will be encouraged.
James P. Price, 865-7711, ext. 7612

NON-MATHEMATICS
A math oriented investigation of words, meanings and understanding.
Joel Gifford
Monday and Thursday, 7-9 P.M.
1139 Bourbon, Apt. 3 -522-8694

LEADERLESS ENCOUNTER GROUP
I've been in encounter groups where we've spent more time relating to the role of leader than anything else. This is an attempt to change that.
Call John, 486-7174

HATHA YOGA
By Peggy White.
Peggy is a member of Amanda Marga Pracaraka Samgha. The asanas, or breathing exercises she teaches are complete in themselves to keep perfect health of mind and body, and to prepare the mind for spiritual practices.
Call 581-4291

EDUCATIONAL ALTERNATIVES
A running review of social action. This is an attempt to establish a continuous switchboard of people and ideas concerning what we can and and should be doing to advance education.
Crazyhorse Mongoose - Call Free U. Info.**

GRINGO IMPERIALISM IN LATIN AMERICA
Find out what William Walker in Nicaragua. Lee Christmas and Honduran banannas.? diplomacy. Woodrow Wilson and Tampico. Pershing chasing Villa. The Platt Amendment. The Drago Doctrine. The Roosevelt corollary to the Monroe Doctrine. CIA in Guatemala. LBJs Marines in the DR. Sandino. Charlemagne vs. the marines. Green Berets in Bolivia. Rockefeller in Peru. Anaconda and Kennecott in Chilean copper. Did FDR really write the Haitian constitution of 1918? Learn the truth about Norte-americanos!!
Frank, 865-7950

SWIMMING*
Kunaga Maitreya
Call Free U. Info.**

HERB CULTURE*
Kunaga Maitreya
Call Free U. Info.**

SCIENCE IN CONTEXT
Historical treatment of the scientific revolution begun by Copernicus; reformation of astronomy. Text: The Copernican Revolution, by Thomas Kahn.
Jim Robinett - 866-5065

BECOMING
Do it yourself course in self-realization and self-reconciliation.
Mike Stark
6:25 and 1/2 P.M.
1212 Royal St. Call Free U. Info.**

TRANSCENDENTAL MEDITATION: A INTRODUCTION TO VEDIC LITERATURE
A course whose purpose it is to stimulate self-awareness by examining the Vedic literatures of India and by chanting of ancient Sanskrit mantras. Group discussion will be essential. The Bhagavad Gita As It Is and Sri Isopanishad will be the texts used as guides to the study of the topmost yoga system - Bhakti. Format includes mantra meditation, lectures, discussion, transcendental art, yoga instruction and spiritual nectar feast preparation. (Yogic foods from ancient recipes)
Nityananda dasa Adhikiry   Mondays, 7 P.M.   7827 Spruce   866-4814

WATCH OUT for the Free U. lecture Series. Free U. is planning an experimental Lecture Series to begin, hopefully, this summer or in the fall. Lectures will be held periodically on various and sundry topics. (If you give a good lecture, or know someone who does, contact us at 895-0317.
When lectures begin, Free U. will post announcements on walls and in NOLA and VCC.

D. H. LAWRENCE AND LUDWIG WITTGENSTEIN
M. T. Blouin
Mondays, 7:30 - 9:30 P.M.
1218 Bourbon - 523-2118

Registration is Saturday, June 19
6-8 P.M. at 1130 N. Rampart at St. Mark's Community Center

REGISTRATION BOOTH AT THE FLEA MARKET - Sunday, June 20

**FREE UNIVERSITY INFO is 895-0317, or (after 6 P.M.) 866-5065

BERKELEY BARB

Published Weekly
MEMBER
Underground Press Syndicate
(UPS)

Intergalacuc World Brain (IWB
Liberation News Service (LNS
New York News Service (NYNS
Zodiac News Service (ZNS)
Earth News Service (ENS)

Editorial & Business Offi
2042 University Avenu
California 94

Blank generation

THE FREE PRESS IS HIT BY THE GLAM EXPLOSION AND WINDS UP PUNK

Paul Morrissey predicts that 'Money will be the next big youth kick' coke-fuelled conspiracy theories glam hits the front pages birth of punk, new wave and the end of the underground

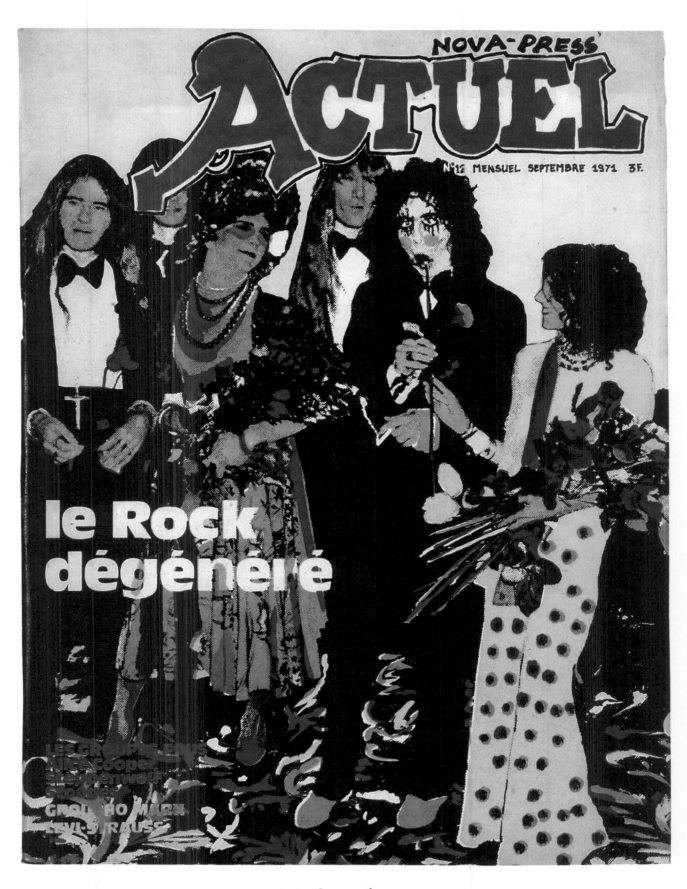

ABOVE: **Actuel**, September 1971. 'Degenerate rock' with Alice Cooper and company.
OPPOSITE: **Other Scenes** in 1970 – is this a prophecy of the yuppie generation that followed?

by subscription only

Wood$$$tock

Who didn't suspect that someone would make a trillion dollars off of Woodstock, all the while lamenting that they'd lost -- to the forces of the people -- an irretrievable fortune?

The movie "Woodstock" is a money-maker. Not just because of the photography -- a tribute to modern technology and some stoned photographers. Not just because the musicians on the screen play fantastic music while the camera shows us magic close-ups of their charisma.

No, the film is a money-maker because it's built on the myth of Woodstock, the myth of a time and a place where 400,000 young people gathered, survived rainstorms and mud; hunger and bad trips, in an atmosphere of love -- forming for three days a city without crime, pollution, or hostility over a common cause: peace, dope, and music. And they didn't even have to pay!

Because the movie theater was dry, because no one was hungry, because the playback was careful to gloss over the fact that it was capitalism, not nature, that made Woodstock a "disaster area", as it was called after the rains came, because of the brilliant editing of the footage, some people left the movie, I am sure, with the myth intact. They went home together on a cold Easter night numb with the need to make it all come true, went home to relive the myth in their own living rooms, with their own friends, dope and stereo.

Women who go to see Woodstock, are you in for a surprise! Woodstock only happened a year ago? is that where most of us were, as women, a year ago?

You should have seen the men building the stage as the movie opened. They were strong, bearded, handsome. They wore old jeans and no shirts, their chests were brown. They deftly lifted the wood and deftly hammered it down. They worked closely together, laughing, sweating, smoking cigarettes, planning the stage on which all of Woodstock would happen.

All of the musicians in the movie were men -- except for Joan Baez, and all she talked about was her husband, David Harris, who is in jail. Before she sang, she told an interviewer that David was a little scared when they shifted him from one prison to another. Understandably. And then the still shots, of Joan and hubbie sitting together (his arm around her), and another of them walking down a lane together (just like Bob Kennedy and Ethel).

So much for Joan.

Wow, what a man Richie Havens is, what a man Joe Cocker is, crazy bastard who really gets into his music. What a man all those men are.

We *know* the cameramen were men.

And what about the women who went to Woodstock, what did they do while the men were building the stage, selling dope, sliding crazily in the mud puddles, playing the music?

Well, the women...some of them had beautiful flowing summer dresses, and walked gently with little naked children, or fed children, or stood in the kitchen tent and served food to Woodstock. That's what some of the women were.

Other women were naked in the cool lake, washing their beautiful long hair, soaping their women's bodies, watching their breasts float, white and pink, on the water. One girl got naked for the camera -- so real to life she had pubic hair! -- and cuddled down with her boyfriend into the weeds and was never seen again.

And there were the girls with liberated nipples beneath clinging rain-flattened T-shirts.

Girls "who were freer" that men came to Woodstock looking for, as one man interviewed in the movie noted.

Girls huddled under plastic, under wet sleeping bags, under rags and sticks, barefoot, with their men, during the storm.

And the girl who was having a bad trip.

And the girl who, when interviewed, said she balled her friend but she wasn't in love or anything.

How'd you like it women? Did the cameras lie? Was Woodstock you?

I stood for an hour on an icy New York street to pay $4 to see what is, I hope, the last incredible episode of a mythic trip called Woodstock. The myth got pasted up all over town. You've seen such posters, months later. They begin to peel, and what's underneath shows through. The posters of Altamont peeled off before the festival was even over.

IT/90, Oct 22 - Nov 5, 1970.

ELEMENTS OF ELEKTRA

ABSOLUTELY LIVE!

ON THE WATERS

Doors
2665 002
double album
Absolutely Live

Bread
2469 005
On the Waters

Incredible String Band
2665 001
double album
U

The Voices of East Harlem
2469 007
Right on Be Free

elektra

Distributec by Polydor Records Ltd.

IT 157
28 June - 12 July 1973

Price 15p.

NEW DYLAN ALBUM - EXCLUSIVE
THE 'X' DIRECTORY
'OTHER SCENES' PULL OUT
WATERGATE - BIRTH OF A LANGUAGE

Nico vit à Paris, devenue la super-star des films de Philippe Garrel. Pendant l'interview, elle tricote, et laisse couler de longs moments de silence : la conversation devra se dérouler à son rythme. Nico aimerait bien chanter plus souvent mais les contrats sont rares. Le monde pop tourne dans un autre univers, et c'est bien dommage pour elle.

Actuel : Que penses-tu de ta période Velvet Underground ?

Nico : C'était très agréable. Avant je n'avais fait que des choses sans intérêt : des photos de mode, par exemple. C'est tellement ennuyeux ! On ne peut pas gagner soixante dollars par heure à ce type de travail et se sentir réel.

Actuel : Tu as fait beaucoup de films avec Andy Warhol ?

Nico : Plusieurs. J'en ai fait un qui dure trente-huit heures. Il s'appelle *Four stars*, et je suis l'une des quatre « super-stars ». Il est passé une fois ou deux à la Cinémathèque et au Musée d'Art moderne de New York. Les spectateurs et les critiques sont restés pendant trente-huit heures, c'est fou ! Le film que je préfère s'appelle *Imitation of Christ*, mais il n'est pas sorti : il n'a aucun rapport avec la réputation pornographique qui fonde le succès des films de Warhol.

Actuel : Tu as mis combien de temps à tourner *Four Stars* ?

Nico : Quelques semaines. Mais nous n'avons pas tourné en permanence ! Le Velvet Underground joue dans le film. Il y a un moment où la police débarque parce que nous jouons trop fort. Ça se passait à l'ancienne Factory, la Silver Factory. Aujourd'hui Andy a une Factory très bien organisée, complètement neutre, super-élégante : c'est la résidence d'un dandy... Andy Dandy. Il arrive un peu tard, ce n'est plus l'époque des dandys, non ? Mais peut-être n'ont-ils pas d'époque.

Actuel : Pourquoi as-tu quitté le Velvet ?

Nico : Le Velvet Underground pensait avoir trouvé un manager meilleur qu'Andy, et ont donc quitté Andy. En fait le type était un escroc, il n'a rien fait pour eux. En plus, il les a monté contre John Cale et moi. C'est pour cela que je suis parti. C'est un démon, je ne l'aime vraiment pas.

Actuel : John Cale travaille toujours avec toi.

Nico : Nous avons les mêmes goûts, les mêmes idées. Il trouve toujours exactement l'atmosphère, la formulation que je désire. Mais je crois que lui aussi profite de notre association. Il lui est difficile de trouver seul l'inspiration. Lorsqu'il fait une musique pour lui-même, elle ne correspond pas du tout à son caractère.

Actuel : Que penses-tu de ton premier disque, *Chelsea Girl* ?

Nico : Mon premier disque ne compte pas. Je commence à partir du deuxième, *The Marble Index*. Je me suis aperçu qu'il est très facile de faire ce dont on a envie. Il n'est pas du tout nécessaire de faire des concessions.

Actuel : Ta musique a-t-elle évolué depuis deux ans et demi ?

Nico : Pas du tout, elle est restée toujours la même. C'est toujours la même mélodie.

Actuel : On a dit qu'elle ressemblait à la musique du moyen-âge.

Nico : Je ne suis pas d'accord. Les gens projettent sur ma musique une étiquette parce qu'ils ne savent pas comment la qualifier. Il y a peut-être une petite ressemblance, mais je me sens beaucoup plus proche de la musique électronique. La musique classique, mais lorsqu'elle est très belle, reste une expression conventionnelle des sentiments. C'est une forme trop codifiée.

Actuel : Le public est-il important pour toi ?

Nico : Quand je suis en face d'un public je me reconnais mieux moi-même, je me découvre des richesses que je ne connaissais pas. Le public est surtout un moyen de communiquer avec soi-même d'une manière plus consciente que d'habitude. D'ordinaire on croit qu'on est assez conscient de soi-même et de son entourage, mais c'est faux. Le public est un témoin, et j'ai besoin de témoins. Sans le public, on ne peut pas sentir que ce qu'on crée existe vraiment.

Actuel : Dans quelle mesure tes chansons sont-elles symboliques ?

Nico : Je ne parle jamais directement des choses, mais les textes signifient quelque chose. « Evening of Light », par exemple, parle des catastrophes naturelles, qui se produisent quand Dieu se fâche. *Desert Shore*, le titre du dernier album, est lui aussi symbolique : le désert et la mer, et entre les deux le rivage, le bord : le bord est toujours un endroit fécond. Le bord permet toutes sortes de naissances, de créations.

Actuel : Si tu expliques le sens cela enlève que que chose.

Nico : Chaque chanson est un film, ou plutôt un ensemble fait à partir de morceaux de films. J'aime la musique visuelle ou visionnaire.

Actuel : Pourquoi as-tu quitté les Etats-Unis ?

Nico : J'habitais chez des amis — j'ai beaucoup de mal à me décider à rester vraiment dans un endroit. Quand on reste dans un appartement, on perd peu à peu son indépendance. Je suis très sensible à ça. Je préfère vivre en nomade, voyager. La plupart des gens ont une famille, même les musiciens. Ils sont organisés. Je n'aime pas l'organisation. (Propos recueillis par Emmanuel Fauconnier)

Illustrations d'Andy Wharol

OPPOSITE AND ABOVE: **it**, 1973, and **Actuel**, 1971: Andy Warhol foresaw the days when celebrity would be everything.
OVERLEAF LEFT: The 1st New York Underground Film Festival, 1970.
OVERLEAF RIGHT: The New York of 1968 anticipates the leather and chains of punk.

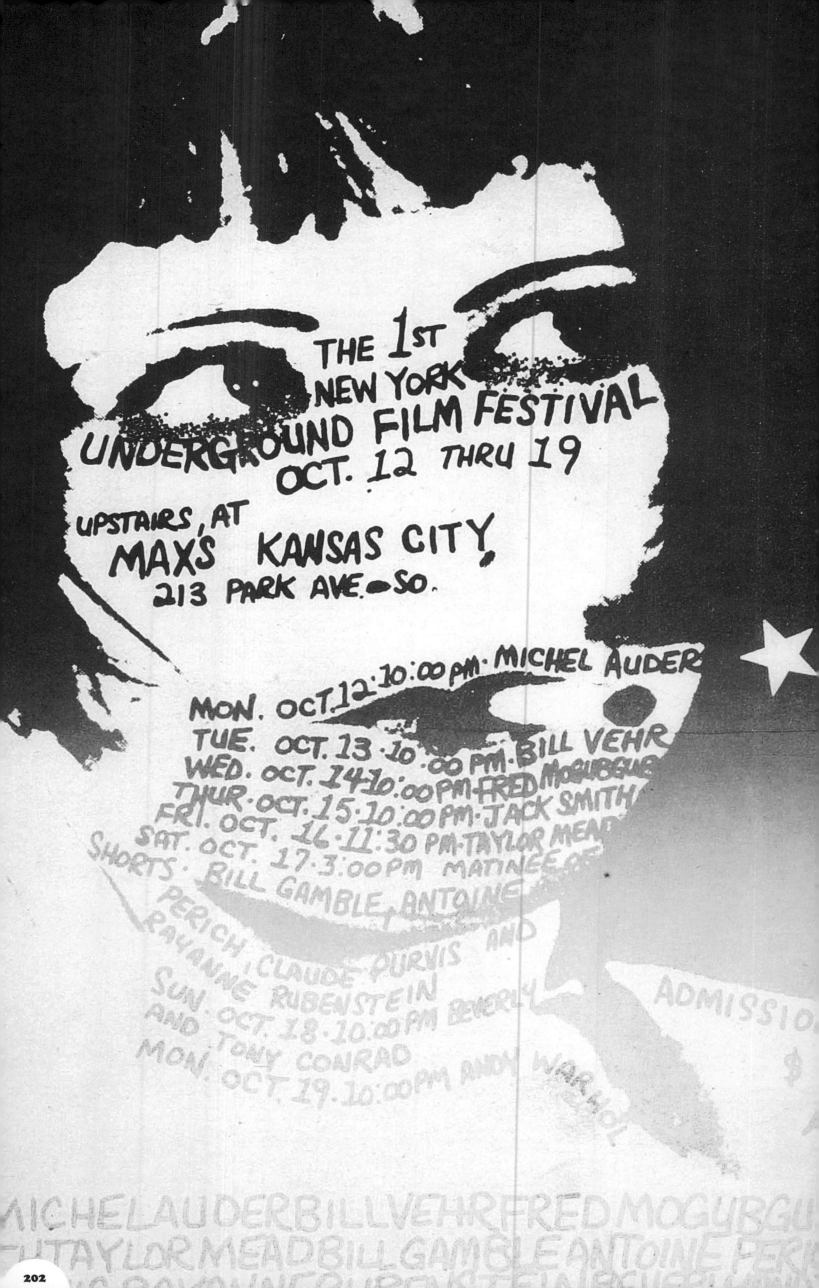

THE 1ST
NEW YORK
UNDERGROUND FILM FESTIVAL
OCT. 12 THRU 19

UPSTAIRS, AT
MAX'S KANSAS CITY,
213 PARK AVE.—SO.

MON. OCT 12·10:00 PM·MICHEL AUDER
TUE. OCT. 13·10:00 PM·BILL VEHR
WED. OCT. 14·10:00 PM·FRED MoGURGUS
THUR·OCT. 15·10:00 PM·JACK SMITH
FRI. OCT. 16·11:30 PM·TAYLOR MEAD
SAT. OCT. 17·3:00 PM MATINEE OF
SHORTS· BILL GAMBLE, ANTOINE
PERICH, CLAUDE PURVIS AND
RAYANNE RUBENSTEIN
SUN. OCT. 18·10:00 PM BEVERLY
AND TONY CONRAD
MON. OCT. 19·10:00 PM ANDY WARHOL

ADMISSIO
$

MICHELAUDERBILLVEHRFREDMOGURGU
TAYLORMEADBILLGAMBLEANTOINE PER

THE east village OTHER

VOL. 3, NO. 45   METROPOLITAN 15¢   OCTOBER 11, 1968

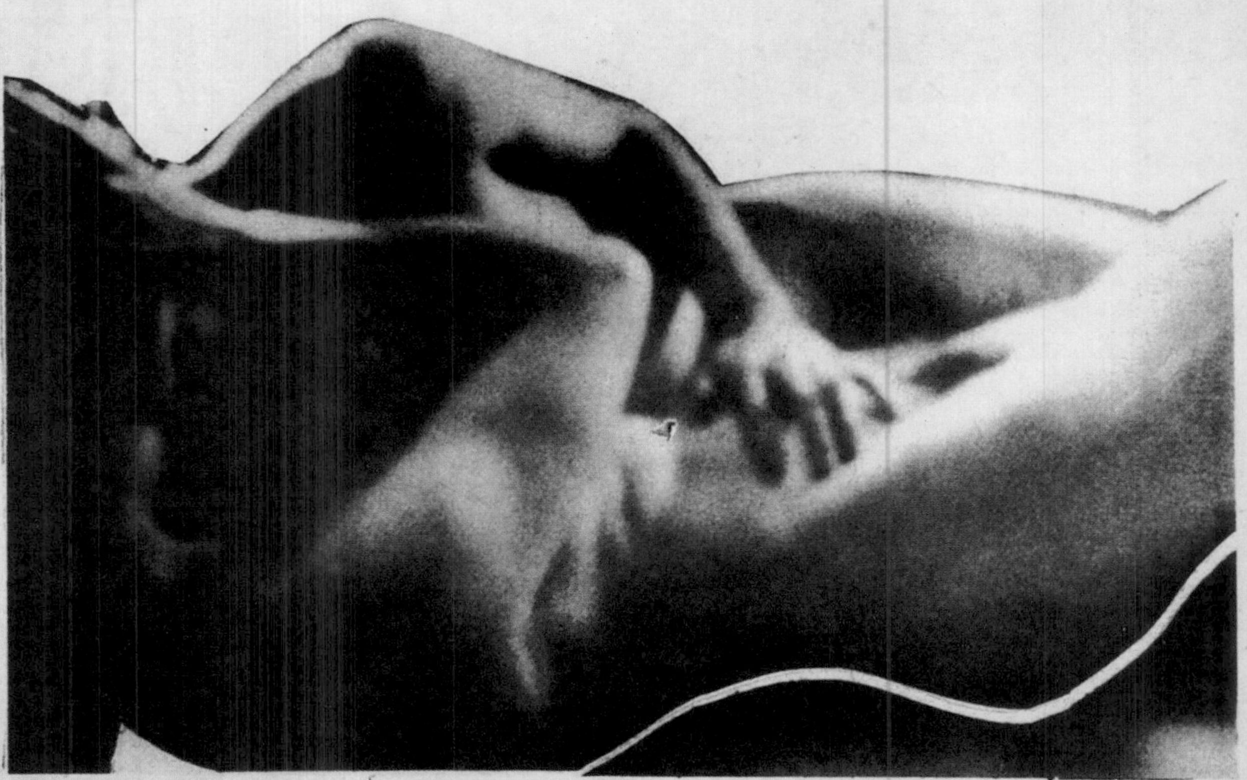

from "Lovemaking"
A film by Stan Brakhage

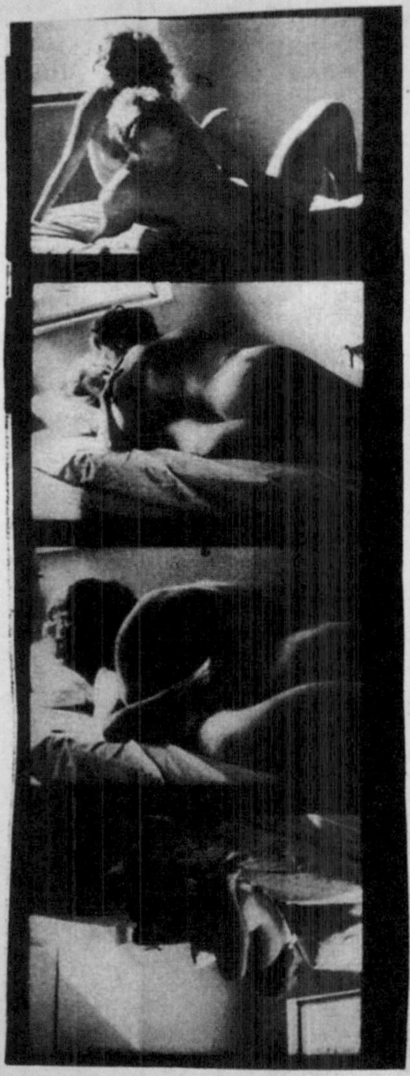

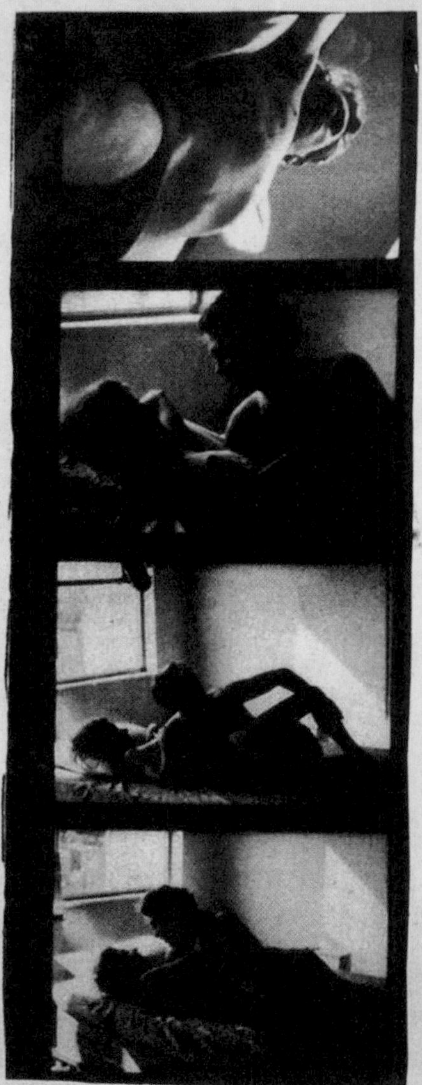

Scenes from
Andy Warhol's
"Fuck" (tentative title)
starring Louis Waldron
and Viva!

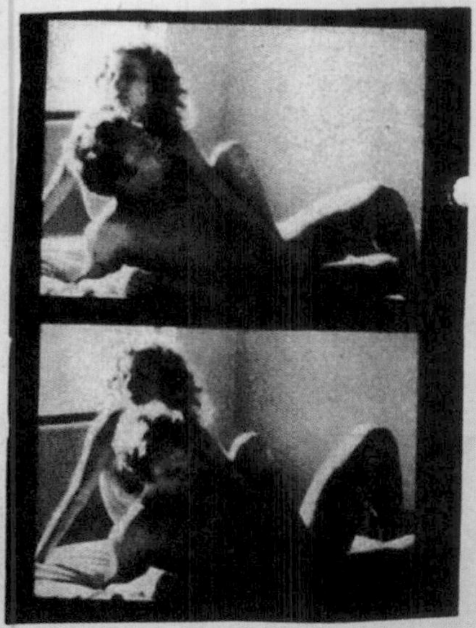

New York in 1969, and underground cinema is breaking every taboo.

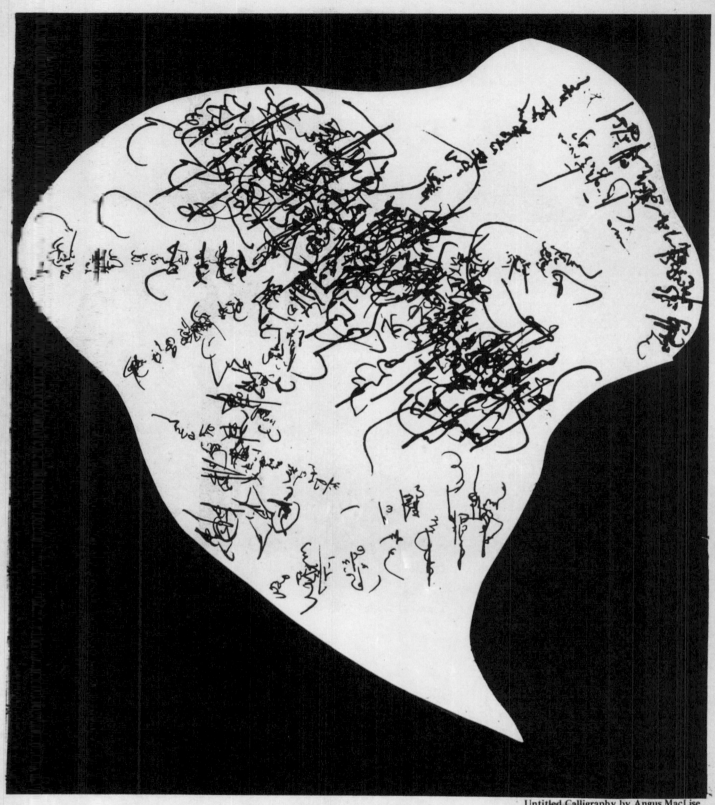

Untitled Calligraphy by Angus MacLise

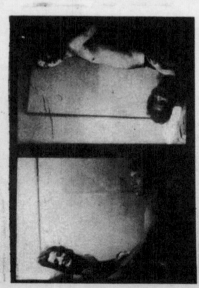
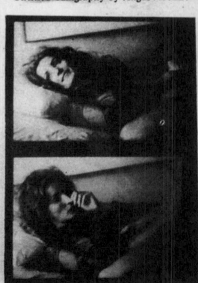

'Q. Would you conclude this interview with an observation on the counterculture of the '60's? I assume that it is less than a node, as you call it, of the coming reversal. A. No, it's simply part of the larger process, the most recent burst of energy in the continuing struggle to create a real revolutionary culture. In its demise as a movement, it too makes its insights to the battle at large, and indeed some aspects of it (like this joint I am about to light) I admire very much. But it just can't last into the dying light of capitalism. It takes more of us than that, and more different kinds of us'.

from An Interview with Donald Duck by David Wagner, *Radical America* Vol7 No1.

The underground never even got a decent funeral. It is simply recorded that something that started out in a duffle-coat in the direction of Aldermaston pegged out in a back room full of unsold comic books and barbiturates. The real, unlikely people who, in pub rooms and over duplicators and behind scaffolding stages made up a movement, have not been asked to comment on the corpse. A new generation of groovers can't see what all the fuss is about. Apart from desultory cries of Bad Dope and Its The Pigs Again, there is no explanation, an almost self-induced amnesia. Which is a pity because no movement can begin again except out of some understanding of its own history. And that history is so personal and intense it has become virtually psychiatry (psychiatrists being simply the historians of the recent past) alone offering explanations of why earstwhile rebels decide to become sheepfarmers, Stalinists, senior lecturers in Deviant Sociology, recluses, 'rock writers', commercial radio hacks or live unhappily ever after in a groovy nuclear commune in the country.

The truth of the matter is not that The-Leaders-Sold-Out or that-something-greatly-beautious-grew-cankered, but that the underground got smashed, good and proper by exactly those forces of which it stood in defiance. It was smashed because it could not, by 1968, be laughed at or ignored or patronised any longer. The underground was able to make really painful attacks on the system's intellectually based forms of power. Of all the intellectual property speculators of the 60's, it made the most sizeable incrusions into capitalism's ideological real estate, the family, school, work-discipline, the 'impartial' lawcourts and the British Broadcasting Corporation. Unlike previous movements of radical arties, it actually transmitted its mood of indiscipline to young people of all classes.

'It is an attack on family life', said Inspector Luff at the *Oz* trial, quite rightly. The popularity of *Oz*'s atmosphere, (no matter how incomprehensible and downright boring the actual magazine) was, especially to working class kids, an index of the end of decades of post war deference, evidence of a new refusal to any longer even pretend loyalty to the Queen, The Law and The Empire. Already the obscenity and dope trials of the sixties look like light comedy compared to the massive police operations around the Shrewsbury building workers' conspiracy trial or the Winchester bombs trial. But they were the first omens of a new legal viciousness, the opportunity for the police to cut their teeth and the Special Branch to enlarge its files. They could take the Angry Young Men out to lunch, but the hairies had to go to jail.

It was not the case that sufficient numbers were ever arrested to halt the movement and that government-organised spies set about wrecking it, as undoubtedly happened in the late sixties in America. Anyone using the word repression about what happened to *Oz* and *IT* literally does not understand the meaning of the word. But the combination of coppers on one hand, the liberal embrace and pampered sensibilities of the groovier merchant bankers, commercial nabobs and corporate impressarios on the other was deadly.

The national papers of the underground had to exist in an almost wholly hostile world where survival alone, each issue, entailed an epic of cheque-bouncing and bravado. They variously stumbled, victims of their own cheerful apoliticism, into a major trial of strength with the authorities simply for the crime of not being hypocritical. The strain and worry and energy drain utterly disorientated their editorial strength and traditions and led to a situation where the papers rocketed down hill in quality just at a time when more people than ever before were showing an interest in them. For although nominally democratic and open, the papers were so dependent on a small improvising editorial aristocracy that the disappearance of a single person at crucial stages could completely alter the paper's atmosphere.

The unstructured, unpredictable production methods of the underground papers, if focused outwards and in contact and in trust with a movement, could produce remarkable committed journalism (*IT* in the acid heighday of '67, *Black Dwarf* after '68, *Frendz* throughout the Mangrove Trial and the last 12 issues of *Ink*). But exactly that structure could become an office coterie bound together only by a passion for self-promotion and unabashed ambition, whilst the general loyalty and openmindedness of their readers was increasingly exploited by

Necrophilia/DAVID WIDGERY

What Went Wrong

For years within the pages of Oz magazine you have been reading about the 'demise' of the alternative press. Here, hopefully for the last time, our author disturbs this wretched corpse in yet another final instalment of the continuing hippy death saga . . .

8

ABOVE: **Oz**, London, 1972. The Last Passion of the Underground Press.
OVERLEAF: The movie *Performance*, starring Mick Jagger, had an impact all over the world.

Photo by Red Saunders.

writers who prided themselves on their resemblance to the Lunchtime O'Boozes' automated copy production, drunkenness and despair.

This desperate hackishness was all the more pathetic in people who actually still had ideas, but simply could no longer find words for them. The beats had been evangelical, CND determined sane but desperate, the Underground capable of great moral wrath; the collapse into plain old cynicism, the oldest crutch in the book, was a real full stop to a movement, however hard you tried to stick spangles to it and call it decadence. Increasingly, elements always jostling around in the underground, the love of fashionable intercourse and the dependence on the good offices of advertisers, became dominant. *IT* became little more than a mouthpiece for the

record companies and, although rock reviews were the only things taken seriously by most readers, their authors could scarcely conceal their own boredom.

This process of defeat was complicated, and often illustrated best, in cultural details. It is a fairly glum tribute to the underground's struggle to be able to express yourself in the clothes you wear that such a counter revolution has been effected by commerce that anyone not dressed like a possum trapper on stilts is trying to look like a Tory tennis player of the late twenties. It is a bizarre 15 years which starts with girls revolting against court shoes and twin-sets in favour of existentialist black sweaters and jeans and ending up having to wear them again. It is strange that the system won't even leave our memories alone, so that people

are obliged to feel nostalgic over experiences they never even had in the first place. It is a pity that music (which alone makes it all worthwhile) being made by English and American musicians now offers solely the choice between mock urban menace (Mott, Bowie, Reed, half the Stones) and a phony countrification (other half of Stones plus everything else). It is quite literally pathetic that a movement succoured by cannabis and raised in electrifying affections of acid should grow old jittering, crying and quarreling with itself on the corners of Gerrard Street or in a mandraxed haze at the back of the classroom. Marx, in a footnote to 'Capital' describes the opium trade as a revenge against imperialism. What more cunningly wrought revenge is possible than for flowerchildren to wind up

Continued on page 66. 9

OH BOY! IT'S ANOTHER SEXSATIONAL ISSUE!

JAGGER'S SADIST MOVIE FINALLY RELEASED

'PERFORMANCE' FOR U.K. SHOW

A HEAVY EVIL FILM, DON'T SEE IT ON ACID

PERFORMANCE, filmed some two years ago, is finally about to be unleashed on the British public. It's probably the heaviest movie ever made – a kaleidoscope of transvestism, sado–masochism, deaths, bad trips etc.

James Fox – Jagger as a retired rock star, and Fox as a thug on the run. Jagger is involved in a three–way relationship with two chicks at his Powis Square pad. Fox moves in and is gradually freaked–out and mentally demolished.

It's a totally illogical movie. A series of seemingly un–related incidents, and complex inter-relationships flashed across the screen at almost subliminal speed– Jagger/Fox Jagger/chicks Fox/chicks, and chick/chick. Chilling and very effective, with superb editing and camera work.

Jagger is outrageous. Any doubts about his acting ability that might remain after "Ned Kelly" are effectively dispelled. He parodies and caricatures himself; pouting, posturing grimacing and generally acting mean and ugly. The music comes from Jack Nitzche, Ry Cooder, and

the Merry Clayton Singers. The soundtrack album is now out and even taken out of the context of

the film it's well worth hearing.

PERFORMANCE is an evil movie.

At times, it's almost pornographic, and the violence scenes are sickeningly realistic. Warner Bros. are warning people not to see it while tripping – they could well be right. It'll be released in October/November this year.

The Stones have just started their first tour of Europe for 3½ years. Jagger was recently interviewed by the Copenhagen paper "Politiken", and came out with the following statement:-
"I want to earn money on our new records, not for the sake of the money but to invest it in other things, such as the Black Panther breakfast programme for ghetto children. We have already set aside some bread for them, in fact." He claimed that the profits of the big American companies went to buy arms and support right-wing organisations. "I want the money to fight this with" he finished.

I who stands watch at the carlton tower?

An individual with a taste for BUTTERFLY PEELS in the closet HE showed me a dump

After the mud dried. What we do is buy our own fruit.

When that easy-going, motorcycle hick cut me down DUST DEVIL'S Two-pronged Bone Pushed out goblin Don't underestimate A

robust and firm 10 Inches It's a TIGHT FIT FOR REAL COMFORT And they say it gets bigger in trucks It's the only mail order come-back gives you juke box butter FOR NOTHING! Could any plastic fore SKIN look prettier CHILDREN, The word is out: Where to go in the U.S.A. DOWN DOWN DOWN

Wild as it sounds, A marriage certificate helped us Fuck Monks Christ Which tears can FESTOON a. MOLE PEOPLE b. SLIME PEOPLE c. GAMMA PEOPLE Even under your End Run Super-Support It doesn't take a Floating head to become MoonHaze eased by drugs ... AND A FANG on his never too sweet Dickie Active Dads RUT after a while. ouch STOP STOOPING!

The trouble starts when they come out where everybody isn't. WHO ELSE WANTS A HE-MAN BODY? in the dark Round trip ANGUISH HAPPENS TO damnably expert PEOPLE all by itself and the NEIGHBORHOOD bully makes her end up with... CHURCH SPONSORSHIP Over a barrel. Why can't a woman's be more like a man's? Take a deep breath.

Pages from Charles Henry Ford's SILVER FLOWER COO to be published by Kulcher Press next October.

ABOVE: **Paranoid puzzle pieces by Charles Henri Ford.**
OPPOSITE: **Fear and loathing on the cover of Ace, 1972.**

EXCLUSIVE: WITH NIXON IN CHINA, P.5
SPECIAL SECTION: N.Y. IS FEAR CITY

NEW YORK

ACE

VOL I NO 5   **FEB 29, 1972**   25¢

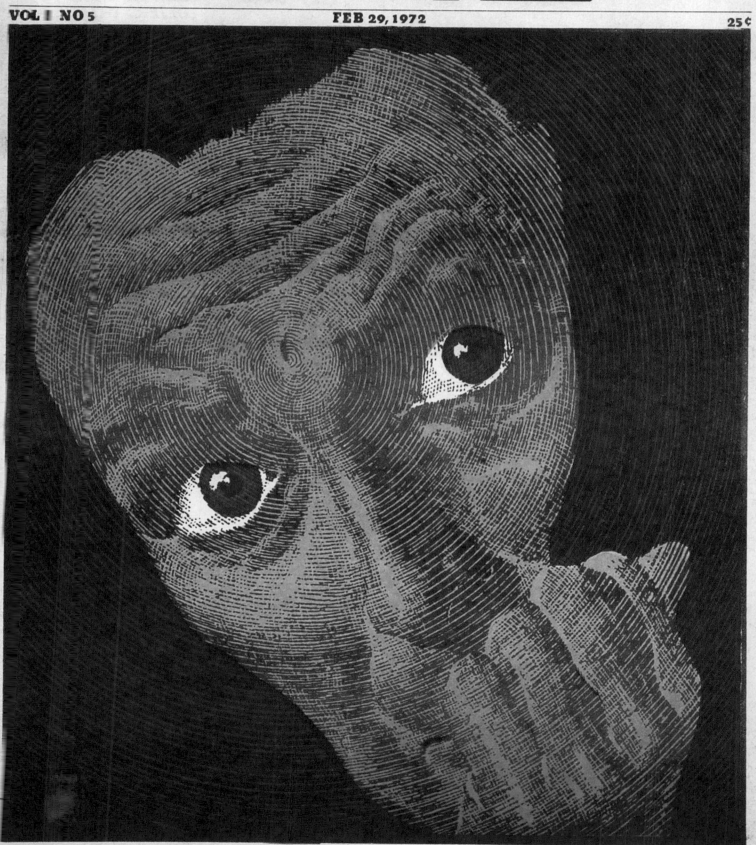

MONSTER ISSUE

Berkeley Barb

Copyright: Berkeley Barb 1976   25¢ BAY AREA, 50¢ ELSEWHERE

Issue 585, October 29 - November 4, 1976

Ball

Hookers'

What Scares

Herb Caen?

Fritz Leiber

Psychics   Predict

Robert A. Wilson

Sybil Leek

Paul Krassner

A division of Poetry On Films, Inc.

inter/VIEW

ON SALE NOW

inter/VIEW

Vol. 1 No.1   A MONTHLY FILM JOURNAL   35¢

INSIDE: CUKOR
VARDA · SARNE
FONDA

Rado, Ragni, Viva in Lions Love

FIRST ISSUE COLLECTOR'S EDITION

OPPOSITE: This Halloween issue of the **Berkeley Barb** looks more like a bad trip. October 1976.
ABOVE: Warhol's sex stars: naked, decadent and bored to tears.

213

Numb's the Word

Cocaine

Sigmund Freud

COPPING THE COCAINE HORRORS

By B.J. GATSBY

On the third day we slept. Or at least part of us slept. It would last a few hours and then the eyes would pop and the brain begin again to savor the unsalivated lining of the mouth and the blood make itself felt squeezing along its narrowing passages in a monumental effort to conduct its business. It seemed obsolete. It was not blood that moved the body, that kept the body in cosmic harmony, that burned the energy of time and space in explosions of omniscience.

It was cocaine and all else seemed beside the point.

The body slept only out of savage primordial need unconnected with the reality of awareness that had been burning bright for three days and held the promise of infinite consciousness. Even in sleep the brain seemed to crank out its infinitesimal observations, fitting them tightly into a scheme not yet revealed but beckoning from beyond some undiscovered barrier to be seen in fragments as the body swelled with the energy of the universe and the mind unleashed its power in fits of incomprehensible magnitude. Coca Cola was all the stomach would consider and so breakfast was brief.

Code Name Warren sat statuesque in the corner, his eyes wide seeing everything and looking at nothing. Movement was not impossible but was not recommended as it was accompanied by a chain reaction of nervous spasms that could last for hours. In front of him stood half a bottle of Scotch and six qualudes, all that was left of the two dozen he had the night before. It was the qualudes that made him shake and the cocaine that kept him up to do it. Code Name Warren was a fiend and this was his meat.

I think it's pertinent to mention here that I am not a coke freak

and, for that matter, neither is Code Name Warren despite his obvious masochistic inclinations No, a true coke freak would not sit like some poor postured Buddha contemplating the various methods of mitigating the pure paranoia of a cocaine induced frenzy. A coke freak revels in the cosmic chill of unreal delusion. Too much coke and he simply polishes his brass bed for a few hours until the brain gets a grip on things. No, this is business and our three day vigil of vice is one of the hazards of the drug world. Without the torture of self inflicted psychosis, the waiting would be unbearable.

Continued to p. 8

ABOVE: The **Berkeley Barb** makes a sly reference to Freud's cocaine connections.
OPPOSITE: Cattle mutilation in Arizona creates a thousand conspiracy theories.

214

Jerry Rubin On The Revolution Of The 80's

Berkeley Barb

Al Trimble

Issue 549   February 20 - 26 1976   Copyright: Berkeley Barb 1976   204   25¢ BAY AREA, 50¢ ELSEWHERE

MUTILATION MYSTERIES

Who needs 1500 cows' ears, eyes, lips, genitals and udders—and why?

Do Satanists pilot U.S. Army Helicopters?

Do coyotes carry knives?

What does the Bureau of Alcohol, Tobacco and Firearms have to do with cattle ?

Who wanted a small town editor looking for answers out of the way ?

Why did law enforcement tell Colorado media to drop the story, and why did they do it?

Are humans next?

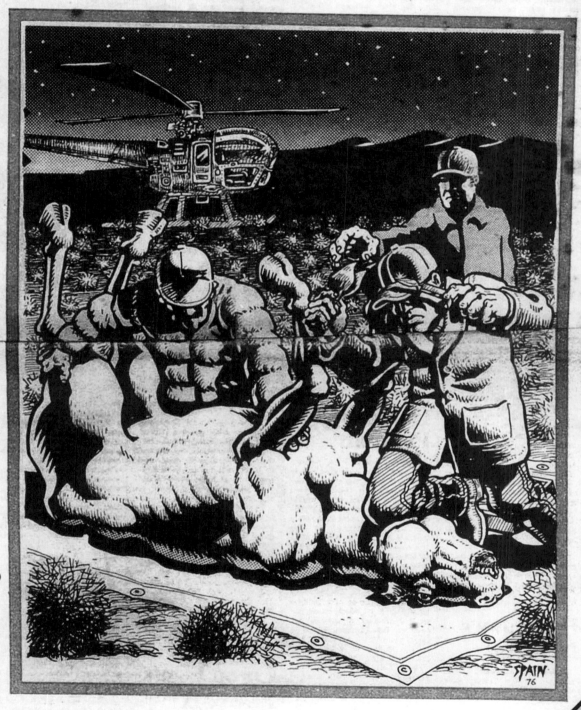

"What emerges in the mutilation phenomenon is much more bizarre and fearful than some revival of a Roman military cult in which parts of bulls were ingested to gain power, or a rash of extraterrestrial bovine collectors. What emerges seems to echo a mentality somewhere between My Lai and Operation Phoenix, with a recurring image of 3,000 dead sheep in Skull Valley, Utah, quivering under the effect of a U.S. Army nerve gas."

Bay Cablevision: 'We Bombed In Berkeley'

NEW YORK ROCKER

#1   75¢

featuring

THE RAMONES
WAYNE COUNTY
TALKING HEADS
MARBLES
MILK 'N' COOKIES
MIAMIS
BLONDIE

MICHAEL BROWN
on the right banke

LA ROCKS
on Iggy, Runaways
and other Stars

PATTI SMITH
on the pix scene

TELEVISION'S TOM VERLAINE

PLUS:

TALES OF THE **HEARTBREAKERS**
IS SAN DIEGO NEXT?
CATCHING MUMPS

~MAP OF THE STARS~

ABOVE: Rock is reborn. **New York Rocker,** February 1976.
OPPOSITE: **Search and Destroy**, California, 1977.
The front and back cover of the best of the punk papers.

SEARCH & DESTROY

No. 1 $1
65P

Search and Destroy

ALLEN GINSBERG
NUNS CRIME

JOHNNY ROTTEN

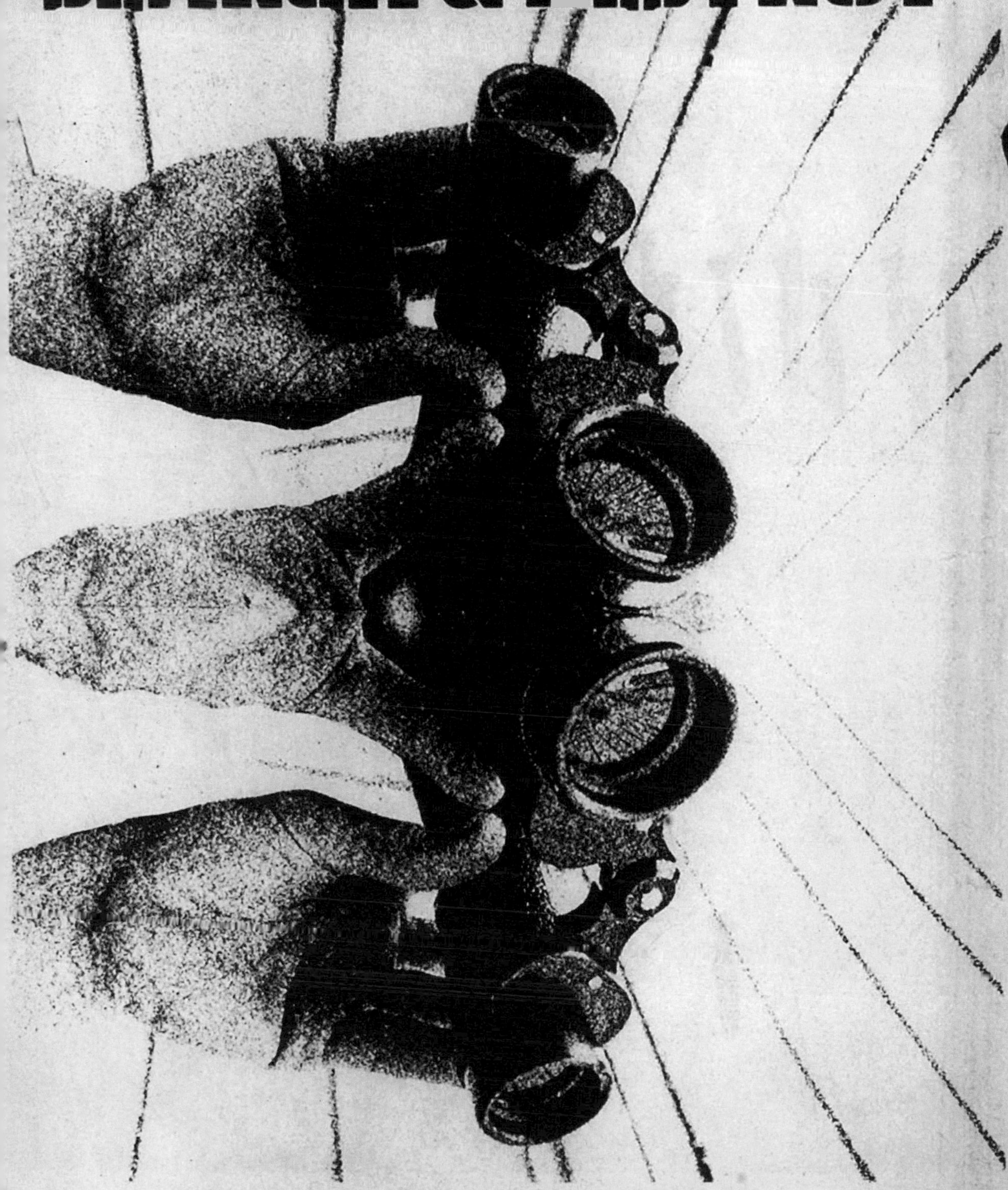

ABOVE: After 1974, everyone seemed to be tightening their belts. **Actuel**, Paris, December 1974.
OPPOSITE: Patti Smith in her *Radio Ethiopia* phase in 1976, a few months before she fell off stage and broke several neck vertebrae.

NEW YORK ROCKER

$1

PATTI SMITH·ROBERT MAPPLETHORPE
ABBA·WAYNE COUNTY·HELL·DICTATORS

ABOVE: The punk design collective Bazooka advertised their own paper,
Un Regard Moderne, in the pages of **Libération**. Paris, 1977–78.
OPPOSITE: The **East Village Other** was replaced by the **East Village Eye**.
Art or fashion was the choice of the new wave.

EaST VILLage
eYE age

SeP-OCT $1.00

ART OR FASHION

FREE ART MUSEUM TICKET-1.30

ABOVE AND OPPOSITE: In the early 1980s, **National Lampoon** and the **East Village Eye** targeted the punk generation.

EAST VILLAGE EYE

CHRIS BURDEN
SLUGGER ANN
U.S. APE
WERNER SCHROE-
TER
RAYBEATS
CLUBS
......

1ST ANNIVERSARY ISSUE!

June 1980   "It's all true."   50¢

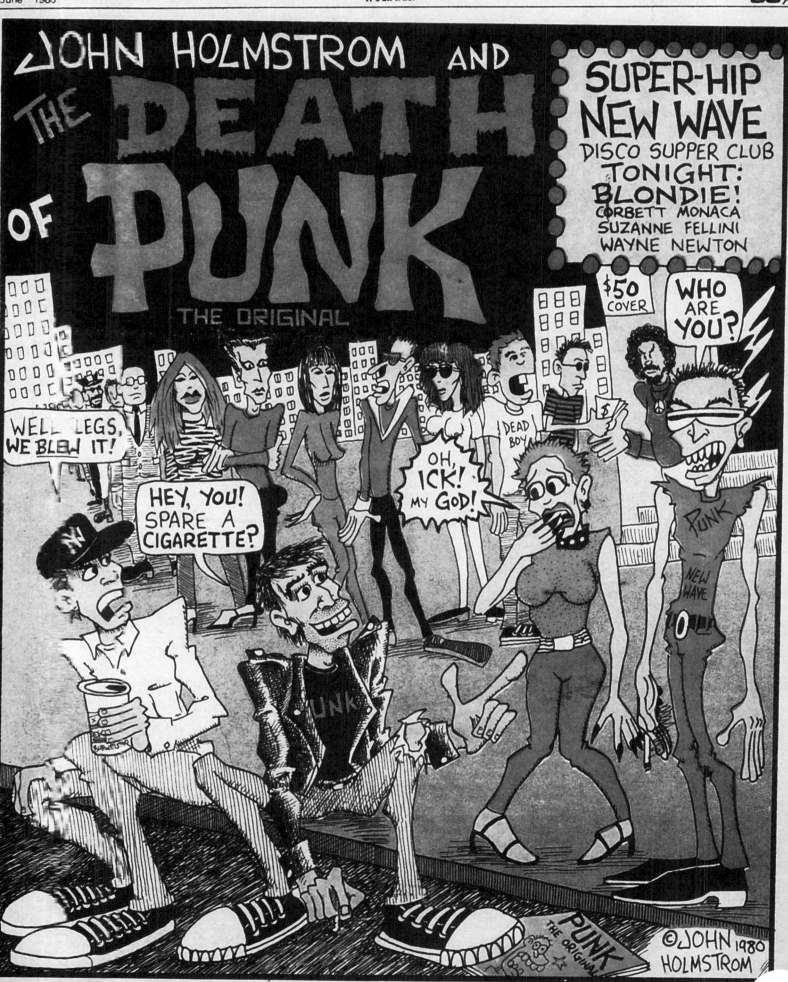

JOHN HOLMSTROM AND THE DEATH OF PUNK THE ORIGINAL

SUPER-HIP NEW WAVE DISCO SUPPER CLUB TONIGHT: BLONDIE! CORBETT MONACA SUZANNE FELLINI WAYNE NEWTON

$50 COVER

WHO ARE YOU?

WELL LEGS, WE BLEW IT!

HEY, YOU! SPARE A CIGARETTE?

OH, ICK! MY GOD!

DEAD BOY

PUNK NEW WAVE

©JOHN 1980 HOLMSTROM

65 75

An enlightening history of the Underground Press Syndicate, as told by Jean-François Bizot

Richard Brautigan, author of *Trout Fishing in America*, whose bittersweet irony was perfect for the anarchist tracts of the San Francisco Diggers in 1966–67.

Max Scherr, former sociologist of the New Left, was over forty when he founded the **Berkeley Barb** on 13 August 1965. The front page kept changing (here, death at Altamont), but the Don Quixote logo was ever-present.

Jim Haynes, born a citizen of the world and Louisiana, co-founded the **International Times** (**it**) in London in 1966. In 1969, he was one of the group that launched **Suck** in Amsterdam – billed as the 'first European sexpaper' and the only source of underground erotica worthy of the name.

Robert Crumb and his colleagues Gilbert Shelton (creator of the *Fabulous Furry Freak Brothers*), Spain Rodriguez, Greg Irons and Ron Cobb gave the underground press a glut of graphic and comic strip art and helped to shape the identity of the counterculture.

An enlightening history of the Underground Press Syndicate

June 1966. In the tiny New York offices of the **East Village Other**, Allan Katzman wrote an article about the benefits of setting up an underground press association, or rather a syndicate, to enhance the impact of the various American publications of the time – ranging from the big guns like the Californian **L.A. Free Press** and the **Berkeley Barb** to the smaller ones like **Fifth Estate** in Detroit. Walter Bowart, co-founder of the project, was interviewed on the subject by *Time Magazine*, and when asked the name of the organization, he looked thoughtfully out of the window. Passing by was a UPS truck – the United Parcel Service, the well-known international delivery firm – and wham! It came to him: UPS, the Underground Press Syndicate.

That is how Abe Peck describes the origins of the UPS in his book *Uncovering the Sixties*. The first meeting took place over Easter 1967 at Stinson Beach. The Black Panthers had just arrived on the scene, San Francisco was becoming the Mecca of the freaks, and there were already more than 400,000 American soldiers in Vietnam. When asked by military leaders to intensify the bombing raids, President Lyndon B. Johnson

wondered 'how long it will take five hundred thousand angry Americans to climb the White House wall and lynch their president.'

The movement was growing so fast that neither the FBI nor the CIA knew where to begin in their efforts to attack it or undermine it. Nevertheless, the thirty or so papers that joined the syndicate could not reach a consensus on policy. On the one hand, for instance, there was Jeff Shero, who campaigned for the abolition of segregated toilets at the University of Texas with one of the great slogans of the sixties: 'Let My People Go'; in 1968, he founded **Rat**, a major left-wing underground newspaper. At the other extreme were the beatnik Dead-head hippies of the **San Francisco Oracle**, also financed by Augustus Owsley Stanley III, the leading maker of LSD, now underground since its prohibition one year earlier. All around were the militants and the freaks, who disliked the phoney, mind-blowing pretensions of the hippies, and were led by Emmett Grogan and Peter Coyote's Diggers – they used to steal food and give it away at free concerts in San Francisco. This culture and shared morality eventually led to the activism of the New Left.

In Europe, London's **it** was a good synthesis of what the movement stood for. The underground press became increasingly powerful, and a few months later it could count around a hundred publications and several million readers, whose shared convictions culminated on 21 October 1967 in a massive demonstration in Washington, with the slogan 'Levitate the Pentagon'.

It was not until after the May '68 revolution that I discovered the UPS, when I met Tom Forcade, who had just started running it. The times were getting violent, and the underground press was beginning to be hounded by the CIA and FBI. Intimidation even extended to the printers, who found themselves forced to raise their prices or even to dowse the print run with the contents of huge stink bombs. Tom Forcade had kept a record of the number of journalists arrested for possession of pot: it was a hundred times higher than the national average.

The Underground Press Syndicate helped us enormously: it was more than just a press agency. You could get a kind of first-hand eyewitness news there, often superbly written, as well as poems, manifestos, collages, the latest news on censorship, and an abundance of illustrations by underground giants such as Robert Crumb, Ron Cobb, Spain Rodriguez, Clay Wilson, Jay Lynch, Martin Sharp and Greg Irons. They were a big factor in the success of **Actuel**, although we also produced home-grown illustrators in the form of Jean-Marc Reiser, Francis Masse and Claire Bretécher, all of whom we published from 1972 onwards. Crumb later said that the underground press 'didn't pay nothing, but you just felt so great that somebody would print your stuff with no censorship at all.' He and the rest lived off the sale of their comic books: *Zap Comix*, *Bijou*, *Fury Freak Brothers* and more.

More underground papers now began to emerge in Europe: **Hotcha** in Switzerland, **Re Nudo** in Italy, **Ding** in the Netherlands, **Parapluie** in Paris, **Vroutsch** in Strasbourg, **Quetton** in Cherbourg, **Le Campin** in Lille.

At **Actuel** we never suffered from any outright censorship, but from 1973 onwards controversy was never far away. We were attacked by thugs, with the connivance of the police, and by a madman on the loose who used to slap the girls as they left the office, and by a dozen or so vicious squatters. There were lots of fights, not to mention several arson attempts, and it finally reached a point where we were so sick of the sneering attitude of the police that we slunk away to the suburbs.

The history of the underground press was drawing to a close. In France, Valéry Giscard d'Estaing had just been elected as president, and immediately jumped on the bandwagon of moral freedom. The age of consent was lowered to eighteen, the right to use contraceptives had already been won, and now abortion was legalized too. Environmentalists had put a stop to tower blocks in Paris, and the Day of the Tree was introduced. To pollute the poetry of sex, pornography laws were also relaxed. Mockery was no longer enough – we were heading for decadence, glitter and cold cynicism in the Warhol style.

In America, the UPS went into decline after 1973, ravaged by revolutionaries facing the apathy of freaks who were drained by debts and lawsuits. The FBI had mounted a campaign against the record companies CBS and Elektra to stop them subsidizing the revolution, which had made the advertising fortune of **Rolling Stone**.

In conclusion, to quote Abe Peck: 'DDT was banned, abortions were legalized, the draft ended, US troops finally left Vietnam, the American Psychiatric Association "de-diseased" homosexuality, and draconian sentences for smoking plants were reduced.' Stake-outs at nuclear power stations had become the province of the *New York Times* and the *Washington Post*, which were now publishing scoops such as Watergate that had formerly been the bread and butter of the UPS. But the movement had been needed to launch this new way of doing things, and without it nothing would have changed.

Thirty years later, the underground press has virtually disappeared. Will the Internet be enough to preserve our liberties? Words may fly by, but the writing still remains.

Richard Neville, Australian student, built like a surfer, activist par excellence, and co-founder of **Oz**, its pages bursting with glorious colour. Find him on his website: www.richardneville.com.au

A self-portrait of **John Wilcock** tucked into a corner of **Other Scenes**, founded in late May 1968 in New York, and very arty. Wilcock had left his previous paper, the **East Village Other**, as a result of a row over a review of Andy Warhol's movies, to which he devoted a book that deserves to be reissued. He is still publishing his own personal paper, the **Ojai Orange**, Ojai being the town in California where he lives. While continuing to indulge his love of collage, he is also an avid collector of quotations, which he reproduces in miniature wallet-shaped books (see below).

Hunter S. Thompson was another icon of the underground press, to which he frequently contributed, and *Gonzo Highway* – a book of his letters – includes a letter to John Wilcock dated 5 January 1967 – paranoia, Vegas style.

We are the future! The free press is everywhere.

PAGE 10. The Realist, New York.

The granddaddy of the underground press, founded in 1958.

From New York, of course, like the **Village Voice** before it (1955), **The Realist** was a real institution. Before 9/11, you could almost imagine that New York was part of the European Union, its roots were sunk so deep in the old continent. New York borrowed the idea of modern art from Europe, after having given refuge to Max Ernst, Duchamp and Breton during the Second World War. New York provided us with an echo through publishers such as Grove Press, who introduced the Americans to Jean-Paul Sartre, Jean Genet, Albert Camus, the *Nouvelle Vague*, and Antonin Artaud. Out of New York, the Actors' Studio produced our favourite screen idols – like Brando in On the Waterfront. New York nourished the iconoclasm of its black and Jewish intellectuals, for it was here above all that, until the end of the 1950s, they found an idea of liberty that was denied to them elsewhere by means of segregation or violence. New York gave us jazz and be-bop, Atlantic and Verve Records by Nesuhi Ertegun and Norman Granz, Dizzy Gillespie, John Coltrane, Miles Davis and Billie Holiday – and there were the beatniks too, and Norman Mailer, Saul Bellow, Philip Roth. In the 1956, Norman Mailer described 'The White Negro' in a pivotal essay of American existentialism. And it was New York that exported one of Simone de Beauvoir's most passionate lovers from the period when she wrote *The Second Sex* – the novelist and playboy Nelson Algren.

Paul Krassner grew in New York and founded **The Realist** in 1958 in the offices of **MAD Magazine**. Like many Jews born between 1928 and 1935, Krassner was anti-establishment, and he sharpened his claws while working on **MAD**. As Patti Smith later commented: 'After **MAD**, drugs were nothing.'

A child prodigy on the violin, Paul Krassner was as skilled with his scathing pen as he was with his scratching bow. **The Realist** was launched on a budget of $500, with 5,000 copies and no cover. Krassner described **The Realist** as a lone wolf howling to see who else was out there. By 1965 he'd found enough others out there to have a circulation of 100,000. He was always ahead of the game: at the end of the 1960s, he was the first to condemn tobacco advertising, and to poke fun at telethons and American reality TV. In other words, he was already condemning these inanities before the rest of the world became contaminated by them.

PAGE 11. Witty collage by Claes Oldenburg, **Other Scenes**, New York, 1968.

The nearly naked truth.

In the late 1950s and early 1960s, the New York avant-garde used to hang out in Le Metro Coffee Shop; there you would find Ed Sanders of the Fugs, the poet Diana de Prima, Allan Katzman – we'll meet him again later – and Tom Robbins, author of *Even Cowgirls Get the Blues*. Young and penniless artists would also wander in and out, including future stars of pop art like Andy Warhol and Claes Oldenburg. They did not forget their friend John Wilcock when he launched **Other Scenes** in 1968.

PAGES 12–13. Collage by Charles Henri Ford, New York, 1966.

Tangle with Chicken 'n Dumplings.

Many artists and poets, like Charles Henri Ford, a central figure in the early counterculture, produced material for the first underground papers.

PAGES 14–15. Greenwich Village, New York, 1970.

News poems by Tuli Kupferberg sum up Greenwich Village in the 1960s.

In the early 1960s, a group of talented drop-outs left Greenwich Village – fast becoming a tourist attraction – and settled in the East Village, then a complete slum, where they squatted until the end of the 1970s, migrating first to Soho, then to Tribeca, and finally to Brooklyn in 1988–90. There Tuli Kupferberg ran the Revolting Theater. They went dancing in St Mark's Place at the Dom, a dilapidated theatre that was later the venue for early gigs by the Velvet Underground.

Tuli Kupferberg was in some ways a quintessential underground figure. He wrote: 'When the mode of the music changes, the walls of the city shake.' And while the rest of us small-time Marxists and Guevarists were singing the praises of the Chinese Cultural Revolution, he had the courage to declare that Marxism was paleopsychological, paleoanthropological, pre-electric and pre-psychedelic. In 1967, he wrote that four revolutions had already occurred in the USA: the sexual revolution which 'liberated the bound-in personal energies of entire generations, of entire nations the automation revolution, the artistic revolution which brought art and life together, and the psychedelic revolution which created new universes. Something that even the young Messrs Bush and Clinton could have dreamed about too.

PAGES 16–17. *Counter Culture*, London, 1969.
Joseph H. Berke, an adbusting pioneer.
Counter Culture was one of the first real books about the underground press.

PAGE 18. East Village Other (EVO), New York, October 1965.
A tuned-in paper for New York.
Berkeley had lived through the revolution of the Free Speech Movement protests of 1964, which gave birth to the **Berkeley Barb** in 1965. In New York, Walter Bowart, with a degree in journalism, spent his youth among the dilapidated warehouses of the area that was to become Soho. In October 1965, with $500 that he had saved working as a barman, he launched the **East Village Other**, the intellectual anti-**Village Voice** of the left. Bowart was influenced by Marshall McLuhan and 'thought of a newspaper as a television set' (quote from Abe Peck, *Uncovering the Sixties: The Life and Times of the Underground Press*, New York: Citadel, 1991). The black avant-garde poet Ishmael Reed beat his drum in Greenwich Village to summon writers who included the poet and philosopher Allan Katzman, the only **EVO** stalwart to survive from the beginning to the end. Looking at all the covers from that period, it's easy to see that they describe all the great themes of the modern underground world.

PAGE 19. East Village Other, New York, April 1967.
A big and beautiful burst of psychedelia.
A response to San Francisco, which was gearing up for the Summer of Love and was supported there by the **San Francisco Oracle**, a paper that was even keener to put psychedelia at the centre of its editorial policy, and which reached a peak circulation of 107,000 copies during the summer of 1967.

PAGE 20. International Times (it), London, October 1966.
London's other underground.
In 1965 John Hopkins and Barry Miles set up a company called Lovebooks – which now sounds like a porn outfit – to publish Beat Generation literature and other countercultural information. Miles was the London correspondant of **EVO** and inspired by that paper, Lovebooks produced an offset news-sheet called the **Long Hair Times** which was distributed on the Easter 1966 Aldermaston CND march. Encouraged by its success, they recruited Jim Haynes, owner of the Paperback Bookshop in Edinburgh and founder of the Traverse Theatre, to join the editorial board. Jim brought his partner Jack Henry Moore with him and they became directors of Lovebooks. They persuaded Tom McGrath, editor of the CND weekly **Peace News**, to be their editor and **International Times (it)** was launched with a big happening at the Roundhouse in October 1966, making it the first European underground paper.

In September 1967, Jim Haynes opened the Arts Lab, with financial support from the Beatles' manager Brian Epstein, and shortly afterwards he exhibited the work of Yoko Ono, other a member of Fluxus, which got John Lennon involved a few months later. To finance his underground multimedia laboratory, Haynes asked eight hundred celebrities to donate cheques. Forty of them responded, including Peter Brook, Doris Lessing and Laurence Olivier. It only goes to show, nothing ventured. In 1969, Haynes put an end to his London dreams and went to teach at the Faculté de Vincennes in Paris, before devoting himself to the sexual revolution and decamping to Amsterdam to launch the 'sexpaper' **Suck**, followed by the first erotic film festival, the Wet Dream Festival. Meanwhile, **it** and its utopian philosophy continued for another five years. Since no revolution had so far managed to change people, there was no choice but to start by changing yourself.

PAGE 21. it, London, October 1966.
it selects the best of the European underground.
Simon Vinkenoog reports on the activities of the Amsterdam Provos, the 1965 eco-anarchist precursors of the modern ecology movement, while Jean-Jacques Lebel, master of the French scene and friend of the beatniks, pays homage to the late André Breton, who was a close friend of his father, Robert Lebel.

PAGES 22–23. Source unknown, 1968–70.

Tributes to Buckminster Fuller.

The first underground wave paid tribute to all things visionary, from Peter Max, genius poster artist, to the early Californian communes such as Drop City, built on the principle of Fuller's geodesic domes. Over seventy at the time (he was born in 1895), Fuller was a physicist and town planner, full of ideas for utopian space colonies and self-sustaining ecosystems, which some of his disciples actually succeeded in creating during the late 1980s in the form of Biosphere II. You will find forums devoted to promoting all aspects of his work on the Internet, along with sites dedicated to the Canadian prophet Marshall McLuhan and his global media village.

PAGE 24. **Other Scenes**, New York, summer 1968.

John Wilcock, the underground globetrotter.

Here his paper reports back on the latest happenings on the London art scene. NASA were getting ready to walk on the moon, and the artistic underground was keen to explore the relationship between art and technology, with exhibitions by Experiments in Art and Technology (EAT) in the US, and culminating in the show 'Cybernetic Serendipity' at London's ICA from August to October 1968.

PAGE 25. Source unknown.

How to be a Magician in Your Spare Time.

This esoteric litany describes ways to free yourself from the chains of oppressive society. The photomontage at the bottom is the work of one Robert Altman.

PAGE 26. **it**, London, June 1969.

The Living Theatre: an open forum.

Their influence on the underground was considerable in the early 1960s, especially through their powerful performances as a poverty-stricken bunch of jazz musicians and artists turned junkies in the face of the contempt of society, in the film *The Connection*, made in 1961 by Shirley Clarke and Jack Gelber, accompanied by improvisations from the Jackie McLean and Freddie Redd quartet. The Living Theatre played a consistent role as cultural agitators with their occupation of the Théâtre de l'Odéon, Paris, in 1968, and also through the controversy created by the on-stage nudity of the play *Paradise Now*.

PAGE 27. **Actuel**, Paris, 1971.

Photo of a performance art piece by Yayoi Kusama, New York 1968.

The New York happenings staged by the Japanese artist Yayoi Kusama often involved performers going naked except for politician masks or painted polka dots. She may not have invented the happening, but she did breath new life into it. When she returned to Japan, Kusama chose to enter a mental institution, which she now only leaves for exhibitions and performances, including one at the Maison du Japon, Paris, in 2004.

PAGES 28–29. **The Seed**, Chicago, 1969.

A double-page rainbow.

According to Abe Peck, it was in May 1967 in Chicago that the poster-seller Earl Segal and an artist named Don Lewis founded **The Seed**, with Peck as editor, along the same psychedelic and political lines as **EVO**. This was shortly after the Black Panther Party was formed. Fraternization between blacks and whites was in full swing in the aftermath of the anti-segregation movement, which had come to a head after ten years of fierce conflict, and it was reflected in the music, with *Psychedelic Shack* by The Temptations, groups like Love, Sly and the Family Stone, and the singer Tim Buckley, one of the few white artists to perform alongside black musicians who weren't just doing it for the money.

The rainbow became a symbol of unity, and went on to be embraced by the 'rainbow government' of Nelson Mandela and the ANC, the rainbow flag of the gay pride movement, and by the pacifist, anti-Bush movement prior to the war in Iraq.

PAGES 30–31. **Oz**, London, 1970 – **Actuel**, Paris, 1971.

The naked truth: who's influencing whom?

May '68 had shaken up the establishment, and the underground were shaking off their clothes. Tired of Marxist-Leninism, **Actuel** took its lead from **Oz**.

PAGE 32. The Avatar, Boston, February 1968.
The first bad guru hits the front page.
Avatar first appeared in 1967 in Boston, mixing sexual astrology with legal advice under the influence of a sort of psychedelic fascism masterminded by the Mel Lyman Family, with Lyman swiftly becoming a notorious cult figure. I experienced this first-hand in New York in his commune, where they confiscated my shoes and tried to hypnotize me in a purifying bath. I escaped barefoot through a window and out into the snow. In late 1967, the **Avatar** journalists took the liberty of criticizing him, but his followers managed to hold of all 35,000 copies and proceeded to pulp them.

PAGE 33. The Berkeley Barb, San Francisco Bay, September 1967.
Death of Hip and Birth of Free America.
Haight-Ashbury, late summer 1967. The Summer of Love brought together tens of thousands of youngsters as naive as a Children's Crusade. American parents panicked. Police, tourists and gurus came flocking. The Diggers, an anarchic guerrilla group whose members included Peter Coyote and the writer Richard Brautigan – their tale is told in Emmett Grogan's book *Ringolevio* – decided to bury hippiedom before it fell into total decadence (remember too that the word 'hippie' was a pejorative term invented by the press) and held the Death of Hippie parade on 7 October. The **Barb** took due note of the public funeral.

PAGES 34–35. Situationist pamphlet, France, 1967 – **it**, London, 1967.
French students embrace activism.
The Situationists protested against the poverty rife in student circles in France. The pamphlet dates from the end of 1967, after protests about female students being banned from male halls of residence at the University of Nanterre, Paris. **it** reprints a strip by Raoul Vaneigem and J.-P. Bertrand on its cover, a great compliment to the French. Situationist writings were also widely translated in the US.

PAGE 36. The Organ, Berkeley, 1970.
Tripping in Taos.
After the Summer of Love, the freaks left the cities, and a favourite destination was Taos in New Mexico, home of the New Buffalo commune. Thirty years later, the commune had become a bed and breakfast but the feeling lived on. I took my first trip there in 1970, in the company of the photographer Eric Kroll.

PAGE 37. it, London, April 1968.
Why Tribe?
A text written by the Zen ecologist-beatnik poet Gary Snyder was on the front page before we French even knew the meaning of the word 'ecology', although we were well aware of the damage being caused by so-called progress. The article is virtually a manifesto for a new way of life:
We use the term Tribe because it suggests the type of new society now emerging within the industrial nations. In America of course the word has associations with the American Indians which we like. This new subculture is in fact more similar to that ancient and successful tribe, the European Gypsies – a group without nation or territory which maintains its own values, its language and religion, no matter what country it may be in.... It's an easy step from the dialectic of Marx and Hegel to an interest in the dialectic of early Taoism, the I Ching, and the yin-yang theories. From Taoism it is another easy step to the philosophies and mythologies of India – vast, touching the deepest areas of the mind, and with a view of the ultimate nature of the universe which is almost identical with the most sophisticated thought in modern physics.... Next comes a concern with deepening one's understanding in an experiential way: abstract philosophical understanding is simply not enough. At this point many, myself included, found in the Buddha-Dharma a practical method for clearing one's mind of the trivia, prejudices and false values that our conditioning had laid on us.... Nationalism, warfare, heavy industry and consumership, are already outdated and useless.... The Revolution has ceased to be an ideological concern. Instead, people are trying it out right now – communism in small communities, new family organization.... The signal is a bright and tender look; calmness and gentleness, freshness and ease of manner. Men, women and children – all of whom together hope to follow the timeless path of love and wisdom, in affectionate company with the sky, winds, clouds, trees, waters, animals and grasses – this is the tribe.

PAGE 38. Action, underground daily, Paris, June 1968.
Industrial unrest comes as a bolt from the blue.
Inspired by the Cultural Revolution and a form of lyrical Communism, **Action** was launched on 7 May 1968, its 35,000 print run selling out instantly. Some of France's best underground artists and designers worked for it, including Georges Wolinski, but it only lasted for a single season, failing to survive its change into a weekly.

PAGE 39. Source unknown, Europe, c. 1969.
No more tears.
The French riot police, the CRS, threw poisonous tear-gas grenades at demonstrators. Tear gas was eventually banned in France, but until 1970 it burned more lungs than a factory full of Gitanes.

PAGE 40. Source unknown, London, c. 1969.
The circus is in town, and everything's moving.
A page taken from the **Actuel** archives. Barry Fantoni's summing up of the late sixties scene in swinging London.

PAGE 41. Other Scenes, New York, November 1968.
Politics is crap.
John Wilcock left **EVO** in March 1968 after defending a review of Andy Warhol's *Chelsea Girls*, a film that Bowart deemed 'too gay'. The co-founder of the UPS then set up **Other Scenes**, famous for its bare-faced cheek.

PAGES 42–43. Other Scenes, New York, September 1968.
Danger and desire in the ghetto.
This collage by the **Oz** artist Philip Proctor is the sum of all contradictions. Armed patrols in the ghettos, 500,000 US soldiers in Vietnam, and all the rioting, passion and hate that followed. After the explosion of liberty came communal unrest.

PAGE 44. Black Panther poster for the presidential elections, USA, September 1968.
Revolution, Revolution.
In 1968, Eldridge Cleaver, co-founder of the Black Panther Party and ex-convict, put himself forward as a write-in candidate in the presidential elections, on the ticket of the Peace and Freedom Party. Nonetheless, it was Richard Nixon who won. Twenty years later, Eldridge Cleaver unsuccessfully stood as a Republican candidate for senate in California! When a true believer tells you his true beliefs, you can't always believe him.

PAGE 45. The Fifth Estate, Detroit, September 1969.
The new watchword: 'Armed Love'.
Fifth Estate, founded in 1965 in Detroit, chose its name to show its opposition to the fourth estate – the US media, growing ever larger but less and less free. **Fifth Estate** was part of the Underground Press Syndicate, whose most recent meeting in July 1969 at John Sinclair's home in Ann Arbor, Michigan, had discussed the rise in police repression. A month later, Sinclair was arrested when he offered a plain-clothes policewoman two joints, and he was sentenced to ten years (though he only served three). Later it became apparent that the FBI were determined to infiltrate the underground press when the **Nola Express** in New Orleans was put under surveillance and bugged. Between 1969 and 1970, the chief editor of the Miami-based **Daily Planet** was arrested 29 times and spent $50,000 on legal fees.

PAGES 46–47. Oz, London, November 1970.
Brave New Morning.
An allusion to both Aldous Huxley's *Brave New World* and to *New Morning, Changing Weather*, a manifesto by the radical activist group, the Weathermen. Founded by the Australian Richard Neville, a talented activist and graphic artist, **Oz** ranked alongside **Actuel** and the Montreal paper **Mainmise** ('Control') as one of the most colourful magazines in the UPS. It was the subject of several obscenity trials – the most famous following its 'School Kids Issue', edited by real school children, who ran a collage showing Rupert Bear with a huge erection.

Freak Out ! First slogan of the free press

PAGES 50–51. Fifth Estate, Detroit, date illegible – **Actuel**, Paris, 1971.
Turn on, tune in, and let it all grow.

After May '68 came trying times in Paris, which left the vast majority of rebels high and dry. Those on the left became radical and saw themselves as the new Lenins and Maos, while the working classes were still locked into Communism and the trade unions. But what could we do?

We all went our own ways and joined up again at the end of 1969. I came back from the USA, my head full of the underground, having seen the beginnings of ecology, the lively and – in both senses – gay scene of sexual freedom, and the seeds of feminism post-Simone de Beauvoir (still alive and well in Paris); Michel-Antoine Burnier dragged himself away from existentialism and the Gramsci version of Marxism; Bernard Kouchner returned from Biafra, his first epic journey; Patrick Rambaud stopped going to the meetings of the Surrealists. We pooled our experiences in order to carry on the fight in the sphere of values and morals, placing our bets on the subversion of youth through dreams of utopia and desire.

The 'first' issue of the revamped **Actuel** was a real underground affair. We also sponsored the first festival on French soil, organized by Jean-Luc Young and Jean Karakos, two musical pioneers. It took place in Biot, mid-summer 1970. We were hanging this very cover on the pine branches of the natural amphitheatre when the announcement came: 'Look over there! The Maoists are coming, hundreds of them!' Chanting: 'Pop for the people!', they broke down the flimsy wire netting, and the festival was a flop, cutting us off forever from those envious saboteurs who were so afraid of the siren call of counterculture. A flop it may have been, but epic and productive too, since it only served to strengthen our liberal convictions in the face of this totalitarian onslaught from the Maoists.

PAGE 52. Other Scenes, New York, September 1969.
A souvenir from the Chelsea Hotel.

A signed gift to John Wilcock from Mimmo Rotella, the famous poster artist.

PAGE 53. The Starscrewer, France, 1970s.
We're all naked under heaven.

Issue no. 6 of one of the best French underground papers, featuring work by Claude Pélieu, the French beatnik, Pierre Joris, Lucien Suel and Charles Bukowski. **Starscrewer** still runs an underground website.

PAGE 54–55. Berkeley Barb, West Coast – **Other Scenes**, East Coast.
Magic wands and ancient charms.

PAGE 56. East Village Other, New York, October 1969.
A penetrating look at new culture?

This impressive column bears the signature of Thilm-Eliscu. The freewheeling subject matter is worth a closer look: it starts off with rock music then takes a detour via Jean-Louis Barrault, whose advice was: 'To be a virgin every morning. To kill (your) self each night and be reborn again each morning.' Then it moves on to John Vaccaro and the Playhouse of the Ridiculous, with its cross-dressing and sexual ambiguity, then to Jerzy Grotowski and the Living Theatre, who revolutionized stage performance, and then on to *Cock-Strong*, a play by the La Mama group which surely provided the inspiration for this page design. All in all, it's a survey of the role of the underground theatre – the San Francisco Mime Troupe, from which emerged The Diggers, Joe Chaikin, and the influence of Artaud and Ionesco, the guerrilla theatre and more…

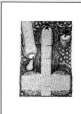

PAGE 57. Oz, London, March 1969.
Letting it all hang out.

Playing around is a serious business, as Germaine Greer shows here for **Oz**, with Vivian Stanshall of the Bonzo Dog Doo-Dah Band. Germaine seems to want a closer look at Viv's masculine credentials. A year later she would become a feminist icon with the publication of the best-selling *Female Eunuch*.

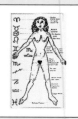

PAGE 58. **Mainmise**, Montreal, 1970.
A tarot that maps out some little-known erogenous zones.

PAGE 59. **East Village Other**, New York, January 1971.
A shot in the head for censorship.
This **EVO** cover reworks a famous Hollywood image, making fun of the seven objects of censorship in the 1940 and 1950s: alcohol, guns, plunging necklines, cigarettes, murder, garters, and you can guess the seventh.

PAGE 60. 1970: Henri-Jean Enu launches **Parapluie** ('Umbrella').
The glamorous cousin of Actuel.

PAGE 61. **Mainmise**, Montreal, 1971.
Ad for a clothing store.

PAGE 62. Parody poster, artists unknown, Berkeley, 1968.
Peacemen, not policemen.
As reproduced in Joseph H. Berke's book *Counter Culture* (London: Peter Owen Ltd, 1969). In real life, it took three years of hair-growing before the FBI came up with cops credible enough to infiltrate the underground.

PAGE 63. Small ad, 1970, source unknown (private collection).
Short-hair wigs for sale.
The clean-cut look is ideal for seeing your bank manager or local police chief.

PAGE 64. Underground press ad, 1970.
A waterbed for all the family.
A bed designed to pick up all your good vibrations.

PAGE 65. **Mainmise**, Montreal, 1972.
Ad with a map of Montreal's underground district.
Can't find a waterbed? Here's your chance!

PAGES 66–67. **Actuel**, Paris, October 1970.
Notes from Paris and beyond.
Michel Le Bris, editor of the Maoist paper **La Cause du Peuple**, was arrested as a risk to French national security; President Pompidou on the defensive; John Cage's MusiCircus mixed up musical styles in the Art Nouveau pavilions of Les Halles, Paris, just before they were demolished; President Pompidou on the attack; the funeral of Jimi Hendrix – like Janis Joplin and Jim Morrison, he overdosed on adulation.

PAGE 68. **Nola Express**, New Orleans, 1971.
Quick-fire cover art.
The FBI didn't take long to put **Nola Express** under surveillance. It survived various half-baked court cases, such as an obscenity charge after a *Playboy* spoof. No matter how jazzed-up Louisiana may have seemed, it was also one of the most reactionary states in the US, and you've got to admire the guts of those who proved that the free press was a mass movement.

PAGE 69. **Baba**, New Delhi, 1969.
In India, 'baba' means sage or spiritual father.
The word didn't travel well, because in France it became the pejorative term for a hippie, 'baba cool'. India was the only place to meet the real thing.

PAGES 70–71. **Mainmise**, Montreal, 1971 – **Actuel**, Paris, 1973.
The fast track to enlightenment.
Psychedelic anarchists were undeterred by the occasional bad trip, and had little time for guru-worship, which they called 'psychedelic fascism'.

PAGES 72–73. **East Village Other**, New York, June 1968.
The Serpent Power.
An example of the delirious delights enjoyed by the freaks, who deconstructed conventional religion to seek the origins of mysticism. **EVO**'s Allan Katzman believed that Christ's ideas were just a carbon copy of the philosophy of a Hindu sage named Charak. Meanwhile, in an issue of **Actuel** from early 1971, Patrick Rambaud played around with the idea that when the disciples witnessed the descent of the Holy Spirit

at Pentecost, they were under the influence of magic mushrooms or some other hallucinogenic. So that's what communion was all about!

PAGES 74–75. Actuel, Paris, 1970.
On a psychedelic quest.
Philippe Caza's comic strip *Kris Kool* pays tribute to Giorgio de Chirico and René Magritte. A heavenly hot dog fails to tempt our hero, but a handful of hungry ghouls send him running into the sunset. Sweet dreams, indeed.

PAGES 76–77 EVO, Nola Express and more, USA, 1969–72.
Practical jokes in a psychedelic style.
Joke ads were everywhere. In the US, peyote was (and still is) permitted for ceremonial use by the Native American Church.

PAGE 78. it, London, February 1971.
LSD was always good for a laugh.
LSD was banned in the US in 1965, after a decade of testing by the CIA, who thought they could turn it into an atomic bomb for the mind. Anyone fancy a trip?

PAGE 79. Oz, London, April 1970.
Crumb blows his mind.
Robert Crumb's artwork echoes the wild and crazy trips he experienced first-hand in San Francisco between 1966 and 1968. You've got to admire the remarkable underground genius that was and is Robert Crumb. This is the man whose drawings made the front pages of all the UPS papers, and who never asked for a cent, until the day when the taxmen took revenge and decided to tax him for the hundreds of pages he'd produced for free.

PAGES 80–81. Oz, London, June 1968 – New York publicity pamphlet, May 1970.
The Great Dope Famine, late 1968.
Grass practically disappeared from the freaks' hang-outs and ghettos of all colours when cheap heroin suddenly came on the market. The underground press attacked this police conspiracy and campaigned widely for the legalization of pot.

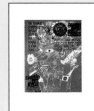

PAGE 82. Actuel, Paris, February 1974.
Repressive tolerance.
Actuel did a drug-based cover in spring 1972, showing Gilbert Shelton's *Fabulous Furry Freak Brothers* smoking a joint. Did it worry us? No, we were just keeping the public informed. By early 1974, all signs were that hash use was in decline, but we still expected to find ourselves hauled up in court, like some of our pot-smoking friends. But it didn't happen. They called it 'repressive tolerance'. Pot was tolerated in the press, but smokers went to jail. Nowadays the courts do the exact opposite: the smokers are tolerated but the campaigners are arrested. Surely a few of these representatives of the people are no strangers to a spliff?

PAGE 83. Mainmise, Montreal, 1971.
Pot's a laughing matter.
Grass just keeps on growing. Clinical trials are currently underway in the UK and elsewhere into the use of the therapeutic form of THC (tetrahydrocannabinol) in the treatment of cancer and glaucoma. Research has also revealed that our brains manufacture a substance very close to THC, which among other things is used to dull bad memories. We're laughing ourselves silly.

PAGES 84–85. Manifesto demanding the legalization of pot, USA, 1970 – **Berkeley Barb**, San Francisco Bay, May 1974.
Meanwhile, thirty years later...
There he was in 2005, Tony Blair – former long-haired Oxford student – talking of strengthening the ban, just to get himself re-elected. And he's not the only one.

PAGES 86–87 Source unknown, **Actuel** collection, 1970.
Psychedelic symbolism.

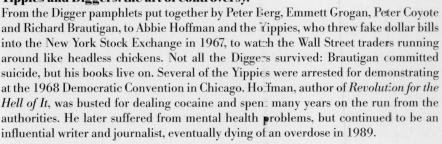

Power to the people! The free press gets militant

PAGE 90. East Village Other, New York, February 1971.
A premonition of a police state?

PAGE 91. Pamphlet, source unknown, USA, *c.* 1970.
Politically educating America.
After 1969, the American underground press became politically radical just as the psychedelic dream was invading Europe. A dialogue between two continents.

PAGES 92–93. Berkeley Barb, San Francisco Bay, 1969 – **Rat**, New York, 1969.
Berkeley up in arms, John and Yoko between the sheets.
The students of Berkeley liberated an area which they made into a People's Park. But the dream turned sour, and the subsequent police clampdown caused an uproar. John Lennon and Yoko Ono, having been turned away at the US border, staged their second 'Bed-In For Peace' in Montreal. Yoko, an associate of the Fluxus group, and John created an image which caused derision and controversy but which nevertheless was seen all over the world.

PAGES 94–95. Berkeley Barb, San Francisco Bay, 1975 – **The Realist**, New York, 1967.
Yippies and Diggers: the art of controversy.
From the Digger pamphlets put together by Peter Berg, Emmett Grogan, Peter Coyote and Richard Brautigan, to Abbie Hoffman and the Yippies, who threw fake dollar bills into the New York Stock Exchange in 1967, to watch the Wall Street traders running around like headless chickens. Not all the Diggers survived: Brautigan committed suicide, but his books live on. Several of the Yippies were arrested for demonstrating at the 1968 Democratic Convention in Chicago. Hoffman, author of *Revolution for the Hell of It*, was busted for dealing cocaine and spent many years on the run from the authorities. He later suffered from mental health problems, but continued to be an influential writer and journalist, eventually dying of an overdose in 1989.

PAGE 96. Nola Express, New Orleans, date unknown.
Questions that every GI should answer.
A little test on the disinformation that proliferated in the Vietnamese jungle. Some of the questions have a surprisingly relevant ring about them, even today:

2. The United States prevented the scheduled 1958 elections...:
a) to preserve democracy there.
b) Because the people in Vietnam were not ready to have elections.
c) Because a CIA report to President Eisenhower revealed that at least 80% of the people would have voted for Ho Chi Minh.
d) To see how mad the people would get.
3. The best statement of the domino theory is:
a) We have to invade Laos to protect Cambodia.
b) We have to invade Cambodia to protect Vietnam.
c) We have to invade Vietnam to protect Thailand.
d) We have to invade China to protect the US.
e) All of the above.
4. The opposing sides in Vietnam are:
a) The forces of good and the forces of evil.
b) Spiro T. Agnew and Abbie Hoffman.
c) The Military-Industrial complex and the people of Vietnam.
d) Mother and apple pie versus godless Communism.
10. The Vietnam war:
a) Is helping the rich get richer and the poor get poorer
b) Is good for the economy.
c) Is helping to fight inflation.
d) Is an inexpensive project.
14. The US move into Laos was a(n):
a) Incursion.
b) Pre-emptive strike.
c) Proactive reaction.
d) Peace feeler.
e) Invasion.

PAGE 97. Berkeley Barb, San Francisco Bay, August 1969.
Neither Bush nor Clinton fought in Vietnam.
There have never been so many wartime draft dodgers and deserters in a western country – not even in France during the Algerian war.

PAGE 98. Other Scenes, New York, April 1969.
An ironic plea for support.

PAGE 99. Ink, London, September 1971.
Knickers to the war!
Ink was launched as a weekly in 1971. The Grim Reaper trots off to Vietnam in her high heels.

PAGES 100–101. Rat, New York, May 1968 – **Rat**, New York, December 1969.
Protests at Columbia University.
Things turned nasty. The police came down hard, but the movement stayed strong. It also gave birth to its own political paper, **Rat**, founded by Jeff Shero, a young man who had already caused a stir at the University of Texas when he and some black students had staged an occupation of the whites-only restrooms. Eighteen months later, in 1969, **Rat** got even more radical and supported the Weathermen, who advocated armed guerrilla action, though their bombs never claimed any victims. The underground once again became the FBI's public enemy number one.

PAGES 102–103.
Berkeley Tribe, January 1971 versus **Berkeley Barb**, March 1973, California.
Skirmishes in the underground.
A juicy pair of front pages. You have to wonder who is ripping off who, the **Barb** or the **Tribe**. The **Tribe** has a swipe at the third anniversary of the Tet Offensive in Vietnam, which resulted in 4,000 American dead during the first quarter of 1968. The **Barb** features a child wrestling with Mao's *Little Red Book*; the **Tribe**, meanwhile, goes up in a big bang.

The story that follows is worth telling, since almost everyone in the free press lived through something similar (in France we had **Actuel** vs **La Cause du Peuple**). The **Barb** had money. Max Scherr ran it well, but increasingly he was accused of peddling flesh, through a flood of small ads for sex and massage parlours. Added to that was a generation problem: Max was well into his forties, and had done his Masters in sociology in 1949. When he launched the **Barb** in August 1965, he was more New Left than rock'n'roll, and the first issue praised *Les Parapluies de Cherbourg* and LeRoi Jones, a black, post-beatnik poet and playwright who later changed his name to Amiri Imamu Baraka. A fan of Cervantes, Scherr used the figure of Don Quixote in his logo. What's more, he had a head for figures, and his satire was cutting enough for him to be accused of cynicism by those who were twenty years younger and were just coming down from LSD and getting ready to dive into the revolution in the aftermath of Berkeley's People's Park. It was around this point that news leaked out. Scherr himself was earning as much as the rest of the **Barb**'s editorial team put together – somewhere in the region of $10,000 a month. Freelance writers were paid 25 cents per column inch, and they were not happy – especially forty of them who were members of the Red Mountain Tribe (named after red wine), led by Stew Albert, a radical hippie, frontline activist, and pal of Abbie Hoffman and Jerry Rubin. Not beaten yet, Scherr told them they could buy the **Barb** for $140,000, paid in instalments (those small ads were a real goldmine). In another time and place, this might have been a good deal, a win-win for everyone involved. But this was not the moment, and Scherr found himself with a militant strike on his hands. Albert was waving placards around, proclaiming 'Max is a pig' – the 'pig media' being the name given to the mainstream press. The whole sordid business ended in the creation of the **Berkeley Tribe**, run by an egalitarian collective which paid each of its staff $30 a month. For the first issue, everyone in the team posed naked, just to show that their pockets were all empty.

PAGES 104–105. La Cause du Peuple, Paris, September 1969 – **Actuel,** Paris, April 1971.
Communists versus Freaks.
Actuel's support of the 'pleasure revolution', with Shelton's *Furry Freak Brothers* on the cover, was the cause of considerable irritation to the leaders of the proletarian left. They saw us as a destructive force who distracted and corrupted youth in the name of egotistical, petit bourgeois freedoms, while we saw them as

mad monks, blinded by the hysteria of the armed struggle. At its peak, in 1971, **Actuel** had no less than a thousand subscribers in France, but even after the issue had been raised with us, we refused to let them be turned into any sort of organization, even a libertarian one.

PAGES 106–107. **The Digger**, Sydney, June 1973 – **it**, London, September 1972.
Watergate sounds the death-knell for the underground press.
Nixon and his Mafia cronies were first exposed by Bob Woodward's scoops in the *Washington Post*. The My Lai massacre, which shook the American army even more than the recent Abu Ghraib prison tortures in Iraq, had in fact been uncovered first by the Underground Press Syndicate in 1969, via Seymour Hersh, a formidable investigative reporter now at the *New Yorker*. With Watergate, however, the mainstream press embraced the anti-establishment spirit.

PAGES 108–109. **Berkeley Barb**, San Francisco Bay, March 1974.
All the President's men.
Here's a charming double-page spread devoted to Nixon's henchmen during Watergate. But switch to thirty years later and they look almost like nice guys, wouldn't you say, Condoleezza?

PAGE 110. **it**, London, March 1973.
Radio silence?
In spring 1973, the French National Front achieved its first breakthrough. Le Pen got 5.22 percent of the votes in the Paris's 15th arrondissement. In Britain, **it** drew a vitriolic portrait of political life among the Frogs. A few pages further on, there was a review of Bertolucci's latest film – or how to enjoy five sex scenes before dinner, courtesy of *Last Tango in Paris*. But the top story was devoted to a look back at the heyday of pirate radio stations, who thumbed their noses at the BBC.

Founded in 1927, the BBC was paid a licence fee by everyone who owned a TV and (at least until 1971) a radio, and its radio programming was mainly dedicated to news, weather, plays and classical music. The youth of Britain listened out for other more exotic channels, branching out to Radio Normandy and Radio Luxembourg, whose broadcasts could be received across the Channel once night had fallen. The BBC held the state monopoly, but was restricted in how many pop records it could play by the Musician's Union, who insisted that in-house bands and orchestras play the top tunes. But rock'n'roll fans wanted the originals and tuned into Luxembourg. At the beginning of the 1960s, when London was swinging, Ronan O'Rahilly, son of an Irish father and loaded with ideas, money and a love of Ray Charles, suddenly burst on the scene. Manager of a rhythm and blues club, he launched Eric Burdon and the Animals, and rapidly caught on to the idea that the best way of spreading this UK underground sound was to have a station of his own. He had also heard of stations such as the Dutch-based Radio Veronica, which had got round the monopolistic transmission laws by broadcasting from a ship anchored offshore.

O'Rahilly became friends with an Australian businessman named Alan Crawford. They bought two 760-tonne ferryboats, equipped them with 10 kW transmitters, anchored them in the Irish Sea, and on 28 March 1964 launched Radio Caroline, ushering in the age of pirate radio. The impact was instant. Twenty thousand fan letters poured down on the bridge during the first ten days of broadcasting. England now had a medium-wave alternative. From the UK up into northern Europe, it was estimated that 39 million listeners tuned into Caroline, with its all-star playlist of Cat Stevens, The Beatles, Cliff Richard, Jimi Hendrix, Donovan, the Monkees, Petula Clark, Sandie Shaw and more. Other DJs didn't hang around on shore, and in the wake of Radio Caroline came a whole armada of independent stations, which furrowed the brow of the authorities and their Victorian monopoly. At the end of August 1967, the government wheeled out its legal cannons to sink the rebellion. Offshore broadcasting was banned, with pirates risking up to two years in prison. The fleet was decimated, and only Radio Caroline survived the bombardment by moving to the Netherlands and later disguising the ship as a free radio museum.

However, thanks to the Internet, which provided a whole new sea to sail, and private donations, the most legendary of all independent radio stations celebrated its fortieth birthday in 2004. Ronan O'Rahilly can now be found at the helm of www.radiocaroline.co.uk.

PAGES 111. it, London, February 1973.
Sunday Bloody Sunday.
One year after the massacre, and a good ten years before U2's hit, **it** revisited the bloody events that made Derry in Northern Ireland the symbol of a state at war. On 30 January 1972, a peaceful demonstration for equal rights for Catholics turned into a riot when the trigger-happy 1st Parachute Regiment opened fire. Thirteen demonstrators were left dead. In reprisal, on 22 February the IRA blew up the officers' mess of the Parachute Regiment in Aldershot, killing six civilians and a soldier. Bloody Sunday was the start of a civil war which mixed religion and colonialism, pitted terrorists against soldiers, and even split up families, and every appeal to lay down weapons seemed to fall on deaf ears.

PAGE 112. Libération, Paris, June 1976.
A joint too far.
Instigated by Frédéric Joignot, this French petition for the legalization of pot was supported by many famous signatories – though not by General de Gaulle, who was unfortunately dead. You have to wonder who would sign such a thing today.

PAGE 113. The Seed, Chicago, 1972.
Mao soup.
Who's smiling now?

PAGE 114. Actuel, Paris, February 1972.
A shout-out to Jean-Marc Reiser.
And thanks for designing the cover of **Actuel**'s issue 17, which contained a list of a thousand of our militant readers. We'd love to know what became of them all. We've tracked down a few: the curator of an ecology museum, a hippie guitarist, Jean-François Pauvros, the producer of the French band Kas Product, Gérard N'Guyen. At around the same time, the actors Coluche and Josiane Balasko were making their debuts with the Vrai Chic Parisien comedy troupe, a stone's throw from our offices on the corner of the Rue de la Gaité.

PAGE 115. Mainmise, Montreal, 1972.
A pie in the face for Che.
Reproduction of an illustration from **Oz**, making fun of the world's most popular T-shirt. Two years later, the same image appeared on the cover of *National Lampoon*, the reigning champion of satire.

Down with male domination! The women's movement and gay liberation

PAGE 118. Rat, New York, October 1969.
Feminist takeover.
Rat, founded in New York on 3 March 1968, was born in the days of student militancy and the strike at Columbia University which ended in police beatings. Jeff Shero, just 25 years old but already a right-hand man to Tom Hayden, patron of SDS (Students for a Democratic Society), was racing headlong to the left.

On a tour of inspection of the American counterculture, I was going dizzy – or at least getting a stiff neck – trying to keep track of everything that was going down. Back in Berkeley in summer 1970, after a year's absence, I found that the whole community of friends I had left behind had turned upside down.

The first time I met Jane Fonda, three years earlier in Paris, she had just shaken off her *Barbarella* image and, now in her thirties, had broken up with Roger Vadim. Infatuated with the writer Roger Vailland, she wanted to do a thesis on 'Libertinism and Revolution'. Then she moved in with Tom Hayden in 1968, and donned seven-league boots to catch up with the revolution; meanwhile, her brother Peter was appearing in *Easy Rider*, which catapulted Jack Nicholson to fame. Tom Hayden and Robert Scheer – who taught me how to be a militant investigative reporter – both in their thirties, decided to set up a commune in Berkeley, naming themselves the Red Family. But in the early 1970s, I suddenly found myself in a world of women – ten or so of them, always having meetings while the men purged their chauvinism by doing the washing and changing nappies. Radical feminism had inverted the traditional roles. In late 1969, having rejected the creed of sexual freedom – which had only benefited the macho male – women seized control at **Rat**: sisterhood *was* power. So now who's changing the nappies?

PAGE 119. Actuel, Paris, January 1971.
Fast forward to feminism.
I felt like I was watching a race between Paris, Frankfurt and Berkeley. In Paris, there were small groups like the Oreilles Vertes holding meetings from which men were banned. In a commune in Frankfurt, the former hero of May '68, Daniel Cohn-Bendit paid the price for his revolutionary fame by watching over the washing machine – well, no, please forgive such a macho suggestion, I must be carried away by memories of the anti-male insults of the time. At the end of 1970, everyone wanted to move fast, and there was a real avalanche of burgeoning movements to choose from: anti-psychiatry, ecology, avant-garde rock, underground cinema, anti-authoritarian communes, and of course, feminism.

The beginnings of the MLF, the French Women's Lib movement, could be found in **L'Idiot International**, the paper run by the eccentric Jean-Édern Hallier, which veered between leftism and dandyism. **Actuel** was not far behind, and we published the one of the most extremist texts – the *SCUM Manifesto* by Valerie Solanas, with SCUM standing for the Society for Cutting Up Men. Solanas later ended up in jail for the attempted murder of Andy Warhol.

Next to appear on the French scene were the Gouines Rouges (Red Lesbians) and the gays of the Fhar (Front Homosexuel d'Action Révolutionnaire), shortly after the advent of the Gay Liberation Front, which was born out of the riots of 27 June 1969 that followed a police raid on a gay bar called the Stonewall Inn in Greenwich Village, New York. Both the feminists and the gay rights movement soon became powerful and autonomous entities, but it took several years for them to take up a regular place in the American underground press, with the exception of the **Berkeley Barb** and **Rat**. In any case, **Actuel** was definitely ahead of the game.

PAGE 120. Actuel, Paris, November 1972.
Tales from the Fhar side.
The cover is by Robert Crumb. The French gay rights organization known as the Fhar was in full swing, and the angel-faced writer Guy Hocquenghem was coordinating their contributions to **Actuel**. The lesbian movement hadn't yet become a fully separate entity, and everyone seemed to be questioning their own (bi)sexuality. The last great crack in what they used to call the moral order.

PAGE 121. Tout, Paris, June 1971.
The family is pollution.
'We are alone in a hostile or indifferent world, where everything is polluted by money, and you can never talk to anyone about the fears that grip you by the throat…You try to construct a little world where you are alone together…and where you can love.' Sexual liberation was finding its feet, and reactionaries were calling us pornographers.

In 1971 the right-wing mayor of Tours, Jean Royer filed a complaint against the paper **Tout** for its alleged promotion of 'homosexual deviance'. **Tout** was an anarchist-communist newspaper run by the group Vive la Révolution, and its editor-in-chief was Jean-Paul Sartre. He later held the same position at **La Cause du Peuple**, the organ of the proletarian left, after the imprisonment of its editors Jean-Pierre Le Dantec and Michel Le Bris. Sartre himself was not arrested.

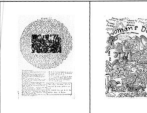

PAGES 122–123. Le Torchon Brûle, Paris, 1972 – **Other Scenes**, New York, March 1970.
Women's Lib strikes straight for the heart…and the stomach.
On the left, a manifesto for the MLF (Mouvement de Libération des Femmes) published in issue 6 of **Le Torchon Brûle**, the French feminist paper. On the right, recipe ideas to celebrate International Women's Day on 8 March.

PAGE 124. Berkeley Barb, San Francisco Bay, March 1973.
A woman's place, past and present.
A **Barb** cover reprints a montage from issue 27 of **Actuel**, including a cartoon by Claire Bretécher.

PAGES 125–127. The Seed, Chicago, 1970.
Sisterhood is powerful.
Another issue devoted to International Women's Day. Overleaf is one of the famous posters that were a key feature of **Seed**. It was not until 1975 that 8 March received the support of the United Nations and became a truly international event. The underground generation was both proud and confused at this official turnaround. Their younger brothers promptly became punks.

PAGES 128–129. Actuel, Paris, November 1972.
Full-frontal freedom.
Jim Haynes, co-founder of **it**, mounted the Wet Dream Festival in Amsterdam – the first erotic film festival, including improvised, orgiastic happenings. We can't wait for Jim to publish his diaries, following on from his autobiography, *Thanks for Coming!* (London & Boston: Faber & Faber, 1982).

PAGES 130–131. East Village Other, 1969 – **Berkeley Barb**, 1970.
Threesomes and 69s... who says romance is dead?
Porno advertising and personal ads were commonplace in the underground press. Because it was all about liberation, nobody saw any harm in it, and since the audience was underground, no one was very shocked. If you didn't like them, you could just skip over them. Often you'd just laugh.
    However, the sex clubs and swingers' orgies began to sow seeds of doubt. I once found myself at Sandstone, a hip Californian club, standing next to a buck-naked sheriff, and I didn't think there was anything so great about it. How did the libertines of the 18th century manage it? There were no X-rated movies in those days – just the desire to imagine what was going on behind closed doors.

PAGES 132–133. Berkeley Barb, San Francisco Bay, April 1976.
Sexism on trial.
The word took a while to reach the front page, but it soon became a politically correct mainstay. Here it is on the cover of the **Barb**, which had long survived off ads for massage parlours. The schizophrenia of modern life, eh?

PAGES 134–135. The Los Angeles Free Press, Los Angeles, February 1976.
Here come the shrinks.
Every good revolutionary has to come to terms with his feminine side. One small question: is he only doing it to make the front page of the **Freep**? After all, confessions will get you a long way. Later Jerry Rubin, author of the anti-establishment bible *Do It* (1970), would end up as a Wall Street venture capitalist.

PAGE 136. Hundert Blumen, Berlin, 1973.
As innocent as babes.
This front page picture, featuring the baby daughter of Jefferson Airplane singer Grace Slick, is taken from an album cover. In Europe, it was Germany, Switzerland and the Netherlands that produced most members of the UPS – **Hotcha** in Zurich, **Ding** in Amsterdam, and **Hundert Blumen** ('A Hundred Flowers') in Berlin.

PAGE 137. Source unknown, *c.* 1972.
Feminist poster: Mona Lisa shows her fangs.

PAGE 138. Berkeley Barb, San Francisco Bay, July 1973.
The abortion issue in jigsaw form.

PAGE 139. Actuel, Paris, October 1973.
Militant Abortion.
In France in 1973, backstreet abortions and abortionists were condemned on all sides – horrors caused by the ban. Militant doctors took the legal risk of carrying out abortions at home, using the Karman method – a sort of embryo vacuum cleaner. Contraception was not yet commonplace. It was time to pass laws that would give women the freedom to choose whether or not they should give birth. Abortion shouldn't have to be a militant issue, as **Actuel** wrote at the time.

PAGE 140. Rat, New York, August 1970.
A good week for gays and lesbians – and not bad for everyone else, either.

PAGE 141. Hobo-Québec, Montreal, 1971.
Free-form poetry.

PAGE 142. Berkeley Barb, San Francisco Bay, September 1973.
Women on top.
The **Barb**, with its unfailing instinct for controversy, offers a mix-and-match selection of female icons: Afro-haired heroine Angela Davis, fresh out of prison; Joanna Leary, wife of Timothy Leary, prophet and prisoner of LSD; Jane Fonda, just back from Hanoi; Marilyn Chambers, one of the first X-rated stars.

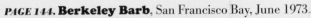

PAGE 143. **The Los Angeles Free Press.** Los Angeles, August 1970.
Glad to be gay.

PAGE 144. **Berkeley Barb**, San Francisco Bay, June 1973.
Toujours gay – parade points way!
San Francisco's first Gay Freedom Day commemorated the Stonewall riots of four years earlier. Back in June 1973, the floats still looked pretty modest – a bathtub, a guy scratching his head, a drag queen – but around two thousand people took to the streets for the parade.

PAGE 145. **Rat**, New York, 1971.
Poster celebrating the gay community.

PAGE 146. **Berkeley Barb**, San Francisco Bay, July 1972.
Naked under the sun.
It took California some time to cotton on to nude bathing. You might wonder what the big deal is and just leave them to get on with it. However, that said, there are a few big questions here. Does nudity increase or reduce desire? How can you stop people stripping by the sea? Should Puritan or Eastern religious beliefs be taken into account? And how can you blame people if all the beaches are packed? Perhaps I'm an idiot, but I'd say that there must be a deserted beach out there somewhere, surely?

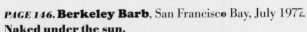

PAGES 147–149. **Actuel**, Paris, January 1973.
Dressed to thrill.
The Cockettes, a transvestite theatre group that included the writer Bruce Benderson, performed in the San Francisco area from 1971 onwards. In New York, drag queens began to appear in the wake of David Bowie and Andy Warhol. Taylor Mead was Warhol's biggest fan and appeared in his films. A great character from long before John Waters and Divine came on the scene. Pages 148 and 149 show him in all his glory, as photographed by Gilles Larrain.

PAGES 150–151. **Berkeley Barb**, San Francisco Bay, November 1973/November 1976.
A brief history of drag.
Transvestism has been around since the dawn of time. With the advent of plastic surgery, transexuals appeared during the 1950s. By the 1970s the time was ripe for a new idea: gay men with male bodies but dressed up as exaggerated versions of women, carnival style, or better still, showgirl style. This was the era of the drag queen. On the west coast, it was at Halloween that these outrageously made-up creatures first appeared. On the east coast, it was all drugs, clubs and divas, the heirs of Warhol and his gang. Gilles Larrain's photography book *Idols* (New York: Links, 1973) is full of boys, effeminate, decadent and made up in different styles, often borrowed from the traditions of burlesque cabaret (the forerunner of the modern strip-show). Meanwhile Liberace in the US and Marc Bolan in the UK camped it up in glam style. The sum of many parts: sex + kitsch + cabaret + showing off + bad taste.

PAGES 152. **East Village Other**, New York, October 1969.
Nothing new under the sun.
Stonewall is regarded as the key moment of gay liberation. But in the underground, gay culture had already been flourishing for a long time. Kenneth Anger's first film was made in 1947. Long before that, of course, was Oscar Wilde, and followed by Jean Genet and friends. This ad appeared in **EVO** well before the Village People.

PAGE 153. **Grabuge**, Paris, 1977.
Pump up your imagination.
Will blowing up the bondage hood make the everyday world go away? French paper **Grabuge** (meaning 'trouble' or 'scandal') took up a radical post-Burroughs stance, and featured work by art historian and critic Gérard-Georges Lemaire. Also aboard the Starship **Grabuge** were the playwright Valère Novarina and René Crevel, the gay Surrealist poet who committed suicide.

PAGE 154–155. **Berkeley Barb**, San Francisco Bay, May 1975 – Source unknown.
Sisters are doing it.
It is still a mystery why lesbian power never had quite the same social impact as gay power. Could it be a hold-over from the male-dominated society?

PAGES 156–157. **Oz**, London. January 1973.

Feminism gets sexy.

Photomontage of Germaine Greer, Australian feminist writer, who showed no reticence about revealing the mysterious forest between her silken thighs. **Oz** was pre-empting the surreal photomontages of Pierre & Gilles at the same time as Pierre Commoy was producing his first photomontages of black bodybuilders for issue 26 of **Actuel**.

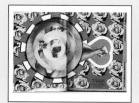

Black Power: The free press fights for equal rights

PAGE 160. Source unknown, **Actuel** collection, *c.* 1970.

In the closet at the FBI.

At the end of 1968, the FBI decided to go gunning for the Black Panthers. In the ghettos, the craze for armed self-defence had become so contagious that even the Puerto Ricans set up their own gang, the Young Lords. In this violent struggle, J. Edgar Hoover, head of the FBI for several decades, had no hesitation in slaughtering dozens of Black Panthers. With hindsight, what seems craziest of all to me is the fact that Hoover was a confirmed but closeted homosexual. There's nothing worse than a reactionary hypocrite. He launched Senator McCarthy and the Communist witch hunt, and manipulated and infiltrated the drug scene, but nobody knew that Hoover was a witch himself.

PAGE 161. **Fifth Estate**, Detroit, January 1969.

The Young Lords on parade.

And while we're passing, here's a brief round-up of the top stories from this issue of **Fifth Estate**: a strike by illegal Mexican American immigrants in the Californian vineyards; the MC5 telling stores that wouldn't stock their records to go fuck themselves; the white left: can you taken them seriously?; is rock'n'roll a drug?

PAGE 162.

The Great Speckled Bird, Atlanta, May 1974 (above)

Inner-City Voice, Detroit, November 1970 (below).

Black power shows its claws.

Since the beginning of the 20th century, in the southern states of the US, strange fruit has often been found hanging from the trees. The KKK had plenty of elbow room. The NAACP (National Association for the Advancement of Colored People, founded in 1909 by W. E. B. DuBois) was limited to working for civil rights, integration and non-violence, while the police went on beating up any African-Americans who dared to stage sit-ins in whites-only cafés. During this time, the UNIA (Universal Negro Improvement Association) of Marcus Garvey seemed to lose themselves on the way back to Africa.

In February 1965, Malcolm X was assassinated. The following summer, the black neighbourhood of Watts in Los Angeles went up in flames. For some, the time had come to hit back, and California felt the full force of the reprisals. In Los Angeles, Huey P. Newton, Bobby Seale and David Hilliard founded the Black Panther Party for Self Defense in October 1966. The underground marketing response was unprecedented. Berets and black leather jackets, Afro hair, military salutes, and iconic poster images (the top image, far left, includes a glimpse of Newton posing as a Zulu king with a Kalachnikov and a zebra skin). The underground press also raised its fist. Self-defence and communal self-sufficiency spawned new organizations such as the IBA (International Black Appeal), which appealed in the pages of the **Inner-City Voice** for donations to help distribute food in the ghettos of Detroit, still smoking from the riots of 1967.

PAGE 163. **Actuel**, Paris, June 1970.

Panther propaganda.

The drawings of Emory Douglas, who designed the first Black Panther posters, are great examples of motivational graphic art.

PAGE 164. **Fifth Estate**, Detroit, June 1970.

Cops versus Panthers on the streets of Detroit.

PAGE 165. **The Great Speckled Bird**, Atlanta, August 1970.

You can't jail the revolution!

The front page of **The Great Speckled Bird**, founded in 1968 in Atlanta, Georgia, features a stylized portrait of Huey Newton, founder of the Black Panther

Party, who has just been released from prison after nearly three years of trials and detentions. The movement had an unprecedented number of supporters, extending as far as Marlon Brando and Jean Genet, and it ended up with a sort of armistice between the BPP and the FBI, which reckoned it had handed out enough beatings.

From the launch of the party in late 1966, the Black Panthers were in deadly earnest, and organized militias to defend the ghettos. Too many blacks had died or were about to die in the Watts and Detroit riots. The first clash with the police came on 28 October 1967, and it left one policeman dead, another injured, and Huey Newton was also injured. Everyone was amazed at the extraordinary power of this movement, whose leaders, Newton and Cleaver, were saved by the revolution from lives as pimps and dealers. After Newton had been jailed, the FBI took regular potshots at the Panthers, killing more than twenty and forcing the majority of its leading figures to choose between exile to Algiers or Cuba, jail or death. Then one day they carried out two murders too many. It happened in Chicago on 4 December 1969: Fred Hampton, 21 years old and a local activist leader, was one of two gunned down in what the FBI called a pitched battle. The law had already tried to bring him in for the theft of 150 ice creams handed out in the ghetto, but had failed. Now the FBI thought they had got what they were after, but the result was public outrage, and thousands of white students got radical. Furthermore, the inquest revealed that the police had fired over a hundred rounds, whereas the two dead Panthers had fired only two shots.

PAGES 166–167. **Rat**, New York, October 1969 – **Actuel** archives, late 1970s.
Black feminists have their say.
In 1993, Toni Morrison was awarded the Nobel Prize for Literature, but African-American women have long used writing as a means of combat:

But listen Black Sisters, we held Black man up for over 300 years
No matter how heavy the Burden, WE HELD HIM UP
And kept the children coming and growing – WE HELD HIM UP
And kept the clothes washed and the house cleaned – WE HELD HIM UP
We worked for the white man and helped pay the bills – WE HELD HIM UP
and while holding him up we kept Faith and Loved him....
But we the Black women of this country have been the tools of men long enough
and it's time they laid these time-worn tools down
Every so-called Great man of this country has come under the Black woman's hands
We raised the white man, changed his diapers and washed his naked dirt
And from our breast flowed all the wisdom of the ages... and he used this wisdom to
destroy our black men and our babies
Now it's time for us to stand up from under and out from behind the man oppression
POWER TO THE BLACK SISTERS OF THIS COUNTRY!
You the white woman must also face the fact that you are not free
You too have been the tool of the white man
Unlike the Black woman, you were put on a pedestal and paraded
And praised as a senseless object of beauty
He made you believe you were not capable of doing anything for yourselves
His politics and livelihood is based on making you more fuckable to him
You, his senseless – Blond-haired – Blue-eyed – White-gloved – LADY...
On the other hand the Black woman never knew how to or had to time to become a
LADY
She was too busy keeping the country clean
Washing for it, scrubbing it – and oh yes, changing its shit
Keeping it nice for company
And when the company came, she went back to her place...
And all the while the white man looked on at his trained LADY
Parading you as he would a prize thoroughbred, but of less value
For when the company left, he snatched your babies from your arms
And gave them to the Black woman
HE SAID – she knew better how to care for them
You were not allowed to nurse or dress your own babies
HE SAID – It would expand your bosom and that's not seeming for a LADY
He reminded you often of your duties as a LADY
– to look pretty and be at his disposal when he wanted you
Not need – just want

And to satisfy your longing for womanhood he gave you the term LADY
And pinned it on your bosom with frills and fancy lace
And you too were forced for hundreds of years to swallow this shit
Even when it gagged you at the thought of another dose
But you were LADIES and it wouldn't be seeming to spit it out
It is time for you to let the white man know
That you'll no longer be the object of his sexual sickness
AND YOU TOO MUST DEMAND YOUR FREEDOM BY STANDING UP FROM
UNDER AND OUT FROM BEHIND THE WHITE MAN'S OPPRESSION.

PAGE 168. Other Scenes, New York, November 1968.
A Presidential manifesto.
During the presidential elections of 1968, Nixon swore that he had a 'secret plan' to end the war in Vietnam. The Democrats tore each other apart, and Humphrey's campaign foundered on the riots in Chicago. The malignant George Wallace set out from Alabama to sow the seeds of hate, while the Peace and Freedom Party put forward Eldridge Cleaver as their candidate. In November, **Other Scenes** entered the campaign with Dick Gregory, a candidate burning with the passion of Martin Luther King, and this page sums up his manifesto:

Moral pollution is the number one problem facing this country today.... Moral pollution permits a nation to wage war in the name of democracy but requires the poor and the black citizens to be nonviolent in obtaining their rights in a democracy. Moral pollution means our leaders cry out for law and order, but limit it to 'crime in the streets', which is America's new way of saying 'nigger'.

The United States has no legal or moral right in Vietnam. There has been no congressional declaration of war.... I propose that if America can decide that you are old enough to die for your country, you are old enough to vote for your leaders and American domestic and foreign policy. Thus the voting age minimum should be set in all states at 18 years old immediately....

It is my hope that the youth of America will be the antidote to moral pollution and will bring this nation back to its senses.... I recommend to the youth who are concerned about what to do for human suffering to go to that poor white hillbilly and help him organize and obtain relief from suffering in this society. Do not be fooled into thinking that all poor white folks live in Appalachia. Poor white folks live in every large urban area in America.

PAGE 169. Re Nudo, Milan, November 1970.
The Angela Davis affair grips the world.
Re Nudo ('Naked King'), an Italian underground paper, took up Angela's words, as indeed we all did. 'The most difficult moment comes after gaining power, when you have to face the problem of building a new world.'

PAGES 170–171. Door, San Diego, September 1970.
Angela bowls over the free press.
The back cover of **Door** promotes the campaign to free Angela Davis, who had been imprisoned for murder and kidnapping. On the front page is the obituary of George Jackson. At the age of nearly 30, he had spent half his life in prison, having been jailed at 18 for stealing $70, and subsequently accused of murder. Behind bars, he founded the Black Guerilla Family, a Marxist organization which established links with the Communist Party and his muse, Angela Davis. She befriended Jackson who, despite being locked up in maximum security for twenty-three hours a day, produced two books of letters: *Blood In My Eye* and *Soledad Brother*. At the beginning of August 1970, George's brother Jonathan, aged 17, died while putting into operation his plan to take hostages in a Bay Area courtroom, with a view to freeing his elder brother and some colleagues. Angela Davis was accused of having supplied him with weapons. The profile of this iconic activist had been rising higher and higher, but now the hunt was on. Angela became the third woman to grace the list of the FBI's most wanted criminals. The windows of houses in black neighbourhoods were full of posters offering her safe refuge: 'Sister, you are welcome in this house.' She was finally caught late in 1970 in Greenwich Village, and was not released from prison until the beginning of 1972, cleared by a jury that did not contain a single black member. But there was no longer any Jackson to fight for. On 21 August 1971, at San Quentin Prison, George had

allegedly made an escape attempt, using a smuggled gun. His rush towards the wall of the compound, emptying the magazine, resulted in five dead, including two guards, and he was killed when the guards fired back.

Prison riots were rife, the most famous occurring at Attica Penitentiary in New York state. From 9 to 13 September 1971, a thousand prisoners rebelled, taking over the compounds, and demanding better conditions. Some 1,700 state police and correctional officers were sent to crush the revolt, and thirty prisoners and eleven hostages (prison guards) were killed. The affair sparked an outcry, and the whole of the underground press took it up. Bob Dylan wrote a song about George Jackson, while Archie Shepp assembled forty musicians for a psychedelic free jazz jam called *Attica Blues* (1972).

PAGE 172. **Re Nudo**, Milan, January 1972.
White Panthers.
John Sinclair was the man who managed the MC5, produced Sun Ra, and founded the White Panther Party in his commune in Ann Arbor, Michigan, a grenade's throw away from Detroit. A born trouble-maker, Sinclair was caught offering two joints to a plain-clothes police officer – it could have happened to anyone between Manchester and Melbourne – and jailed in July 1969. It made him into a cause célèbre, and his story mobilized the whole of the underground press, but nevertheless, he rotted in prison for almost three years. In July 1972 a huge benefit concert, the 'Free John Now Rally', was held in Ann Arbor; it featured Stevie Wonder and the Black Panther Bobby Seale, Archie Shepp and Allen Ginsberg, John Lennon singing *Attica State*…Three days later, Sinclair was released on the grounds that the State of Illinois was about to change the marijuana laws. The free press was now at the height of its power. Today Sinclair, ever true to himself, lives in Amsterdam, that 'free zone' where he plays, poeticizes and promotes Coltrane and free jazz, as well as running an Internet radio show on www.johnsinclairradio.com.

PAGE 173. **Ann Arbor Sun**, Michigan, 1972.
Free Jazz, Black Power.
The Art Ensemble of Chicago were leading exponents of the avant-garde music movement known as free jazz. On the front page of the Ann Arbor Sun, Joseph Jarman, its illustrious and charismatic saxophonist, raises a fist to salute 'Great Black Music'.

After the pioneering work of Max Roach, John Coltrane, Don Cherry, Ornette Coleman and others, the end of the 1960s saw free jazz reach its peak in the perfect balance embodied in the concert performances of this American ensemble – which had actually been born in France, by strange coincidence. In the emptiness of August 1969, fifteen jazz musicians found themselves in Paris. They included Archie Shepp, Sun Ra, the unknown Anthony Braxton and his trio, the violinist Leroy Jenkins, Leo Smith and his trumpet, Marion Brown, Steve McCall, and of course the fulcrum of the future Art Ensemble, Roscoe Mitchell, Joseph Jarman, Lester Bowie and Malachi Favors.

Tipped off by Claude Delcloo, himself a drummer and founder of the first, jazz-based incarnation of **Actuel** in late 1968, Jean Karakos and BYG Records booked a recording studio. Within six months, 52 albums had been recorded, the JazzActuel label had been born, and the Roscoe Mitchell Art Ensemble had become the Art Ensemble of Chicago. Free jazz had reached its zenith in France, far away from the black ghettos of the US, doped up on Motown hits.

Painting their faces, sometimes performing naked on stage, quoting Artaud and borrowing from the Living Theatre and from Albert Ayler, the members of the Art Ensemble of Chicago instilled their music with a mixture of African and European jazz – it was revolutionary, and it got them playing for the Black Panthers and rubbing shoulders with John Sinclair. In November 1970, Joseph Jarman wrote in **Actuel**: 'Great Black Music is a complete thing. It's like a stream: we are in the flow if not at the source – it's the same music everywhere. In the ghetto, I only have to walk a few hundred yards and I can hear black music in all its forms: a guy playing the drums, a choir singing spirituals, a guy banging on a garbage can. Music lives in the streets.' It was the start of the great urban mix. For more details, see *Free Jazz, Black Power* by Philippe Carles and Jean-Louis Comolli (Paris: Gallimard, 2000).

Protect the planet! The free press supports green politics

PAGE 176. **East Village Other,** New York, July 1969.
Coming back from the moon with a new view of the Earth.
Shame there weren't enough people in the Apollo capsule to save the planet.

PAGE 177. **East Village Other**, New York, April 1971.
The Earth teeters on the brink.
Neither the pioneering spirit of the Founding Fathers nor liberalism are a good fit for saving the environment. But in the late 1960s, ecological awareness blossomed underground, and its branches mingled with those of the campaign for Native American rights. Ever the opportunist, Nixon took out his green glasses to try and stop those voters from focusing too closely on the Vietnam disaster. On 22 January 1970, in his State of the Union address, he identified the key issue for the upcoming decade: 'Clean air, clean water, open spaces – these should once again be the birthright of every American.' Such talk was a longstanding conservative tradition, but it was never translated into facts. Nevertheless, under pressure from environmentalist students, the Democrat senator Gaylord Nelson officially inaugurated Earth Day on 21 April 1970. The underground press became the mouthpiece of the new movement. For the second Earth Day, **EVO** put a blue planet on its front page, twenty million Americans went out into the streets and public parks to celebrate... and the Republicans just carried on polluting.

PAGE 178. Dutch poster, Amsterdam, April 1971.
'Amsterdam: The Smurfs of the Revolution.'
The Kabouters (from the Dutch for 'gnome') became the first green representatives on Amsterdam city council, six years after the Provo demonstrations of 1965.

PAGE 179. **Oz**, London, 1971.
Ecology gets sexy.
A poster featuring the title of the cult eco-anarchist book by Murray Bookchin, *Post-Scarcity Anarchism*. Can't argue with that.

PAGE 180. **Actuel**, Paris, October 1971.
What's ecology, anyway?
A brilliant drawing by Ron Cobb, a green cartoonist who later went on to work for Disney. At the time, no one in France knew the word ecology. Three years later, with the support of **Actuel**, which devoted a special environmental issue to him, René Dumont stood as the first Green candidate in the French presidential elections.

Nevertheless, it took over twenty years before the greenhouse effect (anticipated by some visionaries in the early 20th century) and the hole in the ozone layer (discovered in 1973 but ignored by the mass media) became a real cause for alarm.

PAGE 181. **Other Scenes**, New York, 1971.
A mountain of unrecycled rubbish.
It was estimated that an American baby born in 1971 would, in its lifetime, consume 100 million litres of water, 28 tonnes of iron and steel, 25 tonnes of food, 10,000 bottles, 17,000 cans, 27,000 pills, 2–3 cars, 35 tyres, burn 1,200 barrels of oil, throw away 126 tonnes of rubbish, and produce 10 tonnes of pollutants. What about a baby in the 21st century? Will a Chinese baby be any better than an American baby by 2050?

PAGES 182–183. **The Seed**, Chicago, 1971.
Green poster: 'Bring back the buffalo and drive out the cars.'

PAGES 184. **Nola Express**, New Orleans, February 1972.
Water pollution: seems nothing much has changed since 1972...
The free press draws on the Native American nations to illustrate green issues. In New Orleans, **Nola Express** chose Sitting Bull to accompany this article which, prophetically but also disturbingly, raised the issue of water poisoning, denouncing the systematic pollution of the Mississippi by the many chemical works situated along its banks. The source of drinking water for more than 1.2 million inhabitants of Louisiana, the Mississippi was suffering from a septic ulcer near the town of Baton Rouge, where there is a high concentration of oil refineries and factories producing plastics and chemical fertilizers. Upstream, the average weight of solid waste discharged into the river rose from 4,000 tons a day in 1958 to more than 20,000 tons in 1968. **Nola Express** ended by reminding its readers that the Gulf

of Mexico had once been a paradise for fishermen. In the world today, more than 30,000 people die every day from water-borne diseases – a far more serious risk than the petrol crisis. By 2025, it is estimated that a third of the world's population will suffer from a shortage of drinking water.

PAGES 185. Hobo-Québec, Montreal, October 1974.
A collage from Quebec.
All on this poster: a denunciation of greedy multinationals, a spotlight on appalling prison conditions, the threat of famine in Bangladesh, Richard Burton discussing his alcoholism, and an appeal for art to save the working classes.

PAGES 186–187 Poster, 1973 – **Berkeley Barb**, San Francisco Bay, March 1975.
No reservations.
In the mid-19th century, in the great plains that stretched between Montana, Dakota and Wyoming, the Sioux people rose up against the US army and the invading colonists. In 1876, Custer got himself scalped at Little Big Horn. And it was here, into the tepee ghettos of the Pine Ridge Reservation in South Dakota, that the last remnants of a decimated nation were thrown. At the end of 1890, the white oppressors banned the Ghost Dance movement, but the ritual continued. The army was summoned, and the Indian families scattered to avoid pursuit, since they were powerless to wage war. The people of Chief Big Foot, a Lakota Sioux who was to die of pneumonia, hid in a creek at Wounded Knee. The 350 Indians (including 120 women and children) were quickly surrounded by 500 soldiers and their cannons, under Colonel James W. Forsyth. The Lakota refused to fight. On the morning of 29 December, 150 of them were massacred within an hour. Wounded Knee became a shrine to the Sioux genocide and was never forgotten.

The 1960s saw a Native American exodus to the cities, where the younger generation embraced political activism. In 1968 the AIM (the American Indian Movement) was born in Minneapolis. It enjoyed considerable success in combating alcoholism in the reservations, organizing food distribution, and setting up programmes for the preservation of Native American traditions. After 1970, the AIM was classified as a 'subversive organization' by the FBI, and its leaders, Dennis Banks and Russell Means, became enemies of Uncle Sam.

In February 1973, the AIM set about reviving memories of Wounded Knee. The leaders of the movement and a handful of militants joined forces with descendants of the Lakota, and staged a peaceful takeover of the hamlet where their ancestors had been massacred eighty-three years earlier. They were protesting against the regime of terror and police brutality that had been governing the Pine Ridge Reservation since the FBI had rigged an election to make one of its moles, Dick Wilson, head of the tribal council. Two Sioux were killed in the Wounded Knee siege, and in the two years that followed, Wilson's militia killed eighty militant Indians. In March 1975, the **Barb** front page denounced the conspiracy that was threatening the AIM and the continuing police brutality.

Faced with this, one AIM activist made a stand, a Sioux whose ancestors must have worked with French trappers in the 18th century since his name was Leonard Peltier. He organized a resistance movement at Pine Ridge, but when in 1975 the FBI accused him of murdering two of their agents, he had no choice but to flee to Canada. He was extradited and, despite a lack of evidence, was given two life sentences in 1977. Appeals by Rigoberta Menchú, Nelson Mandela, Angela Davis and the Dalai Lama have all fallen on deaf ears. Leonard Peltier is currently incarcerated in the US Penitentiary in Lewisburg, Pennsylvania.

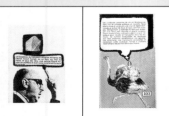

PAGES 188–189. CoEvolution Quarterly, San Francisco, 1972.
Devolving Europe: an uncanny prediction?
Blair's Britain has begun devolution by setting up autonomous Scottish and Welsh parliaments. Catalonia took the whole process in its stride. Yugoslavia exploded. The chains of nationhood are still being loosened all over Europe. This 1972 vision, born of the obsessions of ex-Digger Peter Berg, isn't so far from the truth.

PAGES 190–191. Mainmise, Montreal, March 1971.
Surreal visions of the future.

PAGES 192–193. Vroutsch, Strasbourg – Free University of New Orleans, no date.
Free universities offer off-the-wall courses and events.

Blank Generation: The free press is hit by the glam explosion and winds up punk

PAGE 196. Actuel, Paris, September 1971.
Glam decadence.
Issue 12 of **Actuel** didn't have much time for Alice Cooper. We suspected that their look wasn't a joke. The band were discovered by Frank Zappa, and he'd always had a cool eye for showmanship, so you have to wonder whether he had any influence on their style. Something like that must have gone on, bearing in mind that like Iggy and the Stooges, and the revolutionary MC5, they were originally from Detroit. When Iggy let loose, he projected raw sexuality, like Jim Morrison. When the MC5 performed at the Gibus Club in Paris, several people found themselves with a dose of gonorrhoea. One of the girls from **Actuel** had caught it from the MC5 bass player, and over the next three days she managed to pass it on to the rest of us – and there we all were, thinking we were her one and only!

PAGE 197. Other Scenes, New York, January 1970.
A toast to the future?
The old fox John Sinclair, who had been prominent on all fronts for so long, certainly wasn't lacking in flair. Avant-garde New York, rock and glam parties, meetings of the UPS, trips to see his European cousins, visits to Andy Warhol's Factory – so what could he do to sharpen up his act for the long-haired youth? Paul Morrissey, co-director of most of Warhol's movies, including *Flesh* (1968), saw us all as childish hippies or retarded Marxists, and said: 'Money will be the next big youth kick, with cash, clothes and jewelry replacing peace, love and poverty.' We didn't believe him.

PAGE 198 Rat, New York, April 1970.
Making money from Woodstock.
I can't resist quoting a few excerpts from the interview **Actuel** did with Mike Wadleigh, director of *Woodstock*, in early 1970:

Mike Wadleigh, you've made a very successful film, but a lot of people think it's too commercial.
It's the way it's been marketed that's made them think that. It's nothing to do with me. Look at the Cannes Film Festival: Warners used a whole battery of publicity – big banners, badges everywhere, dreary slogans: 'Anyone who sees the film will be transformed.' The original title was *Three Days of Peace and Music*. Then they added 'and Love', and everything that goes with it. They want you to know that there are naked women in the film, and drug use and weirdos. It's only to be expected, really. Peace and music don't sell very well, but drugs and free love bring in the cash. When we worked on the editing, we had to share the studios with the National Guard, who had hired them over the weekend to practise putting down demonstrations. Some of the guards had disguised themselves as hippies. Did Warner lend them the costumes as well?
Do you think there can be such a thing as pop cinema?
What does that mean, and what's the point of asking? *Alice's Restaurant, Easy Rider,* and *Zabriskie Point* deal with the same subject. I didn't like any of those three. *Easy Rider* isn't a serious film. It's got nothing to do with hippies. Young people aren't fooled by it. They meet some hippies and they go across country on a bike. It's got nothing to do with tripping either. It's too Hollywood. All the same, it does have some great sequences – like the death of the alcoholic lawyer... You can feel the same Hollywood atmosphere in *Alice's Restaurant*. The club and the school where Arlo Guthrie plays are obviously sets. It was better when he was trudging about with his guitar over his shoulder. And *Zabriskie Point* is no better. I'll never forgive Antonioni for the way he ruined the voice of Kathleen Cleaver – Eldridge's wife. When he shows the 'serious' revolutionary students setting out to steal a plane, it's a betrayal. He plays into the hands of the right by trying to prove that the youth revolution can be boiled down to a small irresponsible group.

Now here is a review of *Woodstock*, both the film and the phenomenon, by Patrick Rambaud, published in Actuel, June 1970:

Richie Havens, mouth on the mike, eyes closed, this evening: a hundred million songs that speak of you, that speak of those who are not here, that speak of Vietnam, that speak of the Great Confusion. But Country Joe has nothing to do with the military records burned in marches on the Pentagon, nor the detailed descriptions of the effects of a shrapnel bomb on the body of a Vietcong soldier. The song has replaced the road, and the music conveys some strange sounds. There are cries of all kinds – cries of rage, cries of fear, cries of pleasure, cries of pain, cries that are heard as five hundred thousand lost souls sleep in the mud that is offered to them in the guise of paradise. There are some real apes in paradise. Personally, I think it must be bloody boring in paradise. The damned, in all the paintings, have much more exciting lives than the bored-shitless angels. What can you say about Woodstock the movie? Technically, it's irreproachable and intelligent. There are some great sequences (for example the sequence with The Who, or the one with Ten Years After, and the storm scene). But what stops me from unconditionally supporting the film… is my profound disagreement with the beat pacifism for which it is the mouthpiece. Thoreau has found an audience. The little corner of nature that has been preserved between two buildings makes me laugh. So do the facetious remarks of Bill Gandhi, nirvana salesman, and those of Kerouac, the folklore apostle of revolution. It's a nice enough tradition but it's irresponsible and simplistic. 'Sit down, protest, wave a placard, and don't kill your fellow man.'

Your fellow man doesn't care. He's making a profit. He's selling his cornflakes and his guns. We can put pacifism on trial later. In fact, there is too much shit on the flowers for me to want to pick them… Those who try to break us must pay the price. We won't let ourselves be carried away by the euphoria… Let us remember what Robert Scheer wrote about his friend Eldridge Cleaver: 'Had Cleaver not joined the Panthers, he would have had it made. In America it is possible to be angry and remain safe – in fact, anger is even desirable in a writer so long as it is diffuse and inactive; it can make him entertaining and therefore marketable.' Woodstock is a party… In the days after a party, there's always a nasty taste left in your mouth. And the days after are inevitable… I shall just ask one question: what happens after Woodstock? Between the hope and the cigarette papers, I'm a bit worried about the uses that all this energy might be put to.

PAGE 199 Ad for Elektra Records published in various papers, 1970.
Alternative music goes mainstream.
Apart from ESP Records and then Alan Douglas's productions, few independent record labels managed to establish themselves, and Clive Davis of CBS quickly signed up Dylan and Joplin, and Elektra's Jack Holzman signed up The Doors and Love. Holzman was taken over by Warner. But for three years they supported the underground press, until the government put on the pressure, stopping the ads which had made the fortune of **Rolling Stone**

PAGE 200. **it**, London, June 1973.
Celebrity cover stars.
A story told by Abe Peck in *Uncovering the Sixties* sums up the whole post-1968 situation: Jeff Shero, founder of **Rat**, was a friend of Janis Joplin's, and knowing that she was in New York, he wanted to interview her. She was receiving journalists from *Time* and *Newsweek* at the Chelsea Hotel (the underground hotel par excellence, where artists could pay the proprietor with a painting). Her reply to Shero was: 'Why do I want to do an interview with a li'l ol' hippie publication?' Poor, brilliant Janis, so drugged up and tormented, with such wild mood swings and so easily influenced that the things she took to lift her spirits ended up betraying her.

PAGE 201. **Actuel**, Paris, October 1971.
An interview with Nico of the Velvet Underground, accompanied by Warhol's image of Liz Taylor.

PAGE 202. Ad for the first underground film festival, New York, October 1970.
The cinematic underground.
Fireworks by Kenneth Anger in '47, Markopoulos in '47, Brakhage in '53, *The Pleasure Dome* (not Frankie Goes to Hollywood's version from '84, but Anger's in '54), Shirley Clarke, Bruce Conner, Jonas Mekas and John Cassavetes after '58, Jack Smith's *Flaming Creatures* and Warhol's *Blow Job* in '63….

All of them had seen Buñuel's *L'Âge d'Or*, short films by Man Ray and Moholy-Nagy, Jean Vigo's *Zéro de Conduite*, Abel Gance's work, Léger's *Ballet Mécanique* and Duchamp's *Anemic Cinema*. Isidore Isou and Guy Debord had passed them by, but they were still capable of their own excruciating experiments in wrecking the cinema. In 1970, they found the audience they wanted in New York, and took out their reels which had hitherto been confined to clandestine projection on an old curtain just for their fellow artists. Festivals were organized, and the underground papers were obliged to promote these films that had been liberated from the bourgeois constraints of mere narrative. Avant-garde filmmaker Jonas Mekas even set up a movie theatre with a difference: every seat was separated from its neighbours by a sort of blind that forced you to look straight ahead at the screen, even if for an hour you were being shown nothing but the camera zooming in on various shapes, right into the grain of the film, like a microscope scanning for tiny signs of life.

PAGE 203. East Village Other, New York, October 1968.
New York hardcore
We're not in California any more. The Velvet Underground, sheathed in black leather, played twenty-minute versions of *Sister Ray* in St Mark's Place, with the shrill violin of John Cale and the poet Gerard Malanga whipping himself under the strobe lights. The Velvets were the anti-Grateful Dead. Both played around with hypnotism, sound effects and light shows, but the hallucinations did not come from the same drugs. On one side, ecstatic trips and light projections in saturated colour from the Dead, on the other side, speed and pyrotechnics from the Velvets and the Silver Apples.

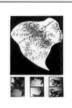

PAGES 204–205. Origin unknown, New York, 1969.
Sex and the cinema.
Some of the scenes in Stan Brakhage's *Lovemaking* were taboo before he filmed them and have probably become taboo all over again. He even shows children innocently playing doctors. In *Fuck* (aka *Blue Movie*), Warhol wickedly and dispassionately shot Louis Waldron and Viva in bed, seen through a haze of dope, as if by an entomologist, the hottest of images filmed in the coldest possible way.

PAGES 206–207. Oz, London. 1972.
The Last Passion of the Underground Press.
Oz realized that the freaks had had their day, and would disappear in a haze of cocaine and Coca-Cola. Let's not forget that Pope Leo XIII drank coca wine as a stimulant, that Coca-Cola contained coca before the First World War, and that cocaine would conquer the world by the end of the 1970s. And it's not over yet.

PAGE 208–209. *Performance* movie soundtrack – **it**, London, September 1970.
'Nothing is true, everything is permitted.'
Nicholas Roeg and Donald Cammell's cult film *Performance* features a classic soundtrack by Jack Nitzsche and Ry Cooder and the ultimate Jagger, fresh from *Their Satanic Majesties Request*. From bed to bed, from twosomes to threesomes, and no standing on ceremony. Mick even lets it all hang out. Made in 1968, the film took two years to get a release, although Mick's genitals had to be snipped in a few places. For the record, *Cocksucker Blues*, a film documentary on the Stones, remains banned from public release.

PAGE 210. Source unknown, *c.* 1971.
Paranoid puzzle pieces by Charles Henri Ford.

PAGE 211. ACE, New York, February 1972.
On the cover, an updated version of a work by pulp illustrator Virgil Finlay.

PAGE 212. Berkeley Barb, monster issue, San Francisco Bay, October 1976.
Bats out of hell.
At San Francisco's annual Hookers' Ball, underground kitsch went overboard. The evidence? Even Paul Krassner was there.

PAGE 213. Ad for the first issue of **Interview**, New York, 1969.
Andy Warhol's glam bible.